THE DISPOSSESSED
An aspect of Victorian social history

The Dispossessed

AN ASPECT OF VICTORIAN SOCIAL HISTORY

BARBARA KERR

WITH 38 PHOTOGRAPHS
AND 18 LINE DRAWINGS

ST. MARTIN'S PRESS

CONTENTS

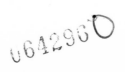

PLATES

PREFACE

In this book an attempt has been made to pick out the salient points of the mid-Victorian scene as they appear in the Thornhill papers. These consist of the diaries kept during the period 1864–1880 by Henrietta Thornhill, the great-granddaughter of Sarah Siddons, and the letters she received over a longer period. As family histories cannot be cribbed within a few decades it has been necessary to look before and after the period 1850–1880 which has been selected for study. Not only do domestic chronicles need a wide sweep of time in which to unfurl but also a wider background than the family circle. Some of the themes which recur in the papers of Thornhill, Beaufoy and Siddons families have, therefore, been supplemented by reference to correspondence of other families. Among the frequently canvassed topics a selection must obviously be made and some omissions are inevitable. For example, the Thornhills were enthusiastic theatre-goers; but, although this taste was shared by mid-Victorians of every class, little reference has been made to it as the intrusion of an outsider into the theatrical world generally proves disastrous. A question to which only indirect references were made, however, is the main theme of this book. Nearly all the young Thornhills growing up in the 1850s were conscious of the 'general cussedness of the upside-down world' as it affected their own interests. That they failed to perceive the basic cause of their discomfiture is not surprising as very few realised that the malaises of the age were due to a crisis in western civilisation. During the mid-nineteenth century, sometimes nostalgically recalled as an age of stability and certainty, industrialism was uprooting families from their natural habitats and forcing them into the wilderness of expanding cities and of untrodden lands. From the complaints of the Thornhills, such as their longings to escape from the fumes of South Lambeth to the sweet-smelling hayfields of Dulwich or from 'uncivilised' New Zealand to country life at home, an attempt has been made to piece together the causes of the uneasiness of those who felt themselves dispossessed from the way of living enjoyed by their forbears.

If any of the principal characters in these chronicles have
come to life so as to throw some light on the mid-Victorian
crisis it will be due to the recollections of Mabel Siddons-
Downe, daughter of Henrietta Downe (*née* Thornhill) and
owner of the Thornhill papers. Although it is disconcerting to
have the gay and sparkling figures of the 1860s conjured up in
exacting or awesome old age, such memories alone can give
substance to the elusive figures of the past. Three of Henrietta
Downe's children carried on the Siddons tradition. Rupert
had a long stage career, while for thirty years (1928–1958) Beatrice and Mabel produced and acted at the Little Bankside
Theatre which they opened in Ealing. Charles looked to the
future and went into motor engineering.

NOTES ON GENERAL SOURCES AND ACKNOWLEDGEMENTS

As the diaries of Henrietta Thornhill and many of the letters she kept were often written in haste, some corrections have been necessary to the text so as to spare the reader distractions of mis-spelling, lack of punctuation, and omissions of minor words. No indication of these corrections is given in the quotations, but square brackets enclose inserted words wherever there is a possibility of an alternative interpretation. For the reader's convenience, also, surnames have often been added after Christian names. Marks of omission generally inspire mistrust; but they have necessarily been frequently used to avoid overloading the quotations with the minutiae of family life. Only those passages which have little relevance to the theme of the quotation have been omitted. As many of these concern purely personal matters, the apprehensions of Henriette (Tal) Thornhill, who wrote: 'One can't write such rubbish as spooney scenes in letters; fancy if anything happened to them', have not been disregarded.

Two final points concerning the presentation of the text must be made. In June 1863 Cudbert Thornhill wrote from New Zealand to his cousin, Henrietta Thornhill, complaining. 'Your letter began with a most powerful lot of "ands". You begin by saying you are sitting in the schoolroom with both windows open "*and* the bees are humming about *and* the sun is shining *and* the birds are singing *and* the flowers are blooming *and* old Jack [the jackdaw] has been talking *and* young Jack is sitting on the window edge putting up his crest *and* enjoying the beautiful heat of the sun *and* you might really fancy it was the middle of the summer." Eight "ands" in seven lines; a very fair amount when you come to think of it.'

Here the pot was calling the kettle black, as most of the Thornhills and many of their contemporaries shared this failing. In some quotations the 'ands' have been pruned as their profusion does not illustrate any syntactical idiosyncrasy of

9

the age but merely that the governesses who drifted through Lyston Hall and Caron Place and the masters at Radley had failed to elucidate the mysteries of dependent clauses.

Occasionally in the interests of clarity a rearrangement in the order of sentences has been necessary. For example, in the letter in which Hazel McDowell Smith (*née* Thornhill) tried to express her joy after marrying 'one of the best' (p. 242), a change has been made to the sequence, but not the expression, of her sentiments.

As many as possible of the line drawings with which Henrietta Thornhill embellished her diaries have been reproduced. Where the diarist's illustrations have not been available, drawings have been made by my sister, Ann Wilson. All the drawings are initialled. Old Thornhill photographs and others which have been kindly lent, and acknowledged in 'Notes on Sources', have been used. All the modern photographs were taken by my brother-in-law, John Wilson.

All the postcards reproduced are those sent home by members of my family at the turn of this century. Help in tracing these and other reproductions and in all questions concerning the history of London has been given by my sister, Eileen Kerr.

For much assistance and for kind permission to reproduce prints and other illustrations I am indebted to a large number of individuals and authorities whose help is gratefully acknowledged in the 'Notes on Sources' on page 245.

Without the sympathetic and wise direction of the late John Baker the Thornhill chronicles could hardly have emerged from the great body of unpublished, and fast disappearing, family papers.

My thanks are due to John Baker's assistant, Donald Kidd, and to Elizabeth Clay. One brought order from the chaos of a large number of illustrations, and the other from an unwieldy MS.

Acknowledgements are made to John Freeman for photographic reproductions of plates 2, 6, 23, 24, 26, 27, 30, 32, 35, 36.

Grants Farm   B.K.
Gallows Hill
Wareham

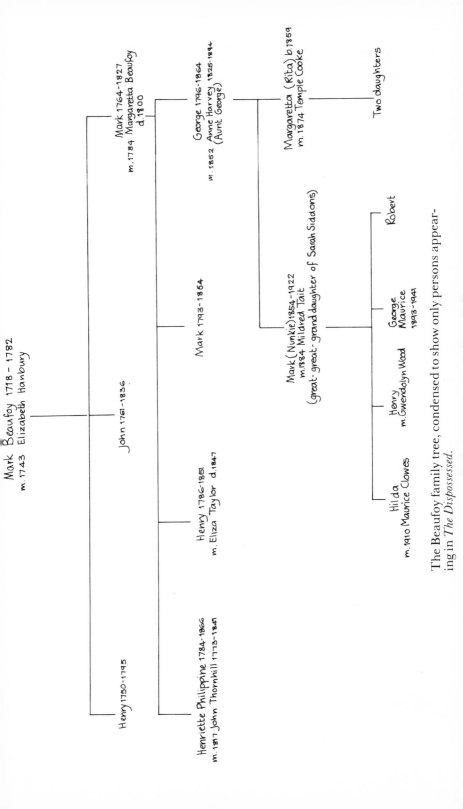

The Beaufoy family tree, condensed to show only persons appearing in *The Dispossessed*.

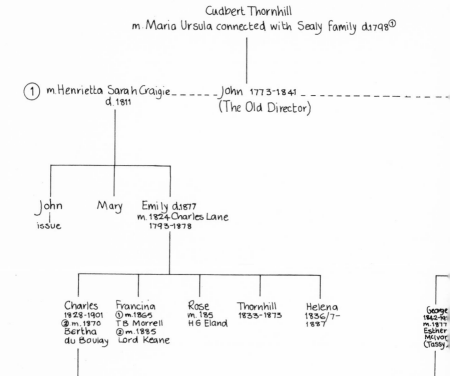

The Thornhill family tree, condensed to show only persons appearing in *The Dispossessed*. Information from a family tree in the possession of Mabel Siddons-Downe.

[1] Bengal Burial Registers show that Harriet Ann Thornhill was buried on 25 March 1798, with no further information. Maria Ursula may have died out of India, but this is unlikely.

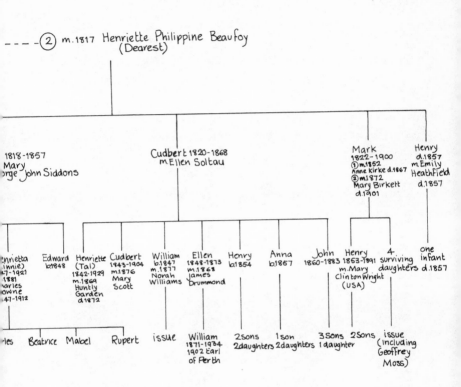

---- ② m.1817 Henriette Philippine Beaufoy
              (Dearest)

1818-1857   Cudbert 1820-1868   Mark   Henry
Mary   m.Ellen Soltau   1822-1900   d.1857
orge─John Siddons   ①m.1852   m.Emily
                                             Anne Kirke d.1867 Heathfield
                                             ②m.1872   d.1857
                                             Mary Birkett
                                             d.1901

nrietta   Edward   Henriette Cudbert   William   Ellen   Henry   Anna   John   Henry   4.   one
innie)   b1848   (Tal)   1843-1904 b.1847   1848-1873 b1854   b1867   1860-1883   1863-1891 surviving infant
7-1921   1842-1929 m.1876   m.1877   m.1868   m.Mary   daughters d.1857
arles   m.1869   Mary   Norah   James   Clinton Wright
owne   Huntly   Scott   Williams Drummond   (USA)
47-1912   Garden
                   d.1872

les   Beatrice Mabel   Rupert   issue   William   2sons   1son   3sons   2sons   issue
                                             1871-1934   2daughters 2daughters 1daughter   (including
                                             1902 Earl   Geoffrey
                                             of Perth   Moss)

CHAPTER ONE

'The Best of Them All'

> The servant, my conductor, screwed his mouth, and shrugged his shoulders, 'Never fear,' says he, 'I will carry you to the best of them all.'
>
> James Bruce, *Travels to Discover the Source of the Nile, 1813.*

The Arab who conducted the seemingly destitute James Bruce was a simple man who considered Cudbert Thornhill the best, because he was the kindest, of the captains assembled at Jiddah. It is fitting that the story of the dispossessed should start with Captain Thornhill (1721/2–1809) as the wanderings of his descendants, by marriages with the Beaufoy and Siddons families, through the no-man's land of the mid-nineteenth century are the main themes of this book. To understand the malaise between the years 1850 and 1880 it is necessary to consider first the times of Cudbert Thornhill when the talents of many of his contemporaries glowed like the Northern Lights in the 'crepuscular skies' overhanging Great Britain. This display was fired by the Romantic inspiration which, since it originated from delicacy of perception and audacity in execution, was manifest in a diversity of activities ranging from the conduct of day-to-day affairs to attempts to express the sublime. This inspiration kindled the benevolence of Captain Thornhill whom Bruce found 'sitting, in a white calico waistcoat, a very high pointed white cotton night-cap, with a tumbler of water before him, seemingly very deep in thought' and prepared to 'have the feeding of ten in India, rather than the burying of one in Jiddah.'[1] The Romantic fervour inspired the transcendental acting of Sarah Siddons; and also encouraged Mark Beaufoy to make the ascent of Mont Blanc in 'a white flannel jacket

[1] James Bruce, *Travels to Discover the Source of the Nile*, 3rd ed. 1813, Vol. II, pp. 168–9.

without any shirt beneath and white linen trousers without any drawers'.[1]

By the mid-nineteenth century the Romantic inspiration was fading and the young Thornhills lost, as did their whole generation, their bearings, or what Nabokov has described as their 'ecological niche'. The sense of timelessness and continuity which had enabled their forbears to live as though eternity stretched before them had gone. In the 1840s the nation started on a journey the end of which is not yet in sight. Men were leaving the villages for the cities, crossing the seas and, above all, moving up and down between the classes which formed the seemingly rigid social hierarchy of the times. The belief, popular on the Continent, that society resembled the English household in being 'a ship where everyone knew his place'[2] was ill-founded. Despite the pious aspiration, neither the rich man stayed in his castle nor the poor man at the gate. Before looking through the eyes of the Thornhills at some manifestations of this revolutionary society, something must be said about their forbears whose activities at the end of the eighteenth century entitled them to be called 'the best of them all'; and also set the pattern which their descendants vainly aspired to copy.

The oriental scene with which Cudbert Thornhill was closely connected began to impinge on everyday life in Britain towards the end of the eighteenth century. This was not the case with other overseas settlements. The impression that North America was a refuge for those fleeing from justice and that the antipodean settlements existed for those unlucky enough to be caught was long lasting. Despite the assurance of the editor of the *Essex and West Suffolk Guardian* (6 January 1854) that Britain had 'at last desisted from the summary practice of throwing snails over the wall into [her] neighbour's garden', the ghost of Abel Magwitch clanking his chains on the marsh was not exorcised until Queen Victoria's jubilees imprinted the imperial image on the national consciousness.

[1] This and subsequent descriptions of the ascent appear in Mark Beaufoy's 'Narrative of a Journey from the Village of Chamonix in Switzerland to the summit of Mont Blanc' in T. Thomson, *Annals of Philosophy*, Vol. IX, 1817, pp. 97–103. Beaufoy was the first Englishman to make the ascent.

[2] H-F. Amiel, *Journal Intime*, 1848–1881, trans. Mrs Humphrey Ward, 1894, p. 196.

Among the cheering crowds on these occasions, however, were many who felt that no place had been found for them in the Empire on which the sun never set. Those who had been unable to take root in the imperial soil included some of the Thornhills who marked time in the colonies in the expectation that some part of Captain Thornhill's fortune might put an end to their half-hearted efforts (Chapter Ten).

Cudbert Thornhill's benevolence, which was a by-word on the sub-continent, was an integral part of his personality, but the position he achieved in India was due to his exertions. His example could have been followed by any enterprising boy before the effects of the Mutiny closed the gates of the 'glorious, glowing land' to the needy and humbly born (Chapter Eight). Family tradition has it that Thornhill ran away from a school in Hull to ship for foreign parts. Records show that after trading with India as a free captain he was established by 1778 in Calcutta where he became, within a decade, Master Attendant at the port (plate 3). Here Thornhill was responsible for the East India Company's schooners, agent's vessels and river boats, amounting in 1804 to seventy-eight craft; and also for their masters, pilots and crews. That he cared for the men as well as the vessels under his charge is shown in the records. One seaman was dismissed for inattention to duty and for 'violence to the Lascars', a pilot was fined a year's pay for turning a boat-swain 'ashore from the *Tweed* schooner and for unmercifully beating George Riley, seaman,' and a master was demoted 'for ill-treatment to Mr Collins, chief officer of the ship *Daniel*'. The casualty lists of the port of Calcutta indicate the great stresses of marine service in India. A large proportion of the casualties were men who, being desperate, bored or adventurous had 'run' or deserted. The casualty list for 1801–2 may be taken as representative: five dead, two superannuated, five 'run' and two dismissed (one seaman for drunkenness and a master for the loss of the *Ganges*).[1] Desertion was the most common escape route taken by overburdened or adventurous men in India. A very few managed to improve their condition by making use of their European skills; but the majority sank into the destitution

[1] Information concerning Cudbert Thornhill's activity as Master Attendant at Calcutta 1785–1809 has been obtained from the Annual Returns of the Bengal Marine Establishment in the India Office Records.

of village life.

As he grew older Thornhill's benevolence remained un-diminished, but his attire grew more conventional. On his arrival at Calcutta the young and forlorn Thomas Twining (1776–1861) was rescued by a 'respectable-looking old gentle-man, dressed in black, with a powdered long-tailed wig, and a cocked-hat in his hand'; and whisked off to the Master Attendant's magnificent residence at Cossipore.[1] His gener-osity and the fact that he knew how to live in the grand style made Thornhill respected among the Indians as well as the Europeans. Among the latter his long and healthy life in India was a matter for wonderment. A glance at the Calcutta burial register for September 1809, when the Captain died, indicates how few Europeans in India achieved either longevity or affluence. Of the six infants among the nineteen recorded burials one was a 'poor boy from the free school' and another a four-year-old pauper. James Barnes, a 'marine pauper' and Margaret Pettie 'a pensioner on the charitable Fund' had stri-ven in vain; and more hopeful prospects had not helped the six adults who died under the age of thirty.[2] The Thornhills had exceptionally strong constitutions. Cudbert's son, John, retired from India to serve for twenty-five years as a member of the Court of East India Directors in London.

John Thornhill (1773–1841) inherited his father's wealth as well as his constitution. After a hard-working career in Bengal, where he became Postmaster General, he retired to settle near his old friends, the Bensleys, at Stanmore. Here the widower married Henriette Philippine Beaufoy; and became the adopted heir of the wealthy widow, Francina Bensley. John Thornhill was, therefore, a man of substance even by oriental standards. The fortune of the Old Director, as John Thornhill was generally called, was to cause ill-feeling among his sons and daughters-in-law, to overshadow the lives of his grandchildren by arousing great, but unfulfilled, expectations and finally to benefit only lawyers at home and in India.

---

[1] T. Twining, *Travels in India a Hundred Years Ago* . . . ed. by W. H. G. Twining, 1893, pp. 77–79 for description of Twining's meeting with Thorn-hill.

[2] As the age of death was not given in three cases the number may have been higher.

While awaiting a favourable settlement of their grandfather's estate, most of the young Thornhills waited expectantly in South Africa, in New Zealand, in India and in North America. The career of the Old Director's youngest grandson and namesake indicates the predicament of the whole family and the fate of many half-hearted emigrants. Young John Thornhill entered the Indian army; but, finding the pay and the climate unfavourable, drifted to South Africa. Here the climate was more to Thornhill's taste, but his earnings were insufficient to support his family. The boys were pushed off to the United States where they managed 'to jog along somehow' and the father withdrew to Leigh-on-Sea where he painted 'very pretty little pictures for calendars', and felt himself to have been ill-used: 'Losses, trials and the general cussedness of the upside-down world are responsible for a good deal'.

Towards the end of the nineteenth century this belief in 'the upside-down world' as one of the chief causes of individual failure was frequently the solace of those whose imperial essays were unsuccessful. Young John Thornhill inevitably remembered how well had fared his connections who had been wafted to India on letters of recommendation from powerful patrons. Among these were John Fombelle (1763–1820, resigned from East India Company) and George John Siddons (1785–1848), who married Fombelle's daughter, Mary (1788–1877). This dark-eyed beauty was reputed to be a scion of the royal house at Delhi. The youngest child of this union, Mary, wed Captain Thornhill's grandson, Robert, in 1839.

At the end of the eighteenth century India acted as a safety valve whereby talent unlikely to be recognised at home could find an outlet, often by the means of patronage. Political equilibrium in Britain as well as prosperity was largely due to the dominance of British influence on the sub-continent. The background and careers of Fombelle and Siddons are not without interest as suggesting that protégés were not necessarily dead weights supported by public money. John Fombelle's arrival in India was due the influence of the Marquis of Lansdowne (1737–1805). Since Lansdowne's artificiality and seeming insensibility offended his equals, he gathered around him at Bowood in Wiltshire humbler men of outstanding, but often unrecognised, ability. Among these were Jeremy Bentham, Henry Beaufoy, the son of a Quaker vinegar manufacturer at Lambeth (Chapter Four) and Pierre Fombelle (1731–1802), John's father (plate 2). Probably as a result of the harassment of the Protestants, Pierre left France for London where his integrity and ability secured his appointment in Lansdowne's household. His position there was described by his great-great-granddaughter: 'Pierre, John's father, was very much liked by the Marquis of Lansdowne who begged him to make Bowood his home after he became old and gave up the appointment of confidential secretary; and Lord Wycombe [Lansdowne's son], also, wrote most warmly and kindly to him. But he preferred to be independent at last, and left Bowood. He was, my Aunt Mary Siddons often told me, a very genial, dear old man . . . There seems nothing to show how he became acquainted with the Marquis of Lansdowne, but he held an important post at Bowood.'

Pierre Fombelle was not self-seeking but he was grateful for his employer's influence on behalf of his son. Patronage took John Fombelle to India; but his ability, acknowledged even by Cornwallis who felt the patronage system was far from beneficial to British rule in India, secured his appointment to the responsible post of presiding over the Civil Court of Appeals and the Criminal Court of the Presidency in Bengal, Bihar and Orissa. Despite the timelessness of the oriental scene, jurists who at home were content to remain entwined in the coils of precedent took on a new lease of life in India. In the early nineteenth century justice in the regular courts established in the areas under the control of the East India Company was often more efficiently and speedily dispensed than at home.

That George John Siddons, a protégé of the Prince of Wales, started his career in the salt customs and ended it in the pepper gardens of Sumatra suggests that service in the East India Company was not without a certain humdrum monotony. The complaint of boredom was often voiced in the early nineteenth century when the initial feelings of wonder and apprehension were waning, and a sense of mission was not generally established among the British serving in India. A short survey of Siddons' career as Resident at

Fort Marlborough in Benkulen on the west coast of Sumatra will illustrate how violence and disorder had become accepted as part of the oriental scene, and how difficult it was for the Company's servants to take any action. Rather than be troubled by a zealous and active official like Thomas Stamford Raffles (1781–1826), who succeeded Siddons at Fort Marlborough, the Company accepted the handing over the settlement to the Dutch.

When Siddons went to Sumatra in 1808 he found himself surrounded by smouldering volcanoes. The Company's pepper gardens were unwillingly worked by forced, often convict, labour, the Sumatran chiefs, or pangerans, were restive and in the Out-Residencies the Company's officials flaunted the Resident's authority.[1] Siddons was obliged, as were many East India Company officials in 1857, to deal with a situation that was beyond control. This is clearly indicated by extracts from the official Proceedings. In the free-for-all methods of pepper cultivation, subordinates often proved intractable: 'Much of the correspondence on the part of Mr Delamotte [a sub-collector] continues marked with a tone of insult and a spirit of litigiousness, which is highly disagreable and censurable.'

Troubles in the convict camps were unending. In October 1813 'Pompey escaped from his irons'; a few years later a more daring escaped convict 'made his appearance in the lines with a long knife or cutlass, cutting at their houses and threatening anyone who came nigh him'. The man was not apprehended as owing to 'neglect and inattention', the sepoys were not at their posts. The dependence of the East India Company on native troops and their officers forced officials to be singularly conciliatory even though 'scarcely a night passed that some burglary or robbery is not committed' in the lines. Here the buildings, like the discipline, were in a state of collapse. In 1814 it was reported that they would be only able 'to stand two or three months longer should no very violent weather occur during the monsoon.' The lines were hardly habitable but the Company's chief concern was that no indents should be made

[1] For description of the Free Garden system and its effects see J. Bastin, *The Native Policies of Sir Stamford Raffles in Java and Sumatra*, an Economic Interpretation, 1957, pp. 80–88.

for sealing wax or tape as 'these articles are cheaper and better in India than they could be supplied from Europe.' Red tape was never in short supply especially in questions of expenditure. Siddons' personal expenses for November 1812 to May 1813 were approved except for '5½ yards of billiard cloth' which was considered 'exclusively of a private nature.'

Siddons tried to check the constant attacks on the warehouses by apprehending the robbers. He was ponderously informed that the Governor General in Council was sensible of his 'zeal and exertions', but the prisoners must be immediately released. The reason given for this order does credit to the impartiality of the Company if not to its commonsense:

> 'The only competent tribunal for the trial of prisoners charged with crimes of magnitude is the Pangeran's Court, and although the authority of the magistrate extends to cases of trivial nature it has always been understood that his decision was subject only to the control of that Court . . .' any infringement 'must therefore involve the introduction of a new law of evidence and a new System of Jurisprudence foreign to the constitution of the country.'

The pangeran released the prisoners who were compensated by the Company; and Siddons wisely concerned himself with matters like the wastage of Glauber salts in the medical stores.[1]

As Siddons was a child of the new age, he was satisfied with service in the East India Company which had filled his pockets with 'plenty much rupees'. The zeal and the enthusiasm for the Malay civilisation which animated Raffles, and his mother's devotion to her art were quite incomprehensible to him: 'I am quite vexed to see my mother continues to perform occasionally, and heartily wish those who value her health – shall I say her character – would prevail upon her to give it up entirely and forever.'[2]

---

[1] Accounts of George John Siddons' activities in Sumatra have been taken from the Diary of Proceedings of G. J. Siddons Acting Resident for the Affairs of the Hon'ble Coy at Fort Marlborough in the India Office Records.

[2] Florence Parsons, *The Incomparable Siddons,* 1909, p. 273, quoting from a letter of G. J. Siddons to his cousin, Horace Twiss, probably written just before he left Sumatra in 1818.

Just as Anglo-Indian activities in the late eighteenth century have been described in some detail to provide a background for the five generations of Thornhills who succeeded
Captain Cudbert on the sub-continent,[1] so something must be
said of Sarah Siddons (1755–1831) if the sense of disenchant-
ment, dominant in the mid-nineteenth century, is to be understood (plate 1). The secret of Mrs Siddons' power was her ability to absorb the emotions of her audience, and to hurl them
back with the shattering effect which Boaden tried to describe:

> 'I well remember, (how is it possible I should forget?) the
> *sobs*, the *shrieks*, among the tenderer part of her
> audiences; or those *tears*, which manhood, at first, strug-
> gled to suppress, but at length grew proud of indulging.
> We then, indeed, knew all the LUXURY of grief; but the
> nerves of many a gentle being gave way before the inten-
> sity of such appeals; and fainting fits long and frequently
> alarmed the decorum of the house, filled almost to suffoca-
> tion.'[2]

These heightened sensibilities were partly due to the stress
of the times. Playgoers, whether in the galleries or boxes, lived
in the shadow of the threatening might of France in the struggle
with this power. As victories and reverses jostled one another in
bewildering succession, the acting of Mrs Siddons provided an
outlet for national grief or rejoicing. That the tears Mrs Siddons
drew as Euphrasia in *The Grecian Daughter* were also shed for the
loss of the American Colonies was not realised by the critic who
scornfully wrote:

> 'Siddons to see – King, lords and commons run,
> Glad to forget that Britain is undone.
> See, of false tears a copious torrent flows,
> But not one real for their country's woes.'[3]

The genius of Sarah Siddons and the heroic scale of

[1] Throughout this work the term Anglo-Indian will be used to denote British residents in India.

[2] J. Boaden, *Memories of Mrs Siddons*, 1837, Vol. I, p. 327.

[3] Nina Kennard, *Mrs Siddons*, 1887, p. 116, quoting from the *Morning Chronicle*, 10 January 1783.

national events called for tragedies, and popular taste demanded that these should be adorned with Gothic trappings.
John Home (1722–1808), an ejected minister of the Scottish
Church, met all these requirements with *Douglas*. In this play
Home's 'principles of virtue, of morality, of filial duty, of patrio-
tic zeal, and reverence for an over-ruling power'[1] and the acting
of Mrs Siddons, who was incapable of portraying even a paste-
board character without passion, prepared the way for the
tumultuous reception of Scott's novels. The influence of these
was so far reaching that Cardinal Newman believed they prepared 'men for some closer and more practical approximation
of Catholic truth.'[2]

If Scott's works had an influence on the Anglican revival
then the influence of Byron was equally marked on the Evangelical movement. Like all Romantics and many Puritans,
Byron was reluctant to drop his burden of sin. His attempt to
explain his predicament is best described in the lines from *Don
Juan*:

> 'A solitary shriek, the bubbling cry
> Of some strong swimmer in his agony.'

Byron's love and detailed knowledge of the Old Testament
and his sad theological exchanges with the polemical Dr
Kennedy on Cephalonia all suggest that his sense of sin was as
strong as had been that of any of his Covenanting countrymen. The stress laid on this consciousness of guilt was the
strength of the Evangelicals until the dawn of the twentieth
century when the show piece of a repentant sinner was beginning to degenerate into W. W. Jacobs' Brother Hutchins
whose claim to sanctity lay in having been in half the jails of
the country.

Closed in controversial combat during the mid-nineteenth
century, the Tractarian and Evangelical parties failed to
notice that the familiar landmarks were being obliterated. The
manor, the guild and the Church had not always protected the
individual from poverty and injustice; but they enabled the
majority of men, however obscure, to fill a recognised place in

---

[1] *The Thespian Dictionary*, 1805, under John Home.

[2] *The British Critic*, April 1839, Vol. XXV, pp. 396–426, J. Newman, 'The
State of Religious Parties'.

society. Many incumbents failed to realise that it was loss of identity rather than faith which kept both agricultural and industrial workers from places of worship. Though most incumbents held firm ecclesiastical principles, few knew where they stood in the changing world of the mid-nineteenth century. In country parishes the effects of the townward drift, the frequent comings and goings of the new gentry and the resentment of farmers often caused inertia to spread 'like a green mould, over a minister's soul'[1] (Chapter Three). The perplexity, if not the inertia, was equally great among the clergy in towns. An incumbent of South Lambeth, one of the reception areas for countrymen seeking urban employment, declared 'People will do any mortal thing for you except go to church.'[2] In this overcrowded and disorderly area, however, clergy of all denominations dwelt on 'the astounding goodness of bad people'[3] (Chapter Five). The Tractarians and Evangelicals were also united in abusing their predecessors in the eighteenth century. Yet it was in this century rather than the succeeding one, that far-seeing men were conscious of the growing complexity of society that threatened to overwhelm the individual. By his philosophy the saintly George Berkeley (1685–1753) tried to lift humanity from the morass of materialism by placing the world in the mind of man, and man in the mind of God. In staking all on the salvation of individual souls John Wesley found, as Mrs Siddons was doing, audiences attuned to lofty words; but William Blake's prophecy of a world in which countryside and humans would be submerged beneath slag was too monstrous for general acceptance.

By the mid-nineteenth century the Black Country was proving the accuracy of Blake's foreboding. As the countryside dwindled a nation of Esaus began to wonder if they had done right to barter their birthright to secure the establishment of industrial society which steadily eroded fields and woodlands

[1] *Report of the Church Congress, 1866*, see pp. 118–142, 'The Church in Relation to Rural Populations'.

[2] C. Booth, *Life and Labour of the People in London*, 1902, Third Series, Religious Influences, Vol. VI, p. 7, although not named it seems from the context that this remark was made by W. A. Morris, Vicar of South Lambeth 1891–1903.

[3] Ibid, Vol. IV, p. 42.

and boasted that, where hands were needed: 'Man is made as a Birmingham button'.[1] To escape from this man-made environment prolonged holidays by the sea or in the countryside became fashionable. (Chapter Six). Once holiday-making became a habit many felt, as Thomas Malthus and Matthew Arnold had forecast they would, that large families and machines were too much with them wherever they went in the United Kingdom, so they sought abroad the recreation and solitude denied them at home. Whether these tourists visited the Riviera, sailed up the west coast of Norway or down the Danube they helped to spread the urban civilisation from which they sought to escape (Chapter Seven). This was especially the case where, as not infrequently happened, they had been preceded by British engineers, mechanics and foremen.

If skilled workers were often without honour or adequate wages in their own country, the path of the early master manufacturers was far from smooth. Their undertakings were threatened by trade fluctuations, depressions and speculation. So hazardous was the course of the trader and the manufacturer that society comforted itself with the maxim, 'that nobody breaks who ought not to break; and if he do not make trade everything, it will make him nothing'.[2] This maxim was disproved by the wide interests of the Beaufoys, vinegar manufacturers of Lambeth. Few members of the family were untouched by the Romantic inspiration, yet in the 1740s Mark Beaufoy (1718–1782; plate 4), a Quaker from Bristol, established an undertaking which remained at Lambeth and in his family for two centuries (Chapter Four). The family temperament, in which fervour and the ability to master detail were combined, helps to explain the success of the Beaufoys in the spheres of politics and science as well as of industry. Perhaps the most gifted, and certainly the most loved, of them all was Mark Beaufoy (1764–1827) whose eldest child, Henriette Philippine, married in 1817 John, the son and heir of Captain Cudbert Thornhill. The activities of the old Quaker and his son were generated by imagination and sustained by disinterested and unremitting application.

Luckier than many founding fathers old Mark Beaufoy had

[1] R. W. Emerson, *English Traits*, 1856, Everyman ed., p. 49.
[2] Ibid., p. 42.

an exceptionally able progeny. That the gifts of his children were fully developed was due to their father's sympathetic understanding; and to the relaxed atmosphere of a household the head of which acted on his belief that happiness could only be attained by those willing 'quietly to acquiesce in every dispensation of Providence'.[1] The Quaker practised what he preached. When his ablest sons showed a disinclination to enter the vinegar business he made no attempt to coerce them. Profits from the Lambeth manufactory, however, enabled Henry (1750–1795) to enter Parliament where he supported parliamentary reform, religious toleration and was responsible for legislation which rehabilitated the British fishing industry, and Mark (1764–1827) to devote his life to scientific enterprises. These included the advocacy of the rifle in the Militia and schemes for reaching the North Pole.

Ardour was the keynote of young Mark's career. A runaway match with his cousin, Margaretta, necessitated a long sojourn in Switzerland. In his letters home Mark was determinedly matter of fact, 'as I have never been inspired you must excuse me not being froze to death on the Jungfrauenhorn or any other of the most elevated mountains'.[2] He achieved, nevertheless, the ascent of Mont Blanc under conditions which could not be described as genial: 'At last, however, but with a sort of apathy which scarcely admitted the sense of joy, we reached the summit of the mountain; when six of my guides, and with them my servant, threw themselves on their faces and were immediately asleep. I envied them their repose; but my anxiety to obtain a good observation for the latitude, subdued my wishes for indulgence.'

To the surprise of the guide, Mark's wife, who came with her first infant to watch the party set off, was as eager about the expedition as her husband. All through her life Margaretta kept in step with Mark's pursuits. To help him she became 'a good mathematician and practical astronomer, familiar with all the details of the observatory, the calculation of eclipses etc; and by method and strict economy of her time, while the domestic arrangements proceeded with perfect regu-

[1] Gwendolyn Beaufoy, *Leaves from a Beech Tree*, 1930, p. 93.

[2] Ibid., p. 169.

larity, she was never at a loss for leisure in furtherance of her husband's pursuits.'[1]

After a few hours' illness, Margaretta died in 1800. Her husband continued their joint studies, but never ceased to mourn for her: 'A few hours before he died, he spoke of her with emotion, which showed time had not caused the slightest diminution in his affection for this estimable woman.'

As well as making astronomical observations, Beaufoy, at the instigation of the Society for the Improvement in Naval Architecture, embarked on a series of experiments at the Greenland Dock which occupied him until the end of his life. The Society started with a fine flourish of encouragement and premiums, both of which soon faded away: 'The whole onus, therefore, of regular attendance from first to last, of conducting the processes (for he never absented himself a single day) was borne by Colonel Beaufoy, the assistant secretary to the Society, Mr James Scott and by Captain John Luard as often as his nautical duties would permit him to attend.' Beaufoy's disinterested zeal inspired those around him. A number of ship builders put their 'mechanical contrivances' at his disposal; but this friendly co-operation suffered a setback when one of the masters emigrated to America and another, whose care of his workers was exemplary, died as a result of a blow during a shipwrights' riot at Rotherhithe. After Beaufoy's death, Scott continued the laborious work of copying the experiments 'by candle light in the evenings after the business of the day was over.' Members of the Society for the Improvement of Naval Architecture were right in their surmise that the most fruitful results were to be obtained by 'ingenious men' meeting informally to 'amuse themselves in friendly conversation upon mathematical and mechanical subjects.'[2] That the French and later the Swedish should study naval architecture so seriously was taken as an instance of the unnecessary flurries into which

[1] Mark's son, Henry Benjamin Hanbury Beaufoy (1786–1851), gave a full account of his parents' activities in his preface to his publication of Mark Beaufoy's *Nautical and Hydraulic Experiments with Numerous Scientific Miscellanies*, 1834, Vol. I; the proposed Vols. II and III were never published.

[2] *Some Account of the Institution, Plan and Present State of the Society for the Improvement of Naval Architecture*, 1792, p. v. Among the 'ingenious men' earlier in the century was at least one woman. In 1762 Elizabeth Taylor took out a patent for tools for making blocks, pulleys and pins for the rigging of ships.

foreigners were constantly throwing themselves. The course of British maritime history at the end of the eighteenth century suggests this belief was not unfounded.

Scientific men at the turn of the nineteenth century could hardly have ventured into the vast unexplored fields before them had they not been impelled by the Romantic inspiration. Beaufoy's last venture proved him a true child of the times. At the age of sixty he made a balloon ascent which was then regarded in the light of a catharsis as well as a scientific exploit. When Charles Darwin considered the pros and cons of marrying, one of the objections he envisaged was that he would never make a balloon ascent.[1]

Beaufoy ended his days at Bushey and was buried in the churchyard of St John's, Stanmore. In this church and yard can be seen memorials to three families – the Thornhills, the Beaufoys and the Bensleys – whose lives and fortunes were to have a significant bearing on the destinies of the Thornhills (plate 7). One other memorial besides the skyed epitaph in St John's remains to Mark Beaufoy: an obelisk at Bushey, almost hidden by trees, showing the mean variations of the compass for neighbouring landmarks and the bearings and distances of more remote ones.

Many had difficulties in finding their bearings during the decades after Beaufoy's death in 1827. The hopes that peace would enable the nation to fulfil a noble destiny by reforms at home and by the wise direction of subject peoples in the ancient and new worlds were not altogether achieved. The dislocations and discontents of a changing society in Britain seemed beyond the reach of reform. Too often those seeking to find overseas a less trammelled way of life took with them the bitterness of religious controversy, the itch for speculation and the greed for land which had created the social scene from which emigrants were seeking to escape. With one exception the Thornhills who made their way in the 1860s and 1870s to India, New Zealand and the United States fell between two stools. They had lost the curiosity and the passionate urge for self-fulfilment which had drawn the young Cudbert Thornhill to sea; and their upbringing at Lyston, where Henriette

[1] *Autobiography of Charles Darwin (1809–1882)*, ed. Norah Barlow, 1958, p. 234.

Thornhill cared for the children of three of her sons (Chapter Two), and at Radley had not fostered the self-assertion and tenacity which might have enabled them to succeed overseas.

Though ridiculing the romantic sentiments of their grandparents, young people growing up in the 1850s did not find 'the practical spirit of the age' altogether to their taste. This was shown by the frantic enthusiasm which greeted Garibaldi on his visit to England in 1864. At every turn he was greeted by 'lusty, ringing cheers' and by bands playing 'Cheer, Boys, Cheer' and 'See, the Conquering Hero Comes'.[1] Young people resented the tendency to ridicule seemingly impractical heroism. Through the prism of mockery Byron's doomed heroes were distorted into Dickens' Augustus Moddle who was convinced 'that the sun had set upon him; that the billows had rolled over him; that the Car of Juggernaut had crushed him; and also that the deadly upas tree of Java had blighted him.'

Sarah Siddons, the arch-portrayer of the Romantic theme, was also responsible to some degree for the determined practicality of the mid-nineteenth century. If Mrs Siddons superbly voiced national emotions on momentous occasions, she could also call for beer in equally heart-rending tones. Despair became fashionable and penetrated into the parlour and the garden. As Mrs Siddons' garden was filled with: 'Evergreens, which, together with a few deciduous shrubs, were of the most sombre, sable and tragical cast, such as Box-trees, Fir, Privet, Phillyrea, Arbor Vitae, Holly, Cypress, the Red Cedar, Laurel, . . . Cneorum Tricoccum, or the "Widow-Wail"'[2], the popularity of mournful, and often dripping, shrubberies was established. When Mrs Elton wished to impress Emma with her gentility she alluded to the profusion of laurels around her brother-in-law's seat at Maple Grove.

This penetration of the tragical into domestic minutiae was open to ridicule. It was only too easy for Hablot Browne to portray Boz's 'poetical young man' sitting in a corner of the parlour and 'staring with very round eyes at the opposite

[1] *The Lambeth Observer and South London News*, 16 April 1864. Lambeth's welcome to Garibaldi was repeated wherever he went.

[2] T. Hogg, *A Concise and Practical Treatise on the Growth and Culture of the Carnation . . .* , 1824, p. 107.

wall'; and for Cruikshank to depict Gothic tales as the solace of a general servant sitting amidst the chaos of unwashed dishes.

The suppressed longing for heroes and excitement would have made the 'Age of Equipoise' a time of revolt if dissatisfied youth had not found an outlet overseas. This drain of the young and energetic meant that the pace at home was set by men like Gladstone, who were more concerned with the nation's book-keeping than its vision. Such an outlook, though economically justifiable, produced a cribbed and humdrum way of living which encouraged emigration and also generated fierce outbreaks of dissension and protest. As well as the values of their fore-fathers the generation growing up in the mid-nineteenth century lost the feeling of stability which, despite the prophets of woe produced by the French Revolution, had not been seriously threatened in a predominantly agricultural country. By determinedly maintaining the social groupings of the pre-industrial age the mid-Victorians were able to close their eyes to the fact that the rises and falls of individuals between the classes were making a mockery of the old distinctions. These eruptions were indeed encouraged by the great importance attached to individual effort: self-help, self-improvement and self-control. The rallying cry of the age was expressed by an ambitious young coster: 'Gee up Johnny, and away we go.' The trouble was that at the end of the century so many were uncertain in which direction they wished to travel.

This was the predicament of Captain Cudbert Thornhill's great-grandchildren. Of one thing, however, they were certain: that the happiness they had known with their grandmother, Henriette Philippine Thornhill, at Lyston in Essex could never by recaptured. As they roamed disconsolately through the world the young Thornhills regarded with favour only those aspects of the countryside which reminded them of their old home. When gazing over the luxuriant forests around Penang, Tal, Mrs Thornhill's eldest granddaughter, wrote that the scene:

> 'carried me back to dear old Lyston completely for the air was laden with the scent of flowers so like the spring at home when the seringa was all in blossom. It made me

think more about our happy old days there than I have done for a long time; when the boys used to come home for their holidays and poor Uncle George used to help Dearest cut down the dead wood and Aunt George used to sit out with Rita in the garden as a baby. . . . Dear me, how long ago it seems. I don't think we half realised what a happy time we had till those horrid days came when everything as at loggerheads and the poor boys left home and that was our first break up. Fancy it is ten years ago in September [1871] since that.'

CHAPTER TWO

Lyston Hall: 'Ideal Sweetness'

> . . . that at each season's birth,
> Still the enammell'd, or scorching earth
> Gave, as each morn or weary night would come,
> Ideal sweetness to my distant home:
>> Robert Bloomfield, *On Revisiting the Place of my Nativity*

Only when he started shoemaking in London did Robert Bloomfield (1766–1823) realise the extent to which the seasons had governed his life in Suffolk. Those who worked in the country took it for granted that the months should dictate their ploys. When Bloomfield died a hitherto unknown half-and-half world, neither town nor country, was beginning to emerge. Most of Henriette Philippine Thornhill's life was spent in these marchlands around London. Visits to Devon had given her a longing for the country, but only the last ten years of her life were spent in the promised land. In 1854 Mrs Thornhill moved to Lyston Hall,[1] on the borders of Essex and Suffolk, where she found a peace which helped her to bear the loss of two sons and their families in the Indian Mutiny and to establish for her surviving grandchildren the happiest home they were ever to know. To understand why Henriette Thornhill was called Dearest by all her grandchildren some account must be given of her life and surroundings before she reached the haven of 'dear old Lyston' (plates 9 and 10).

The first child of Mark and Margaretta Beaufoy, Henriette Philippine was born during their long visit to Switzerland; and as an infant she was carried to see her father start his ascent of Mont Blanc. The death of her mother left Henriette at the age of fifteen in charge of the household and of her

[1] The Thornhills often described their home as Liston, but throughout this work the current Post-Office spelling has been used.

brothers, Henry (1786–1851), Mark (1793–1854) and George (1796–1864), and sisters, Margaretta, Julia and Laura. The relationship of the children with their parents had been a happy one; absorbed in their common interests Mark and Margaretta had given their family a sustaining but undemanding affection. The loss of such a mother dimmed, but could not extinguish, the well-founded happiness of the home at Hackney. Mark's deep and lasting grief drew him even closer to his children to whom he was 'the dear Pip'; and caused him to place great reliance on his eldest daughter. Henriette managed the house-hold, tended the young ones, made shirts for her elder brothers and undertook all the little offices which are only missed when they are unfulfilled. Her life seemed one of unruffled calm and usefulness. This contentment was not achieved without a strug-gle. That Henriette, particularly in her old age, added to the gaiety of every assembly is explained by her philosophy of life. An expression of this appears in an undated letter written to Minnie for her birthday:

> 'Many returns of the day may the Almighty vouchsafe you. If you are His servant every day will bring you nearer to your Saviour. If you love Him with all your heart you will in every word and action try to obey His commandments. It is this alone will bring you near to Him and by which you can yourself certify that you are a Christian indeed; not in name only like the guest at the Great Supper. It is idle, therefore wicked, to bid you expect much happiness. Happiness is only found in doing, and in trying to enter the Strait Gate. Your home is in Heaven try to be worthy to enter in through the living Saviour, our Redeemer. Be wise while you are per-mitted to choose. Never say or do a thing you would not like to be known. My dear child, I wish I could warn you from those evil things I so deeply deplore having done and which all had their origin in the forgetfulness of God, our God, our exceeding joy. May His love be ever with you; His peace always in your heart.'

This peace enabled Henriette to throw herself whole-heartedly into the pleasures of her grandchildren during the winter before her death: 'A new set of books from Coombs' came yesterday. Dearest and Miss Ward read to us all the evening; we began *The Chelsea Bun House* . . . 'Dearest came downstairs into the drawing room this evening to see us dance. She did enjoy it so much and said it was the happiest evening she had spent for a long time' . . . 'Ellen had a gallop with Lethbridge [Willy's schoolfriend from Radley]. I danced with the small fry' . . . 'Aunt George danced away like anything' . . . 'we had a jolly dance after dinner then played grab and had singing.'

Henriette's movements before she settled at Lyston in July 1854 help to chart the chief stages not only of her life but also those of the steady outward movement from London by townsmen seeking to combine drinking syllabubs with their City avocations.

From Great George Street, where they settled on their return from Switzerland, the Beaufoys moved to the rural seclusion of Hackney Wick. Here sheep grazed on stretches of marshland and, according to Thackeray, 'every green rustic lane' led to a ladies' seminary[1] or, he might have added, a young gentlemen's academy. These ranged from Dr Newcombe's establishment for the sons of gentlemen and noblemen, to the Protestant Dissenters' College at Clapton. Here learned men, who included Joseph Priestley (1733–1804), endeavoured 'to extend the rays of science over the darkest region of ignorance.' But Priestley's gases often proved inflammable especially in an establishment where the masters were disputatious and the boys unruly. The college was closed and Priestley, having sought scientific and religious truth in chapels at Leeds and Birmingham and in Lansdowne's library at Bowood, moved to America 'In search of a soil *less* contaminated by despotic ferocity.'[2]

As his own and his brother's experiences at dissenting academies had left Mark Beaufoy with a poor opinion of formal education, he was not attracted by the academic renown of Hackney but by its proximity to the Greenland Dock where he was conducting his nautical experiments. Also Beaufoy felt

[1] W. M. Thackeray, *Miscellaneous Essays, Sketches and Reviews*, 1885, pp. 285–304 'The Professor' appeared in *Comic Tales and Sketches*, 1841.

[2] W. Robinson, *The History and Antiquities of the Parish of Hackney*, 1842, Vol. I, p. 140 for account of Dr Newcombe's establishment and Vol. II, pp. 290–293 for description of the Dissenters' College.

the whole family might enjoy the society of learned men and women who often appeared to a better advantage in a private than public setting. Henriette never forgot the description she heard from a traveller 'who had watched the movements of *two* great sea serpents that were fighting in the waves for about ten minutes' off one of the West Indian islands.[1]

In Hackney, as in other parishes near London where the influx of new men and ideas had been too rapid, local disputes were endemic. A sham fight arranged by the Hackney Volunteers with a neighbouring parish developed into an ugly riot; and the officers of the Hackney Militia were divided into two camps. As one of these formed an independent rifle corps,[2] the rift was probably not unconnected with Mark Beaufoy's enthusiasm for this weapon. The martial ardour displayed by Beaufoy, who later had a command in the Tower Hamlets Militia, was marked in all the Old Quaker's sons.

Not only did the plodding rustics often show unexpected spirit in the environs of London, but the countryside was also changing. At Hackney water power had attracted cloth mills which, when they utilised steam power, increased both their production and the turmoil of the district. In 1815 when his militia duties and practical work at the Greenland Dock were drawing to a close, Mark Beaufoy moved to the calmer realms of Bushey Heath, near Stanmore (plate 8). His son, Mark, was delighted with his sisters' description of the 'new residence: it apparently unites all the necessary requisites for happiness, comfort and gentility; besides the country is beautiful about Bushey Heath, and is I suppose a most excellent neighbourhood. The distance from London is not great and stage coaches probably pass and repass continually, and why cannot gentlemen ride in stages? I know not one objection.'[3] The young guardsman could not envisage the changes which the continually passing stage coaches were to bring to the countryside.

The metamorphosis of villages like South Lambeth, Hackney and Stanmore into suburbs indicates the pattern of

[1] Agnes Giberne, *A Lady of England*, the Life and Letters of Charlotte Maria Tucker, 1895, p. 129.

[2] W. Robinson, op. cit., Vol. I, pp. 244–5.

[3] Gwendolyn Beaufoy, *Leaves from a Beech Tree*, 1930, p. 221.

urban development in the first half of the nineteenth century. This growth was marked by the obvious spread of buildings and by the less immediately detectable emergence of a new mentality. The new houses were more easily described and accounted for than the adoption of new values.

Although the environs of London could not boast of country seats on the scale of those established in the more aristocratic counties, like Rutland, Staffordshire and Dorset, large landowners held considerable acreages around the capital. As the value of land rose in the second half of the eighteenth century, property owners were unwilling to sell, but were not averse to augmenting their incomes by letting long-established houses, often old farmhouses detached from their land, or by building new ones. Sometimes, however, creditors were so pressing that landowners were forced into making sales. Such occasions benefited men like Andrew Drummond who was able to buy Stanmore Park early in the eighteenth century. The Drummonds were then making their name and wealth in India where a century later they were still entrenched as officials, and also as landowners in Stanmore; but the family was becoming anxious to secure heiresses. There was little rejoicing therefore when in 1868 the Honourable James Drummond of the 1–14th Foot married Mrs Thornhill's granddaughter, Ellen, at Allahabad. After the Drummonds the Duke of Buckingham and Chandos was the chief landowner in Stanmore at the time of the Tithe Apportionment in 1839. As the duke was taking a headlong course to bankruptcy, he was lucky in having found a wealthy tenant, Robert Bensley, for the Manor House and fourteen acres of land. Providing they retained some vestiges of business sense, landowners around London found the letting of old houses or the building of new ones a profitable source of income. The search for semi-rural establishments was so general by the 1850s that letting and selling could no longer be conducted through newspapers or by solicitors, but were undertaken by the pioneer estate agent, George Robins, who disposed of 'earthly paradises' in the Cape Colony as well as in the United Kingdom. In districts where the well-to-do settled shops, highways and railroads soon followed. After a passage of a few years an amateur naturalist visited in 1859 his old collecting grounds within half a mile of Marble Arch: 'Looking northward, I could see nothing but houses . . . looking eastwards and westwards nothing but houses in course of erection and houses built. Looking to the south the railway embankment shut out the prospect as before. The hedges were gone, so were the song birds: the sharp click of the bricklayer's trowel was now the prevalent sound. The grass-field was turned into a square, laid out with flower-beds and fenced with an iron railing.'[1] The development had been profitable for the landowner but not for the bird-catcher: 'It's hard for a poor man to go to Finchley for birds that he could have catched at Holloway once, but people never thinks of that.'[2]

The falling value of agricultural land after 1875 accelerated the pace of urban development. By the 1880s the wooded heights of Stanmore had given place to: 'Such a peculiar country, neither country nor town. Here and there one comes on a lonely-looking secluded place as Stanmore Common, but directly afterwards one finds oneself in an interminable broad high road bordered by second-rate dilapidated houses . . . I can't think who lives in all those second-rate houses, there do not appear to be many inhabitants about.'[3]

This apparent lack of inhabitants was one of the most striking features of newly developed areas which experienced neither the bustle of the city streets nor the constant comings and goings of the village. The sense of unreality which was often engendered in such districts produced an outlook which Frederick Denison Maurice (1805–1872) described as Cockneyism. He used the term to describe his particular *bêtes noires*: those who lived in Hampstead cottages, lectured at the Surrey Institute, drank weak tea and indulged in Jacobinical principles and in criticism for its own sake.[4] Maurice was feeling his way towards describing a new community which was little concerned with either seasonal changes or the city ploys of

[1] *Once a Week*, 6 August, 1859, pp. 117–119, Albany Fonblanque junr., 'Sebastopol Villa.'

[2] H. Mayhew, *London Life and the London Poor*, 1851, Vol. II, p. 65.

[3] *The Journal of Beatrix Potter*, 1881–1897, transcribed by Leslie Linder, 1966, p. 99, the journey described was from a Hydropathic Establishment at Bushey to Kensington.

[4] *The Life and Letters of Frederick Denison Maurice*, ed. F. Maurice, 1884, Vol. I, p. 62.

buying and selling. A thoroughbred countryman, Robert Surtees (1805–1864) who tried to make his living in London, was equally critical of this half-and-half world. When the eponymous hero of *Mr Sponge's Sporting Tour* (1853) visited the country around Edgeware he found little farms with the appearance of 'inferior "villas" falling out of rank', and with 'a half-smart, half-seedy sort of look.' Those who cultivated the little holdings had an equally indeterminate aspect: 'They have the clownish dress and boorish gait of the regular "chaws", with a good deal of the quick, suspicious, sour sauciness of the low London resident.'

As the number of her grandchildren steadily increased Henriette felt justified in escaping from the world in which the less pleasing qualities of the town and country seemed combined. Even before the mid-nineteenth century home-keeping relations were pressed into imperial duties. The tasks of those who manned the rearguard posts by tending the children of absent parents were not without minor hazards. Amidst the cramped cottage elegancies of Westbourne Farm, Mrs Siddons found the exuberance of George John's children overwhelming, and the unpredictable behaviour of their ayah, or 'Black Patty', a source of constant anxiety. If guardians had their worries, the little Anglo-Indians in their charge often had sorrows which were almost unbearable. The feeling that they were quite abandoned which haunted the charges of Mrs Pipchin in *Dombey and Son* and of Kipling's Mrs Jennett was general. Many shivering children from India might have preferred to face the hazards of cholera, dysentery and sunstroke than those of home care. The fate of the young Thornhills was exceptional as the happiness of their Lyston days illuminated their whole lives. Whether they stood beside the Ganges or the Rangitata in New Zealand they noticed only those aspects of the scene which reminded them of the 'dear old place.'

The compilers of Post Office Directories were understandably cautious in their references to country mansions; they well knew that if omissions were resented, descriptions were seldom to the occupier's taste. The parish of Lyston, covering 643 acres with a population of 95 souls in 1861, only boasted of one house of substance: 'Lyston Hall, a handsome seat, is the residence of Mrs Thornhill.' County chroniclers were willing to concede that Lyston Hall was handsome, but preferred to dwell on the more eye-catching events associated with the history of the manor. These put into the shade the building in the mid-eighteenth century of a red-brick Italianate house, even though it was erected by the brother of a duke.

William Campbell, brother of the fourth Duke of Argyll, had the ability to carry out successfully an ambitious scheme. He adapted a style of architecture suited to a strong light and open countryside so that it appeared at home in the cloud-shadowed and wooded landscape of the Essex-Suffolk border. Built of red brick Lyston Hall with its four wings connected by arcades to the central square building was both comfortable and handsome. The Hall remained in the Campbell family until the 1840s when a Campbell heiress married Richard Lambert who added the property to the 300 acres he already held in the parish. Though long occupied by servants and short-term tenants, the Hall regained something of its former consequence with the arrival of Mrs Thornhill and her large family. This revival was short-lived as soon after the Thornhills departed in 1866 the Hall was burned down. The flames also consumed the last hopes of the exiled Thornhills whose happiest thoughts dwelt on Lyston and the possibilities of their acquiring a similar home in the English countryside. From New Zealand young Cudbert wrote: 'It is wretched to think of dear old Lyston being burnt'; while in Penang with her sick husband, his sister wondered how the Hall had survived the careless handling of candles by their old nurse: 'It is strange to think how Anne Jackson used to go on and nothing used to happen. I'm sure for Dearest's sake there must have been a special mercy against fire all that time. Often and often I have lain awake in a fright that she would be setting fire to something.'

Lyston Hall was rebuilt and reoccupied; but the Second World War brought deterioration of the fabric and then demolition (plates 9 and 10). Now only two wings remain to suggest the appearance of a house, enshrined in the hearts of all the Thornhills who grew up there. Trees have been felled in the park; but the lay-out of the walled kitchen garden remains much as it was when Minnie took visitors 'round the kitchen garden and they enjoyed the peaches very much.'

Before considering the activities of the grandchildren who filled but did not overcrowd the Hall during the school holidays, a muster of the inmates is necessary. This task can be facilitated by following in the footsteps of the census enumerator who, in June 1861, had a rough passage at the Hall. Of the twenty-four persons in the establishment, ten had been born in outlandish places. The enumerator sometimes made a dash at a name like 'Mysifroozie', but generally played for safety with 'East Indies.' The head of the household, Henriette Philippine Thornhill, spared him Neuchâtel and gave her place of birth as 'Switzerland, British.'

Staying with Mrs Thornhill were her son and daughter-in-law, Mark and Anne Thornhill, and eleven grandchildren. Mark and Anne had with them their six surviving children, Henry Mark, Edith, Annie, Margaret, Kitty and Ellen. Also at Lyston were the offspring, Henriette, Cudbert, William, Ellen, Henry Beaufoy,[1] Anna and John, of Cudbert and Ellen Thornhill, who were still in India; and the orphans, George, Minnie and Edward. The shadow of the Mutiny still hung over the gathering. In the summer of 1857 rumours of unrest in India had reached the relations at home of Anglo-Indians; by the autumn few believed the Government's assurances that the situation was under control. Only rumours reached the waiting, hoping and praying families in Great Britain until on 20 February 1858 when *The Suffolk and Essex News* and other local papers announced: 'A supplement of the *London Gazette* has been published containing additional lists of killed or wounded by the rebels in India, received at India House. This list fills nearly sixty pages of the *Gazette*, more than three of which contain names of those who were so inhumanely murdered at Cawnpore.'

Among those murdered at Cawnpore were Mrs Thornhill's eldest son, Robert, with his wife and two infant children; her youngest son, Henry, was shot with his wife and baby at Sitapur.[2] Some rhymes Robert wrote in India about his mother

---

[1] Always known as Henry Beaufoy to distinguish him from his cousin, Henry Mark Thornhill.

[2] For an account of the part played by the Thornhills in the Indian Mutiny see Chapter Eight.

suggest that Henriette Philippine had established with her sons
the same happy relationship she had known with her parents:

> 'And such a mother seldom shows her form
> To cheer us up, and drive away the storm.

           *   *   *

> Her form of late has grown rather stout
> Some 7, 8 or may be 12 feet about
> But all the same she is lovely to behold.'[1]

The death of Robert and Mary left their three surviving
children under the charge of Mrs Thornhill and her son, Cudbert. Their other grandmother, Mary Siddons, was also concerned about the orphans. The widow of George John lived at
Oldfield Cottage at Hampton Wick, where she was visited by
her numerous grandchildren and managed by her old cook.
When the home at Lyston broke up in 1866 she offered a home
to Minnie and Eddie: 'I write to ask where dearest Minnie
and Eddie are to reside and with whom? I often asked dearest
Mrs Thornhill if I could be of any use, either in a pecuniary,
or in any other manner, and her answer always was that her
son Cudbert had so entirely taken the orphans under his care,
that nothing more was required of me. I renew the offer now.'
The offer was not accepted. Minnie went to live with her Aunt
George Beaufoy in South Lambeth and Edward sailed to join
his brother and cousin in New Zealand.

While Mark and Anne Thornhill were in India, their children resided with a governess who sent Henriette Thornhill a
report concerning Henry Mark which forecast the fates of
nearly all the Thornhill boys: 'Poor little Henry Mark has
broken the small bone of his ankle . . . he says he was up a tree
when the boys cried: "Scramble for an apple!"; and, in getting down, his foot slipped between two branches and he
twisted his ankle. He cannot walk and is carried down to the

---

[1] Under this effort Robert Thornhill wrote: 'A fragment, composed in a
momentary fit of inspiration and filial affection on the receipt of his first
letter from his Mother after his marriage, which he read in the Cutcherry
[courthouse] and then forwarded to his wife.'
The date was probably early in 1840.

sea beach to sit there.' Somehow, when advantageous opportunities arose neither Henry Mark nor his cousins were able to
jump for them.

Although diffidence inhibited the young Thornhills, except
Henry Beaufoy, from prospering overseas, their life at Lyston
well prepared them for the rigours of foreign parts. The interests of the whole family, girls as well as boys, were centred on
out-of-door activities. These were pursued almost as a matter
of course since in Lyston and the neighbourhood, life still kept
in step with the seasons. By 1865, however, the pace was beginning to quicken: 'The train has been running all morning
between Lyston Mill and the Paper Mill. There are only
trucks at present; but it is horrid to have it so close, and we
can see it for some way in front of the house.'

The young Thornhills resented the intrusion on this stretch
of land beside the Stour. The boys bathed in the river, the girls
gathered forget-me-nots on the bank and the little ones were
always importunate in their demands to accompany them.
Their grandmother remained on good terms with all her
neighbours, even those responsible for the trucks. On 28
August 1865: 'Mr Hunt from the Paper Mill, Mr Baker from
Lyston Mill and Mr Ardley from Borley Mill all sent up some
eels today.' The attention rather than the offering was
appreciated; for a few days later Minnie noted: 'Ellen rather
seedy and sick; it must be the eels we had the other day.'

The onset of the machine invasion of the natural world was
accompanied by a frenzied enthusiasm for pet keeping which
was the only common interest of prince and pauper in mid-
Victorian England. Queen Victoria had her favourite bullfinch and, according to Mayhew, about 30,000 of these 'bold,
familiar, docile' birds were caught yearly for sale in the meanest streets of London. Loth to let her pets out of sight Anne
Beaufoy on a visit to her sister-in-law at Lyston 'brought her
three bullies; John, the footman, came down with her and
took care of them.' Later the bullies were to give place to a
parrot. Birds, animals and insects were kept as pets and also
collected as specimens. Butterfly collecting was considered
especially suitable for girls. The little princesses at the
Russian imperial court shocked the old Countess Tolstoy

by pinning their live trophies on their straw hats.[1]

That pet keeping with all its ancillary activities of hutch, cage and pen building should have so bewitched Victorian youth was largely due to the influence of *Swiss Family Robinson*. Written by a Swiss pastor to entertain, instruct and elevate his children, this book deservedly became a household favourite after its publication in English in the early nineteenth century. Its day-dreaming quality enabled *Swiss Family Robinson* to take the place of the eminently practical and down-to-earth *Robinson Crusoe* as the handbook of boys anxious to be prepared for every eventuality from candle making to finding a bride in the tree tops. The fascination of this tale of a family shipwrecked on an uninhabited island lies in the skilful blending of the exotic and the practical. Surrounded by giant creepers, palms and bamboos, the handy family Robinson constructed terrestrial and arboreal homes for themselves; and pens, cages and stalls for the wild buffaloes, asses, turkeys, jackals, monkeys and parrots which they had tamed. The ease with which settlements were established and surrounded with lowing, bleating and neighing stock turned the thoughts of boys first to pet keeping and then, often, to emigration.

At Lyston the boys and their Radley schoolfriends employed themselves during the holidays by digging ditches, building hutches and frames, training dogs and levelling a cricket ground; but these ploys which occupied them so happily in Essex lost their charms when they became bread-and-butter tasks in New Zealand. That life neither in India nor in New Zealand came up to the standards of the island on which the Robinsons were wrecked is suggested by two letters which Cudbert Thornhill senior wrote to his niece, Minnie: 'If persons described their life in India, they would simply say "we perspire" and that is the sum total' . . . 'the days pass so much alike that looking back from one week to another, I can hardly think of anything to tell you.' He then proceeded to give news of his nephew and his son who had just arrived in New Zealand. They could only find 'scanty accommodation,' the food was 'loathsome' and they had been obliged to dig a ditch

[1] Marie, Queen of Romania, *The Story of My Life*, 1934, Vol. I, see p. 20 for description of the Queen's bullfinch, 'such an angry little fellow'; and p. 103 for the entomological interests of the princesses.

which was 'beastly dirty work.' When Cudbert observed that 'I am certain it was not less cleanly than some of their amusements at Lyston,' he failed to perceive the great difference between getting covered with mud for fun and from necessity.

Dearest may not always have understood what pleasure her grandchildren could have found in many of their outdoor ploys or in their large collection of pets, but she regularly reported to the absent ones the progress of their birds and animals: 'The pigeons are well and Ellen feeds them; but the jackdaw has escaped and wisely refused to listen to the whistle, and the bits of meat intended to lure him into his miserable prison cage' . . . 'The turkey is better. I saw her just now settling like an invalid lady.' When writing to Minnie and Ellen, who were devoted to their ponies and to any horses which came their way, Dearest teasingly referred to the short-lived craze for horse meat: 'Poor old Dolly will tremble if, dear Ellen, your capabilities extend to horse meat on your return' . . . 'The Reverend Henry Bull [rector of Borley] and his lady took the opportunity of leaving their cards just now. I see Mr Bull rejoices in a horse . . . the horse's ears were pricked with great spirit, my Minnie.'

Henriette made no reference to the canary whose family cares Minnie made her own: 'Canary with topknot hatched one egg, she had five.' Advice concerning this anxious time was given by the editor of the *Boy's Own Paper* (11 November 1880) to a correspondent: 'No; leave the cock bird in while the hen is sitting so long as he conducts himself like a gentleman.'

One pet was to be found in every country house and also wherever the English travelled or settled: the tiresome dog whose misdeeds kept him continually in the limelight. At Lyston Rollo chased everything from the peacocks in the park to the neighbour's fowls: 'When we got to Mrs King's he went into the hen house and nearly killed one of the hens and Charles' pet cock.' Not content with these minor achievements he attacked sheep in the lane and 'pounced on a little lamb, the poor little thing lay down just as if it was dead; luckily Rollo did not bite it.' In his exuberance he knocked over a little cousin and also Minnie herself: 'Rollo in his delight at coming for a walk rushed up to me and knocked me down, rather too much of a good thing.'

Minnie and Ellen gave much time to their outdoor occupations which they sometimes permitted the 'small fry', or Anna and John, to share. Their happy potterings would have been restricted had not Dearest been a true Beaufoy in her opposition to intensive and systematic education. Between the departure of the fascinating Sarah Cookson in 1862 and the arrival of Miss Fricker in 1865, Anna and John only had spasmodic lessons: 'Dearest has been hearing John his lessons'. . . 'I have been giving Anna and John their first lesson in English Grammar, they have been very good and quiet . . . that lazy Ellen has been asleep on the easy chair in the schoolroom.' The imparting as well as the acquiring of knowledge in the mid-nineteenth century had a certain hit-or-miss quality which could spur earnest scholars to advance by their own efforts, but often resulted in the less industrious leaving the class or schoolroom remarkably ill-equipped. As she thought '£70 per annum a small stipend', Henrietta Fricker did not over exert herself with her teaching duties at Lyston Hall. These, however, were not onerous: 'Miss Fricker takes Anna and John in the morning directly after breakfast for almost an hour; then we have our singing lesson and on each alternate day one of us has a music lesson' . . . 'Miss Fricker came this morning and give us each a new song; mine is "I cannot sing the old songs" and Ellen's "Sweet is true Love though given in vain" '.

At Lyston lessons like other activities were regulated by the weather; on wet days studies were industriously pursued; the coachman cleaned the harness and, in the absence of the revealing sunlight, the household dusting was not done so carefully as usual.

Allowing for the vagaries of the weather, the seasons set the timetable for the year. In spring the church was decorated for Easter, the bees swarmed, rook shooting and croquet started. As the nights and days grew warmer the Thornhills could hardly bear to come indoors: 'Ellen and I thought we would stay out all night, it was so jolly'. Croquet continued through the summer, often by moon and candle light, the boys bathed in the river and the girls were 'very busy bottling and preserving the blackcurrants; we have filled six bottles and made eleven pots of jam,' and picking mushrooms. Before the boys returned to Radley in late September shooting had started and the Harvest Home Supper was celebrated. Though Tal and Ellen joined in the fun at one gathering, they felt rather neglected: 'We only had that one dance the whole time, Ellen did not dance at all . . . Then we went back to the tent and looked at the people dancing. Old Sturt wriggled about and made everyone laugh. Eddie, Willy and Richards [a Radley schoolfriend] came in the evening. They danced a good deal with the poor people . . . We did not come home till past twelve; we left the tent after they played "God Save the Queen", having had a most enjoyable day.'

The pace always slackened when the boys with their friends returned to school: 'Willy went back to Radley; it is horribly dull without him.' Their mild escapades made the whole household feel they were seeing life. Once the boys returned late to find themselves locked out: 'Ellen and I had to go down in our dressing-gowns and unlock the door for them. We had an awful scuffle to get upstairs again as they rattled the handle of the door to make us think they were coming; but they promised to give us so much time for going upstairs. I think it was past one.'

The Guy Fawkes celebrations opened the winter season. After being shown in Melford the Guy was brought up to the Hall: 'Mrs Jackson was very much amused by the old man telling her that last year poor Guy's white gloves were burnt, and they were obliged to get him a new pair.' Gathering round the bonfire on the gravel in front of the house was an occasion which the whole household could enjoy without being numbed by the cold which often spoilt the Christmas festivities. The children tried to play snowballs but 'John came in crying with the cold;' and his elders sometimes felt inclined to do the same indoors: 'We have done all the Christmas decorations in the hall this year and we found it a very draughty place, nearly everybody has had colds in consequence.' It is not surprising that 'Ellen and Mr Lethbridge [a Radley schoolfriend] had a game of shuttlecock and kept it up 354 times.' Dancing – waltzes, galops and lancers – was the favourite indoor exercise: 'I had several waltzes with Will, he is quite a swell.' Will was also, until he settled in New Zealand, remarkably hardy; on 12 December he 'had a bathe in the river before breakfast.' The season of coughing, sneezing and rubbing chilblains drew to a close with St Valentine's Day. Lively Ellen with her glorious auburn hair had bowled over the Radley schoolfriends one after another so, according to Minnie, the 14 February was the one day of the year when she rose early:

> She hastens down on the wings of love
> Her bed has no charms that morn
> Her sleep has been restless and disturbed
> She woke long fore it was dawn.

> Here's one from Will and one from Ned
> But here – and here's *the* one,
> I knew he'd send it as he said
> Well 't might have been for fun.'

It is strange that Henriette Thornhill most of whose life had been spent in the outskirts of London should have been as conscious as the psalmist of the roll of the seasons. This awareness is apparent in the instructions she left her grandchildren:

1. To Read Isaiah Chapter 58 every Saturday night.
2. To have furmety on the fourth Sunday in Lent.
   [Refreshment Sunday]
3. To have goose on Michaelmas Day.
4. To have, if possible, a bonfire on Guy Faux Day.
5. To have, if possible, roast beef and plum pudding for Sunday dinner.

That these ordinances were regularly carried out at Lyston Hall helped to impart to the young Thornhills a sense of timelessness and of security which they were never again to experience.

Regardless of the seasons the girls visited the cottagers of their little parish which, though seemingly remote from the stress of the world, knew all the cares of dwindling employment and low agricultural wages. Until she died, 'poor girl Eady' was visited almost daily by the Thornhills. This household well illustrated how the Indian summer of farming prosperity in the 1850s and 1860s did not always warm the cottage hearth. At forty-four the head of the household,

Charles Eady, was resigned to earning as an agricultural labourer a wage too low to support his family. That his son was obliged to face the same hopeless future was a shadow on the home, which was held together by Eady's wife and his three daughters under twenty. They all earned a pittance by straw plaiting. In the 1840s prices for twenty yards of straw plait varied between 3d and 10d;[1] but, though the numbers of straw plaiters were increasing two decades later, prices were beginning to fall. By the early twentieth century only the elderly could remember the distinctive smell of steeping straw which pervaded homes like the Eady's.

New opportunities did not come readily to men like Charles Eady who was born at Foxearth and had probably been working in the fields since he was ten; but his neighbour was more fortunate. Although Ambrose Snazell also came from a labouring family, he was a younger man and able to put himself within the orbit of opportunity in a way that had not been possible in Eady's youth. Railways may not have contributed so greatly as was once imagined to economic expansion, but they opened the world to the poor man. In 1861 Ambrose Snazell was employed as a porter in the best country labour exchange, a railway station. By 1867 Thomas Fisher was writing to Minnie that Snazell and his wife were off to London: 'He is to drive a van at 25s a week. I shall be sorry to lose the children out of our day school at the Lodge of Lyston Hall.'[2]

If an agricultural labourer wished to live comfortably by his craft he had to go as far afield as Upper Canada before he could earn £62 10s a year and write: 'I have my house free, firewood, the use of four cows and all the fowls, and one acre of land.'[3] Had this Glemsford man moved only to the nearest town he would have found a distress as great as in his own parish for his fellow villagers were walking to Sudbury to earn 7s 6d a week at velvet weaving. The once thriving velvet and silk industries of Sudbury could not compete with the north-

[1] *The Victoria History of Essex*, 1907, Vol. II. See pp. 375–379 for an account of the straw-plaiting industry.

[2] As Fisher omitted the date, the year has been estimated from the events to which the rector referred in his letter.

[3] *Suffolk and Essex Free Press*, 31 January 1856, quoting a letter by an emigrant from Glemsford, Suffolk.

ern textile factories; and the weaving of bunting was all that remained of the town's woollen trade. Despite the depression men still stuck to their looms with the cry 'anything . . . rather than go into the Bastille Union House.' The public acclaimed men who refused to leave a sinking ship, but seldom recognised the heroism of those who stood fast to the craft which for generations their forbears had practised. In 1866 eight to nine hundred silk weavers refused to leave their Sudbury looms to become absorbed in the textile factories of Derbyshire.[1]

Living from hand to mouth, weavers, shoe binders and straw plaiters dared not contemplate the future; but the shopkeepers of Sudbury were beginning to feel the warmth of the Gulf Stream of city wealth which was steadily flowing outward from the capital. The Thornhills were not the only emigrants from the city who seldom let a week pass without making some purchase in 'dear Sudbury.' The drapers in particular started to move with the times. In his old age Ichabod Nagg found himself able to employ five assistants; while parasols 'fashionable needlework, fancy beads and embroidery' appeared in the windows of his younger rivals, particularly in those of George Bridgeman who was much patronised by the Thornhills. New life was flowing into the shops: 'Tal and I went into Sudbury, we met all the world and his wife in the shape of three or four carriages and pairs.'

A similar renaissance of the shopkeeping interest was apparent in most country towns within fifty miles of the capital. Bromley in Kent lost its importance as a coaching centre, but gained the patronage of wealthy families, like the banking Normans, who were settling in the district; while the 'splendid parks and residences' around Basingstoke helped to give the town 'an air of comfort and thriving.'[2] Something of this appearance is still retained in the centre of Sudbury where the ornate Corn Exchange and the handsome proportions of the brick residences show that the burghers had no mean opinion of themselves or their town. But its fortunes had been founded by those who dwelt in the small stud-and-daub houses still standing in Weavers' Lane.

[1] *Suffolk and Essex Free Press*, 21 February 1856 for the weavers' fear of the Union House and 10 May 1866 for their refusal to emigrate to Derby.

[2] R. Mudie, *Hampshire*, 1838, Vol. II p. 37 and p. 40.

As the profits of small-town shopkeepers increased so did their aspirations to have a voice in local affairs. Vestry meetings were for minor local notabilities what the petty and quarter sessions were for the gentry: occasions on which they could make their weight felt. All parishioners had the right to meet yearly with the incumbent, usually at Easter, for the despatch of parish affairs, the most important of which was the election of church-wardens. As custodians of church property the wardens were officials of considerable consequence which had increased when they were made responsible for poor relief and, in many parishes, for paving, drainage and other activities concerned with sanitation.[1] Vestry meetings, at which outgoing wardens presented their accounts and new ones were elected, provided a useful forum for the airing of local opinions. Nonconforming parishioners had the right to attend these meetings until the abolition of the compulsory church rate in 1868 deprived them of this opportunity of polemical display. That few of these chances were missed is suggested by the brisk verbal exchange at a Lavenham Vestry meeting:

Mr Peek: 'No wonder that men, who only judge Christ through such institutions as state churches, should exclaim like Voltaire, "Crush the wretch." '

Mr Hitchcock: 'Well, Mr Peek, we confess you have taught us something.'

Mr Peek: 'Then, as honest men, you ought to pay me for the information imparted.'[2]

At the vestry meeting of St Gregory with St Peter, Sudbury, in 1856 John Sikes, a wine merchant and landholder, opposed the restoration of the church, for which he had subscribed £100, on the grounds that 'Popish chairs' had been substituted for the benches in the original plan. To this John William Henry Molyneux, perpetual curate 1855–1879, peremptorily replied that the question at issue did not concern the type of seating but whether all seats should be free, as he was determined they should be, or only a limited number. After an acrimonious discussion in which Samuel Higgs, a Nonconfor-

---

[1] The vestry's responsibility for poor relief was transferred to Boards of Guardians by the Poor Law Amendment Act of 1834.

[2] *Suffolk and Essex News*, 24 April 1858.

mist master weaver, played a prominent part and legal objections were raised, Molyneux declared with true new-broom vigour that his scheme should go forward and 'he cared for neither Bishop nor Archbishop.' He had early caught the tone of the district where the Independents had been prominent in the seventeenth century.[1]

The resurgence of country towns in the mid-nineteenth century is illustrated not only by the flowers of rhetoric at vestry meetings but also by the variety of public entertainment. The inhabitants of Sudbury had opportunities of hearing George Grossmith lecture on *David Copperfield* and Sir Charles Lyell on 'the Agency of Ice in the Transportation of Rocks', Spurgeon preach at the Baptist Chapel and Fanny Kemble, niece of Sarah Siddons, give readings from *Henry IV*. Spectacles were equally varied. They ranged from a clown being drawn 'on the river in a common tub . . . by four geese' to a grand Historical Panorama and views of India 'embracing representations of the principal cities of the Empire, and the chief features of the present Mutiny – events which have arrested and still continue to absorb so much of the public attention.[2]

Although she continued to show all her old interest in her grandchildren's activities, Henriette Thornhill's thoughts towards the end of her life often turned to India. Nothing gave her greater pleasure than a visit from Charlotte Tucker (1821–1893) whose family had been almost as long associated with India as the Thornhills: 'Dearest is but poorly; Miss Tucker has cheered her up very much. She is very kind and sits with her nearly all day.' Charlotte Tucker had lost the most gifted of her five brothers in India; and, when over fifty, she left England to continue the missionary work he had started. Her lively tales, published under the pseudonym A.L.O.E. (A Lady of England) proved as popular with Indian children as they had been with English ones; perhaps even more so as by the 1870s her simple fervour was losing its charm for children who were becoming accustomed to the more indirect approach of Mrs Gatty and Mrs Ewing. After the death of her old friend

[1] *Suffolk and Essex Free Press*, 27 March 1856, for report of vestry meeting.

[2] *The Essex Standard*, 7 January 1859; the *Suffolk and Essex News*, 13 February 1858 for description of the clown who was drawn by the geese for one mile in half an hour.

Charlotte Tucker wrote: 'It is a blessing, dear Minnie, to have known her, to have been loved by her, to have her example left behind! For how truly she was one of God's saints! . . . She seemed like one of the holy women of whom we read in the Bible.'

As well as recalling old friends and events with Charlotte Tucker, Dearest had long talks with her sister-in-law, Anne Beaufoy, on whose sense and capability she came greatly to depend: 'After lunch Aunt George sat with Dearest – private conversation – no admittance.' To avoid causing alarm when Dr Image was called from Bury St Edmunds, Henriette arranged for him to see also Henry Beaufoy, whose constant attacks of faintness and sickness were as taken for granted by the family as was his good temper. On 14 February 1866: 'Dearest had a Valentine from Henry Beaufoy, Ellen had four, I had three – from Ned, Willy and Henry B, Anna and John each had three, Miss Fricker two.' A month later Minnie wrote:

'Dearest Grandmama died this morning at quarter to seven. She passed away without a struggle, she seemed only in a calm and peaceful sleep . . . Ellen called us all at about half past six. Dearest was then breathing very gently. The breath gradually got shorter and shorter and then it ceased. Dearest seemed as if she had fallen into a quiet, peaceful sleep, her eyes shut and she looked so calm and tranquil – no expression of pain.' . . . 'It is such a dreadful blank we don't know what to do, so went round the garden and down the Park.'

The sense of loss and blankness increased the next day when a clerk arrived to take the inventory. On 20 March the whole household, including Anna and John, attended the funeral: 'Marky Beaufoy put the cross on the coffin as it was lowered and dear little Johnny a wreath . . . our little church was crowded. Dearest was beloved by everyone who knew her.'

The old, happy, protected world was breaking up completely: 'We have been packing nearly all day it is a fearful break up . . . our room is in an awful mess' . . . 'Poor old Dolly and Cheddy were shot; I felt so sorry particularly for dear old Doll.' . . . 'It makes me feel beastly to think we are going to leave this dear old place; it does look awfully pretty, such lovely weather and beautiful moonlight nights. . . . the house begins to look so desolate.' . . . 'Anna has given Mrs Foster her little canary.'

As they were driven away Minnie and Ellen leaned out of the pony chaise to keep Lyston in sight for as long as possible. They were conscious, as were all the Thornhills, that the golden days had ended. George and Cudbert were already in New Zealand, where they were soon to be joined by William and Edward. Tal was not finding life with her parents in India to her taste: 'I am sorry to say we have all to go out to fry and grill in those horrid plains . . . Goodness knows one feels slow enough'; while her little brother and sister, Anna and John, felt life to be equally slow with their Soltau relations at Clapham. Minnie and Ellen left Lyston for their new home at Caron Place in South Lambeth.

Occupied with their own sorrows and trials the Thornhills could not realise that a whole way of life, ruled by the seasons, was also passing. New tenants came to Lyston Hall, but few new families filled the homes which Lyston cottagers were leaving. Some of these houses crumbled into ruins and disappeared; others were replaced by Richard Lambert with the four-roomed brick cottages which still stand in Lyston Gardens and opposite the church. By the 1860s villages were ceasing to provide employment which would enable men and women to continue the slowly moving round of rural activity. The desolation took longer to reach the country towns; but by the end of the century there were signs that the distinctive small-town outlook was giving place to the half-and-half values described by Maurice and Surtees. Villagers, the inhabitants of small country towns and the Thornhills were all being forced, for better or for worse, into a wider sphere of activity. They could view themselves as either the dispossessed or the inheritors of a new civilisation.

CHAPTER THREE

The Country Parson

> The Country Parson is exceeding exact in his life, being holy, just, prudent, temperate, bold, grave in all his ways.
>
> G. Herbert, *A Priest to the Temple; or the Country Parson . . .* , 1652

> I have also played my part in the usual manner, as doctor, justice, road-maker, pacifier, preacher, farmer, neighbour and diner-out.
>
> Sydney Smith, writing on 1 June 1820 from Foston Rectory,
> York.

In considering the duties of the country parson both Herbert and Smith set their sights rather high. Few attained either the standard of piety prescribed by Herbert or the social eminence achieved by the rector of Foston. Even allowing for the exuberance of his fancy, Smith was right in setting such wide bounds to the country incumbent's sphere of activity. So long as the village was an important strand in the social fabric of the country, the parson was, as Herbert maintained, 'all to the parish and not only a pastor, but a lawyer also, and a physician'. It might be said that as his lay activities were circumscribed his spiritual influence declined. During the seventeenth and eighteenth centuries the country parson was a greater force in the parish than his successor in the late nineteenth century was to be.

Many reasons for the decline in the spiritual and social influence of rural incumbents were put forward at the 1886 Church Congress held at Wakefield.[1] Some familiar Aunt Sallys were resuscitated: 'the unsatisfactory character of the rural clergy . . . for at least two hundred and fifty years after

[1] *Report of the Church Congress 1886*, pp. 118–142, The Church in Relation to the Rural Populations.

the Reformation' . . . 'the terrible laziness which a quiet country parsonage is apt bring out, like a mould, over a minister's soul' . . . 'Nothing is harder on the country clergy than that they should have to go about begging or demanding . . . tithe payments' . . . 'the comparative failure in many places to enlist the co-operation, and kindle the enthusiasm of the laity in practical religious work.'

Also new targets for criticism appeared. The tennis-playing parson took the place of the fox-hunting one: 'The time, covering many months, spent by many appointed guides of souls *in lawn tennis would suffice to visit every farmhouse in England.*' Lack of imagination rather than lack of learning was blamed for many clerical failures: 'Dullness in a country pulpit is little less than a sin'.

The sense of dissatisfaction among many clergy, who felt they had been 'put into a parish where everything is green-mouldy and half a century behind', ranged from a feeling of malaise to suicidal despair. The basic reason for this green-mould syndrome was a dislike of country life. Some incumbents felt with Sydney Smith that such an existence 'might have done very well for Adam and Eve in Paradise, where the weather was fine, and the Beasts as numerous as in the Zoological Gardens, and the plants equal to anything in the Gardens about London; but I like a greater variety.'[1] But many rural incumbents were both happy and steadfast in their work; and a few were so happily rooted in their parishes that they were concerned to establish clerical dynasties. The widow of John Foster, rector of Foxearth 1845–1892, wrote in 1905 expressing the hope that a Foster would continue in the living: 'It is now about 60 years since it first came into the family and so many of our dear departed are laid in the churchyard and beside the memorial of a beautifully restored church. Lyston is still occupied by a Fisher; Borley and Pentlow by descendants of old Mr Bull.'

Minnie Thornhill passed through many country parishes as a visitor, and took an active part in the daily work and life of others. She watched the parochial wheels turning at Lyston and Foxearth, at Maxey in Northamptonshire and at

[1] S. Smith, *Selected Letters*, ed. Nowell C. Smith, World's Classics, 1956, pp. 242–3.

Bedminster, a suburb of Bristol. In the 1870s Bedminster still came within the definition of a country parish as being in 'the region beyond lamp posts', but it was fast becoming an urban slum. Before following in Minnie's footsteps through these parishes, something should be said about the predicament of even the country-loving rural incumbents in the mid-nineteenth century.

By the 1870s Sydney Smith's do-all parson was no longer administratively concerned with the poor, the roads and the schools. He was beginning to find himself in an isolated position, often deserted by the villagers, neglected by the squire and resented by the farmer. The second wave of dissenting enthusiasm was sweeping through the countryside leaving a trail of new or enlarged chapels and schools. These were supported by those who wanted to take a responsible part in the management of their church affairs and to hear preachers who were intimately concerned with the working life of the parish. Nonconformity was fostering a village aristocracy as surely as the Reformation had encouraged a landed one. This is illustrated by events in Iwerne Minster, a village in North Dorset, where Anne Beaufoy rented for the summer of 1873 Iwerne House from Thomas Bower the principal landowner in the parish.[1] This letting of their mansion was the sad prelude to the Bowers selling the conventual property they had purchased in the sixteenth century. Among the tenants able to purchase their holdings was Charles Short who belonged to a prominent shopkeeping family closely associated with the Baptist Chapel which had been enlarged in 1860. Equally a portent of the new age was Lord Wolverton, a member of the Glyn banking family, who purchased the greater part of the Bower estate. Though the genial and sociable John Acton, vicar of Iwerne 1860–1899, was able to adapt himself to the changed order, many incumbents found it hard to work with the new squires who often resented a rival power in the parish. With new men owning the old acres, with enterprising villagers becoming increasingly drawn to the chapel and with the need to approach, hat in hand, farmers for their tithe payments the country parson's lot was not a happy one.

[1] As a friend of the Thornhills at Radley, young Bower had stayed at Caron Place in South Lambeth.

Minnie's outlook on parochial and clerical activities reflected the lasting influence of her grandmother, Dearest. Although the parents of Henriette Philippine Beaufoy had joined the Established Church, she grew up in a household which retained the Quaker custom of a direct and spontaneous approach to God. When Minnie attended a Mission Service at Bedminster on 9 March 1879 she noted: 'Mr Ives took the first Mission Service. It was *quite perfect*; no one since Dearest died has so much made me think of the heartfelt, earnest prayers she used to say with us, as Mr Ives did that night, he made you *feel* all he said.'[1]

Although a governess refused to enter the Lyston household 'on the grounds of our being very High Church', Henriette Philippine Thornhill read Latimer's sermons as well as Froude; but the heartfelt love she felt towards God and her fellows lifted Dearest above controversial issues.

Their upbringing and the proximity of the church to Lyston Hall made it inevitable that the young Thornhills should play a considerable part in its affairs (plate 11). Their numbers and enthusiasm were rather overwhelming to the retiring Thomas Ruggles Fisher, rector of Lyston 1857–1893, though he was thankful for the support of Mrs Thornhill, whom he described as 'that grand old lady whose like I never did see'. To meet the wishes of the Hall Fisher arranged weekday services but sometimes his congregation failed him. In September 1865 Minnie wrote: 'We met Mr Fisher in the park waiting for his congregation, but as we had not dined none of us were going. We went for a turn in the moonlight after dinner. Mr Fisher had the church to himself. He is going to give it up on weekdays for the future.'

Minnie and Ellen took the lead in holding choir practices at the Hall, but often Fisher had other calls on his time: 'Little Smith and Ayer came up to practise but Mr Fisher did not, nor did any of the little Fishers.' This was not surprising as Fisher's seventh child, and fifth daughter, was born at 8 p m.

Throughout England changes were taking place which

[1] The sensibility of R. J. Ives was well used by the Church of England. He served in three parishes with outstanding social problems: Clewer near Windsor, Bedminster and the industrial parish of Roath near Cardiff. Ives' singleness of purpose impressed all classes of men from the labourers to the Earl of Devon whose domestic chaplain he became.

substituted the little Ayers and Smiths for the old village choirs. The desire to improve church music was general. The choral revival in the Anglican Church left little place for the village choristers and 'musicianers', drawn mainly from the artisans of the parish. Whatever their failings the old choirs with the clerk represented an active parish participation in church services. When the humble had no hope of playing an independent part in church affairs, many made their way to the chapels; and all the energies of churchmen in the second half of the century could not lure them back again.

After the Thornhills left in 1866 Fisher felt that 'so many empty pews look dreary'; but when they were filled by the new tenants of Lyston Hall, the Palmers, Fisher could hardly call his church his own. The Palmers were those enthusiasts for restoration whom Hardy described as regarding 'a church as a sort of villa to be made convenient and fashionable for the occupiers of the moment'.[1] When Minnie revisted Lyston in 1875 she found, as revenants often do, 'the lanes seem to have grown much narrower', and the church 'wonderfully improved, the Palmers have done so much for it.' They had, indeed. Between the Norman chancel and nave a screen was erected, a marble reredos was placed behind the altar on either side of which paintings of the apostles had been executed by Miss Palmer. A more serious assault on the ancient fabric of the church was the construction of a Palmer mortuary chapel to the north east and a vestry to the south east. But there were limits even in the 1860s to the tunes which could be called by those willing to pay for restoration. In March 1870 a notice had to be affixed to the church door announcing that additions, according to a plan of Henry Woodyer, had been made to the church by Lieutenant-Colonel Frederick Palmer; H.M. Scots Fusilier Guards, with the consent of T. R. Fisher, and that neither were aware 'that any licence or faculty for the works aforesaid were necessary.' The Thornhills were not guiltless of unlicensed alterations. A fourteenth-century piscina was covered with a marble memorial to Robert and Henry who, with their families, were slaughtered during the

[1] T. Hardy, *Personal Writings*, ed. H. Orel, 1967, p. 217, from Hardy's paper on Memories of Church Restoration read to the Society for the Protection of Ancient Buildings, June 1906.

Indian Mutiny. The glass in the east window, in which a Reckitt's blue was the predominant colour, was inserted in memory of George Beaufoy who died at Lyston in 1864.

Even more lavish restorations were carried on at the neighbouring church of Foxearth (plate 12). Though these were undertaken by Joseph Clarke, the whole of the astonishing interior reflects the Italianate taste and English sorrows of John Foster, rector of Foxearth 1845–1892, half of whose family was carried off by consumption. Foster's Low Church neighbour, Henry Bull of Borley, who considered that Popery 'was a translated Paganism',[1] may well have felt that Foxearth parish church had been given over to heathen deities. The interior walls were almost completely covered with paintings of saints, mostly female, in subdued colours on a gold background. To see these ranks of pale and attenuated figures is to hear a long, low sigh. Happily the figures of the rector's moving requiem have been restored so that future generations may know how effectively Victorian design could, but seldom did, recapture the 'strange disquietude' which Ruskin considered the great characteristic of Gothic art.

Although he had not Foster's means and sensibility, Fisher was determined not to be left in the Protestant wake with 'old Mr Bull'. But between high-handed patrons and apathetic villagers the going was hard. The same old sad cares continued to occupy the minds of his parishioners. To cheer Minnie after she had left 'the dear old place', Fisher sent her local news: Mrs Snazzle's baby had died from whooping cough, Mrs Tyler had lost her child, and the baby of the eldest Eady was born dead. Mrs King was 'no worse', but Miss Gibbons was failing and Miss Almack 'dangerously ill'. The vicar had little heart left for the pleasures – croquet, singing and social gatherings – which he had enjoyed with the Thornhills; and he concluded by describing himself 'as stay-at-home as ever'.

Fisher had succumbed to the mould of the long, low rectory built of purple-hued bricks. But Foxearth Rectory, despite the many sorrows of the Fosters, had the welcoming appearance of a house much used for entertaining. The

---

[1] *Essex Standard*, 1 July 1859, reporting Bull's speech to the Sudbury Protestant Association.

Fosters sheltered families, like the Merciers,[1] in difficulties and entertained the whole neighbourhood. Villagers enjoyed the Harvest Home suppers where 'a sufficiency of good brown ale, with tea, buns and cake, good music and plenty of harmless fun were provided.'[2] The well-wooded rectory garden was ideal for young people. Willy Foster was not pleased at being noticed 'sitting with a young lady under a tree; he pretended not to see us. I think he must be engaged to her as they were so awfully spoony, the whole time he never left her side.' Three years later Willie died in Italy.

Though as young men Fisher and Foster shared the concern to add to the dignity of their offices and the dimensions of their churches, their differences in temperament and income drew them apart. In 1875 Minnie found 'the Fosters and Fishers don't visit now.'

The incumbents of Lyston and Foxearth were both susceptible to the trends of their times, but these hardly touched Charles Cookson, vicar of Maxey in Northamptonshire 1833–1881. Minnie frequently visited the vicarage as she was close friends with the vicar's homekeeping daughter, Minta. Cookson's formative years were passed at Oriel College, Oxford, at a time when church reform was discussed as an academic rather than a spiritual exercise, so that the warning cries that the Church of England was being undermined by 'the emissaries of the Great Harlot' or by 'odious Protestantism' left him unmoved. He drove regularly into Peterborough, where he had been a minor canon and a prison chaplain, and into Market Deeping, where he was shaved; he restored his church with loving care rather than by ecclesiological theories, he cared for the poor and enjoyed his nightly rubber.

Outwardly Maxey was an idyllic village of irregularly placed thatched cottages. The rambling stone vicarage, which still remains, overlooked to the south a small stretch of parkland where in April 1871 'the dear nightingale was singing all morning.' To the north stretched the watery pastures of the fens. Their antiquity and their stillness gave an elegiac quality to the small farms on the boundary between

[1] See p. 161 *infra.*
[2] *Essex Standard*, 16 September 1859.

Northamptonshire and Lincolnshire. In April 1871 Minnie visited Crowland.

> 'in the very heart of the fens. The country is as flat as it is possible to be with such long straight roads. The little town itself is most wretched; nothing to be seen but the very poorest people and such wretched houses. The men stood and gaped at us with open mouths and their hands in their pockets. There was a funeral going on when we reached the abbey so we walked back into the town. There is a wonderful bridge in the town, it has three arches joined into one centre (the clerk told us it was meant to represent the Holy Trinity). Mr Cookson says the streets used to be ditches, so the bridge was made that you might cross the water. He remembers it. The abbey is very fine; it is still the only church they have.'

There was more hope in the overcrowded and clamorous alleys of South Lambeth than in the still and melancholy villages of the Fens. Even in the large and comparatively thriving Maxey it was impossible to escape from the mournful aspect of the countryside. The massive blocks of grey stone gave the isolated parish church of St Peter the appearance of a fortress built in a desperate attempt to stay a fast oncoming assault from humans or from water. Attempts to check the onslaught of misfortune in this desolate area seemed unavailing to John Clare, a native of the district. To him the very willows stood 'like the remains of a wreck telling where their fellows foundered in the Ocean of Time.[1] Many incumbents felt that their poorest parishioners were destined to sink and rot like the trees, so that the controversial issues around Peterborough were social rather than ecclesiastical. Because of its social implications, the provision of free seating in churches was discussed with such prolix and vehement dialectics that on 28 November 1874 the editor of the *Peterborough Advertiser* ruled that: 'Any further communication on this subject must be paid for as an advertisement.' Foremost in the fray was Henry Burgess, vicar of St Andrew's, Whittlesey. With rolling periods and scriptural texts he denounced alike churchgoers 'who could not endure the contact of broadcloth with fustian', far-

---

[1] *The Prose of John Clare*, ed. J. W. and A. Tibble, 1951, p. 241. The line appears in a description of the countryside around Maxey in the autumn.

mers who employed gangs of children in the fields and those who opposed the formation of agricultural unions. That on this last issue he offended many, including William Magee, Bishop of Peterborough 1868–1891, was no deterrent to Burgess who was determined to escape the condemnation: 'Woe unto you when all men speak well of you'.[1] Burgess considered that the agricultural rot set in with the gangs of children who worked in the fields for nine months of the year. These 'children of Hell' often started work when they were five years old and could be seen on Saturday forlornly 'going from one beer house to another, seeking their driver for their week's wages at 10 o'clock at night.'[2] The children were paid off in their early teens when they had grown too unmanageable for any prospect of regular employment. During his lifetime few listened to John Clare who had shared the sufferings of his fellow labourers:

> 'Toiling in naked fields,
> Where no bush or shelter yields,
> Needy Labour dithering stands,
> Beats and blows his numbing hands;
> And upon the crumping snows
> Stamps, in vain, to warm his toes.'

Winter invested even the thick walls of Maxey Vicarage where in the bitter November of 1874 it was 'awfully cold . . . Yer Pa [nickname for Charles Cookson] feels the cold very much and has taken to his warm cloak indoors'. Cookson's winter sufferings made him feel for his parishioners and he left £98 in consols to buy coal for the poor widows of Maxey. In the 1870s the strong and able suffered with the weak. It was not only in Crowland that men stood around with their hands in their pockets. Even before the depression of the late 1870s farmers relied on gangs rather than regularly employed day labourers. Determination rather than profit enabled some cottage cultivators, among whom was Clare's wife, to retain their small holdings. But it was clear even to these dedicated toilers that their children would have to work

---

[1] *Peterborough Advertiser*, 28 November 1874.

[2] *Peterborough Advertiser*, 20 August 1862, letter from Thomas Hutton, Stilton Rectory.

off the land. But where? Once the railways had been built they absorbed mainly imported labour. In 1861 of the six railway officials at Helpston, Clare's birthplace, only one came from the immediate neighbourhood. Shoemaking had not spread into the north of the county and even in the 1840s was barely sustaining the home workers of Northampton where the long-haired and bearded shoemakers worked in rags;[1] and lace making was confined to the south of the county. Even that great concern of the Shires, hunting, brought bustle and trade mainly to the district lying south west of Peterborough. Here in the 1870s the Empress of Austria hunted with the Pytchely, but her attempts to outride care were as vain as those of the poorest labourer in the district.

After the restoration of the church, Cookson's chief concern was the school. Maxey village school was established in 1833 by John James who had been headmaster at Oundle and took a busman's holiday by occupying himself with village education while vicar of Maxey. The original school was probably enlarged under Cookson as the gables and pointed windows have the appearance of nineteenth-century Gothic. Since no school master or mistress was resident in Maxey in 1851 or 1861 the burden of teaching must have fallen on the vicar and his daughters. Though attendance in schools was often resented in clerical households as forced labour, the Education Act of 1871 which brought the possibility of an order of release was far from popular. By this act locally elected boards, on which the incumbent generally sat, were empowered to establish schools where none existed or where existing establishments failed in efficiency. The dilemma of a self-assured and illiterate board member examining the children provided *Punch* with jokes for many years. Maxey school was taken over by a board and Cookson shared the general opinion of the new managers: 'Yer Pa was amused with a board meeting'.

That age mellowed the vicar's outlook is suggested by the two photographs of him in the vestry of Maxey church. In middle age he is shown with a set and lowering expression, which was probably due to his anxiety to maintain the image

[1] *The Family Economist*, 1851, Vol. IV, pp. 87–88 quoting from an article in the *Morning Chronicle* where the author attributed the squalor of shoemakers' dwellings to 'the dissipated habits of their occupiers'.

of a hard-headed Yorkshireman, and wearing a high, stiff collar and highly buttoned waistcoat. In old age his whole appearance was more relaxed, his hair was longer and the former stiff set of his clothes softened by his 'warm cloak'. Clearly as an old man Cookson enjoyed the champagne sent by friends and his evening games of écarté and whist.

As in most well-to-do households, the days at Maxey vicarage were regulated by a timetable: prayers at 9 a.m, breakfast at 9.10, dinner 1.30, tea 6, supper 9 and bed at 10.30. Only the presence of servants made it possible to prescribe these set hours for meals, the times of which might vary according to the household but not the regularity with which they appeared. Into this timetable Minta had to fit parish visiting, teaching in Sunday school, playing the harmonium in church and taking choir practice. Had the old choirs been retained villagers would have shown greater interest in church services and clerical households would have been relieved of a constant intrusion. When 'Minta had a lot of her little school children in to sing this evening to practise', the whole of Maxey knew what the Cooksons were having for supper. Time also had to be found for reading, sketching, shopping expeditions, sewing and the daily walk of four miles prescribed by a London doctor as Minta had been 'suffering from her heart for sometime'. During Minnie's visits to Maxey, the girls read *The Tale of Two Cities, Adam Bede, Don Quixote*, 'as it was considered the thing to be done', Wilkie Collins' *Poor Miss Finch, Rob Roy*, George Lawrence's *Guy Livingston, Breakspear* and *Toilers of the Deep*. Not content with reading in the carriage: 'Minta behaved very badly in the night. She woke up, lit a candle and read Shakespeare for over an hour'.

The most well planned timetables were disrupted by domestic crises. John Clare had been 'very fearful' of the 'haunted spots' around Maxey, so there was some excuse for the alarms of 6 May 1872: 'We had such a fright at about half past 8 by both the maids rushing and tumbling downstairs, screaming with all their might, and saying that, as they were turning down the bed in Minta's room, a figure came out of the cupboard. Mr Cookson went boldly upstairs and we all followed, Minta and Miss Young each with a poker in their hands. After looking about, under the bed etc. we opened the cupboard and out walked the cat!' The vicarage cat caused trouble below as well as above stairs. Shut in the cellar at Christmas time, the cat in jumping on a barrel turned on a tap so 'enough beer ran out to flood the floor'.

This accident was particularly vexatious as Christmas was near with its bustle of extra choir practices and church decorating which had assumed massive proportions. As early as the 1840s 'Christmasing' had become a big event for city costers: 'Then look, . . . what's spent on a Christmasing the churches . . . I hope there'll be no "No Popery" nonsense against Christmasing this year. I'm always sorry when there's anything of that kind afloat, because it's frequently a hindrance to business . . . St Paul's . . . would take £50 at least, aye, more, when I think of it, nearer £100.'[1]

The 'No Popery' men lost the day and flowers invaded the church. At St John's, Bedminster, during the octave of St John the Baptist, twelve 'beautiful vases' mainly filled with roses stood by the altar; while 'on the ledge of the reredos were four smaller vases of flowers upon a mat of ivy leaves.'[2] The increasing use of flowers in vases helped the florist and did no harm to the church. But the hanging of heavy holly branches and of red flannel showing 'texts and devices in holly or ivy' was a serious menace to the fabric of ancient buildings. Thomas Hardy commented on the harm done: 'The battalion of young ladies to whom the decking with holly and ivy is usually entrusted seem possessed with the fixed idea that nails may be driven not only into old oak and into the joints of masonry, but into the freestone itself if you only hit hard enough'.[3]

At Maxey Minnie became familiar with the day-to-day activities of parsonage life. During her travels, and particularly when Anne Beaufoy swept her entourage into south-west England, she realised how many variations could be played on the country-parson theme. At Iwerne House Mrs Beaufoy enjoyed all the attention due to the friend and tenant of a well-liked landowner. Among the leading families of the district who called on Mrs Beaufoy was Archdeacon Huxtable, rector of

[1] Henry Mayhew, *London Labour and the London Poor,* 1851, Vol. I, p. 141.

[2] *Bedminster Parish Magazine,* Vol. I, July 1873.

[3] T. Hardy, op. cit., p. 213.

Sutton Waldron 1834–1883. It was hard to imagine that this frail and kindly old man had once set the county in an uproar with his 'rural sums'. Scientific farming was Anthony Huxtable's answer to the problems of both labourers and landowners after the repeal of the Corn Laws.

On a desolate sweep of chalk downland he established a farming unit that would not have looked out of place in Manchester. A tall chimney dominated 'an extensive range of buildings' and a steam engine was kept constantly at work driving machines for cutting, grinding, bruising and winnowing. At night the remaining steam cooked roots for the pigs. Like the Manchester mill workers, pigs, cows and sheep had to adjust themselves to a mechanical life; their days and nights were spent on 'sparred boards' or concrete. As Huxtable never revealed whether his experiments made a profit or loss, controversialists had a field day.

Once the farms were in working order Huxtable relinquished his constant supervision of the project which he considered 'lawful for a clergyman only under exceptional circumstances.' Having brought farm management up to date, Huxtable started to pull the local clergy off their shelves where, as a speaker remarked at the 1886 Church Congress, they had grown 'a little dusty.' Feeling that in a questioning age rural incumbents did not always give a good account of themselves, the archdeacon established debating clubs to secure 'both theological and exegetical improvement'. Having shown the farmers how to make profits and the clergy how to return ready answers to their disbelieving questioners, Huxtable turned his energies to church restoration and overseas missions. It is not surprising that the archdeacon was subject to those 'accesses of nervous prostration' which attacked so many mid-nineteenth century pastors. By 1873 Huxtable only passed the summer months in his cure, little thinking that his indoor farming would cease to be a parish joke and become a national reality.[1]

[1] Details of Anthony Huxtable's life appear in the *Dorset County Chronicle*, 27 December 1883, *The Western Gazette*, 19 December 1883; and of his farming experiments in the *Journal of the Royal Agricultural Society*, 1854, Vol. XV, pt. II, pp. 389–454, L. H. Ruegg, 'Farming in Dorset', and in his own controversial pamphlet, *The Present Prices*, 2nd ed. 1850, 34 pp.

So well was Aunt George satisfied with her excursion into county society that she determined to repeat it. For the summers of 1876 and 1877, years of crucial importance as her son, Mark, came of age in 1875 and Rita came out a year later, she rented Donhead Hall on the Dorset-Wiltshire border from John du Boulay (plate 13). The earnest outlook of this Huguenot family was shown by Bertha du Boulay who, as wife of Charles Powlett Lane, provided tea and Bible readings for the British soldiers in India.

The handsome proportions of Donhead Hall provided a suitable setting for Aunt George and Rita when they sallied forth 'looking fearful swells in their Goodwood dresses.' This splendour was not unconnected with the fact that at a not distant village had settled Mark Thornhill with his second wife and lively daughters who were also anxious to shine in the county firmament. No gathering was too humble to afford opportunities for display; and both families attended the feast of the Donhead St Mary club on 10 August. The box with the weekly subscriptions from working men for the year was 'broken' to provide a frolic, when club members pushed aside for a day their fears of old age, accidents and sickness. As the club was supported by the local gentry, the celebration was unusually festive. 'The bells have been ringing and the band playing all the morning. The band came and played up here just before luncheon. Aunt George gave them £1 1s 0d. It is a grand day for the rustics. The festivities today were held at Mrs Graves' Charlton House. They had dinner at 3 o'clock. We went . . . about 5.30. They danced on the lawn . . . The gentlefolk did not join in the round dances. Nearly all our maids went to join in the fun . . . We had supper about 9 o'clock. The old rector escorted in Aunt George and Rita, . . . We came home about 10 o'clock.'

The old rector, Richard White Blackmore, had succeeded his father, whose incumbency started in 1817. Some of Blackmore's parishioners, including Minnie, envied the go-ahead activities in the neighbouring parish of Donhead St Andrew: 'I do wish this was our church instead of Mr Blackmore's. He is so very Low I must say, though I dislike the term.' Both the Blackmores followed in the footsteps of their famous predecessor, Praying Ince, who, ejected from

Donhead St Mary after the Restoration, continued his ministrations in barns and under hedgerows.

As a young man, Richard White Blackmore had struck out for himself, and he spent twenty-two years in Russia as chaplain to the Russia Company. The onion-shaped domes, the 'sumptuous' rites of the Eastern Church and the 'brave and hardy' peoples of Russia bewitched the young chaplain. Above all Blackmore admired the ancient and sure foundations of the Eastern Church which 'counterbalanced all the evil consequences of any partial deficiencies in the men themselves . . . may not we clergy of the Church of England learn something from this example?'[1] It was too late to teach the old dog new tricks for since its foundation the Church of England had produced men who were convinced that 'any partial deficiencies' arose from the establishment rather than themselves.

The Rectory, Donhead St Mary.

Though they were unfashionable in the 1870s, 'very Low' incumbents were often architectural blessings, as they saved church antiquities from the destroying hand of restorers determined to clear away ecclesiastical lumber. The Blackmores left untouched the splendour of their rectory and the simplicity of their church.

[1] R. W. Blackmore, translation of A. N. Mouravieff, *A History of the Church in Russia*, 1842, pp. XV–XVI of translator's preface.

In St Mary's were memorials to the two Burlton brothers, both of whom had been well known to Mark Thornhill during the Mutiny. Francis died from the effects of his sojourn in 'the beleaguered fortress of Agra'; while Philip 'was basely murdered by a party of his regiment employed as treasure escort under his command at Muttra'. Philip Burlton's body lay unburied until Mark Thornhill found it 'lying on its back with the arms upraised, the hands were untouched; surmounting the fleshless arms they had the appearance of gloves, and gave to the skeleton an air of ghastly masquerade . . . The picture was very horrible, but I could not dispel it – for some days it continued to haunt me.'[1]

Perhaps the course of Empire-building is more clearly charted in church memorials than anywhere else. One memorial in Bath Abbey is also a reminder of the numbers of children's lives which were lost as their parents spread over the globe. In May 1860 a mother returning home from India lost two infants at sea, her husband died at the Cape of Good Hope 'from the effects of exposure during the Indian Mutiny', and her youngest daughter died soon after the family's arrival in England. India was a recognised graveyard for children but they did not always thrive in more invigorating climates. A settler who lost her child in New Zealand was told in a matter-of-fact way that 'infants born in Christchurch during the Autumn often die.'[2]

The same could be said of infants born at any time of the year in Bedminster, a dockside and industrial suburb of Bristol. Here Minnie frequently visited her cousin, Rose, who had married Henry George Eland, vicar of Bedminster 1852–1881.

To meet the spiritual needs of a district notorious for body-stealing and for the 'low debauchery' of the Bedminster Revels on Whit Monday, the Parliamentary Commissioners made a grant early in the nineteenth century for the improvement of the 'mean edifice' of St Paul's. Henry Eland went further and rebuilt the church; the new building, with the addition of a handsome carved reredos, was ready for consecration in

---

[1] M. Thornhill, *The Personal Adventures . . . of a Magistrate during The Indian Mutiny*, 1884, p. 75. J. W. Kaye, *The History of the Sepoy War*, 1876, Vol. III, p. 241, gave the name incorrectly as Boulton, *Quandoque bonus dormitat Homerus*.

[2] Lady F. N. Barker, *Station Life in New Zealand*, 1870, p. 53.

August 1855. Those concerned with the Anglican revival constantly stressed the fact that they were restorers rather than innovators. But the seemingly radical changes they often advocated gave their proposals a revolutionary aspect which was far from unpleasing in cities which, like Bristol, had a long history of turbulent opposition to authority. Eland with his moderate Tractarian sympathies, would not have been averse to a reredos; but the whole charge of the installation of this 'novel feature' in the restored St Paul's was borne by two wealthy and influential parishioners, W. Fripp and Robert Phippen, a High Sheriff and a former Mayor of Bristol. The immediate emergence of two parties, those supporting and those opposing the 'richly sculptured reredos' was inevitable. Though officially deploring that 'the smouldering contention between the two parties . . . burst forth into a fierce flame' at the stormy meeting at the Bedminster Temperance Hall on Wednesday 1 August 1855, the reporter of the *Bristol Mercury* obviously enjoyed himself more than he would have done in reporting the usual run of Temperance meetings. A member of the Pinney family, long connected in Bristol with slaves and sugar, led the 'anti-reredosites' and presided over the meeting which soon ran 'into brawling excitement, turmoil and rancour.' Pinney and his supporters were vehemently opposed from the floor by Robert Phippen who refused 'to act like a gentleman . . . and behave like a man' by speaking from the platform. He was not unwise as none of the speakers could be heard through the 'noise caused by shouts, groans and stampings' and by members of the audience jumping on forms, some of which 'gave way with a loud crash'. But all this heat was not entirely generated by religious zeal. The reredos only gave an air of respectability to the old city quarrel between the conservatives and radicals. The cloven hoof showed itself when Pinney likened Phippen to Orator Hunt, and Phippen responded by attacking 'puritans of the modern days' who denied the working man his Sunday recreations, and by declaring that: 'He had always resided among his poorer neighbours, and was never afraid or ashamed to appear amongst them (cheers and groans).' Much steam was let off and the reredos remained. Eland's church was destroyed by fire in the Second World War. The white-washed simplicity of the new church, dedicated in 1958, the plain wooden altar and the absence of a reredos suggest that the last word was with Pinney rather than Phippen.

When Rose came to Bedminster in 1857 the smoke of the battle for the reredos had drifted away. Eland's church tower dominated one of the main approaches to the city and the new vicarage, 'such a pretty house', stood in its shadow. Although now the offices of a funeral director and quite unapproachable across the fields as it was in the 1870s, the grey stone vicarage still has considerable charm. The front aspect with its gables and bay windows is pleasing, but the rambling and gloomy rear quarters suggest both inconvenience and discomfort. A fine beech and parts of a stone wall remain from the garden which Rose loved and tended more carefully than her house.

The vicarage and a few surrounding streets of Southville, reputedly built on earth thrown up during the excavation of the Cut, formed an island of stability in the surging sea of Bedminster. When Phippen declared he would stand by his poorer neighbours he was thinking not so much of those living in the vicinity of his home in Church Lane but in the alleys and courtyards branching off the main thoroughfares and straggling into fields and market gardens. The meanest of these alleys were often inhabited by labourers, many of whom were drawn from the countryside. Unless they had some means, countrymen found few openings except as labourers in the docks, tan-yards, sugar refineries and glue factories. But the heavy and dirty work in these concerns was hard to secure as Irish immigrants would accept lower wages than even agricultural labourers from the West of England.

Local men fought, not unsuccessfully, to keep their hold on the more skilled work in the shipyards, engineering works and sugar refineries, though here they faced some competition from German immigrants. The aristocrats among the artisans were the coalminers almost all of whom were local men. The increasing output of the Bedminster coalmines between 1870–1900 meant that the coalminers could live more comfortably than other labouring families. With the vicar, Minnie visited in March 1879 a coalminer's family in Parson Street where: 'One cottage was quite a picture; a great fire, wife and dear baby, young collier husband and old blind grandfather'.

The vicar who trudged almost daily on his visiting rounds probably knew his poor neighbours better than Phippen did. Though not an orator Eland could always find words to speak to his parishioners; and Minnie wrote 'it does me good to hear how he talks to them with such extreme gentleness and yet with so much force'. Walking in the streets of Bedminster was not pleasant. The atmosphere was enervating and 'such smelly streets! Almost as bad as Rome'. This could only be expected as despite the three miles of main sewers constructed in the 1850s, the most usual outlet for sewage was in the waterways. The vicar could bear anything for the sake of his church and his people, but his fellow-workers sometimes caused him to despair. In September 1880: 'The vicar gave himself up to be quite miserable with his cold and trouble about his curates.'

Downtrodden in the mid-eighteenth century, curates were coming into their own a century later. By their intransigence, their spiritual crises and attacks of physical prostration at busy times many of them amply revenged the slights, snubs and drudgery inflicted on their predecessors. The resurgence of the curates was largely due to support from the incumbent's wives many of whom, like Rose Eland and Trollope's Mrs Proudie, stepped ahead of their more steady-going husbands. The scope of Rose's activities may help explain the vicar's trouble with the curates.

Eland worked steadfastly and quietly; Rose threw herself with a splash into Girls' Guild activities, church teas, parish visiting, and sustaining the curates. Meetings and classes were held almost nightly in the vicarage. The peace of the home, where the vicar might have rested, was further shattered by domestic eruptions. One maid ran away and another threatened to do so: 'Wet, wet. No progress, all in confusion . . . Alma Mabery[1] told Rose in a fearful voice and with a ghastly face that she saw a "figure" in white at the foot of her bed last night, and nothing would induce her to sleep in that room again – this being bed time. Consultation with the vicar and she was persuaded. I slept in the vicar's dressing room, as it made Rose feel happier about me. My feet were

[1] The new parlourmaid who, from the surname, appears to have come from Rose's old home, Badgemore, Henley-on-Thames.

very cold; I was awake about 1.30 to 3.' The next day matters hardly improved: 'Wet-rain-rain-rain. Mabery slept better and fancies she was over-tired on Monday night . . . Rose had such a talk to me about her scruples; she really seems a Roman Catholic at heart. All one can do is to pray for her; she seems exceedingly troubled and only waiting . . . (sic)'.

Eland, too, was 'in dreadful trouble about his curates'; the two most restive in the vicar's team of five curates were Sidney Williams and Augustus McNeile. In the wet and dismal October of 1880 Williams insisted on taking a rest when he was most needed in the parish and McNeile returned unexpectedly early from his leave so that Eland had had little time in which to relax in the absence of this stormy petrel.

Williams' temperament was perhaps better suited than his vicar's to the down-to-earth needs of the inhabitants of Bedminster. Eland's sincerity and selflessness impressed the individual, but his more worldly-minded curate realised that a carved reredos would hardly attract those who never entered a church, but that bustle, noise and the prospect of a meal might. Confident in his beliefs, Williams directed the mission services during Lent 1879:

> 'Rose gave a big tea to about 80 people (the Sisters asked most of them). They all went to church afterwards (Mr McNeile did not come, he does not like the idea of teas in Lent). The church [St Paul's] was full . . . there was quite a little congregation waiting outside after evensong but they were very shy and only hung about the door . . . Then there came quite a rush of the very poorest, dirtiest ragged boys (regular street arabs). Several looked as if they had been in prison with their hair cropped as short as possible. Their clothes were all torn and one was without any coat . . . All was stillness in the Church when Mrs Williams recognised her husband's voice and then in the distance we heard the hum of a crowd. As they came nearer we could distinguish that they were singing; it grew louder and louder. Then Mr Williams (in his surplice) came into the church leading the people in a mission hymn, and drawing after him a mass of poor half-starved (in body and soul) ragged people. The procession reached the chancel and still they kept coming in. No need of pressing now they entered as

their right and were shown into the best seats all still echoing the refrain: "I do believe I will believe"; old women in their cracked voices as well as young men and little children. It was a most imposing sight. Mr. Williams seemed like a faithful shepherd seeking his sheep and then leading them to the fold'.[1]

By the following year Williams was not only exhausted by his efforts, but was exacerbated by criticism that he felt rather than heard. Even Minnie, who whole-heartedly supported his work, thought: 'Mr Williams quite *rants* when he gets excited, but he is so eager and . . . set on doing good to the poor that one feels he must succeed.' Williams did not feel so confident and in October 1880 had the inevitable 'long interview with the vicar. Mr Williams goes for a change [to Teignmouth] tomorrow, quite broken down. Vicar very worried about this, but more especially about Mr Burnett's behaviour. Then Mr McNeile came in . . . to tell the vicar he has had to leave his lodgings . . . Rose has acute rheumatism.' Williams eventually found a place well suited to his talents, St Gabriel's Mission House in Poplar.

A scholar and prizeman of Queens' College, Cambridge and a former curate of All Saints, Clifton, Montague Burnett, another of Eland's curates probably showed little sympathy with Williams' efforts; and his attitude was shared by Augustus McNeile. Like the war horse, McNeile could smell the battle smoke from afar and readily plunged into controversy. One evening during the vicar's black October he preached, with evident satisfaction, on the theme that 'there are and always have been storms in the Church'. Face to face with the individual he could be counciliatory: 'Mr McNeile took the baptism. He holds the babies so nicely and rocks them if they cry.'

Some of the storms which were stirring the parish concerned the House of Mercy in Bedminster where Mrs Eland was a frequent visitor. On the 1 September 1874 Minnie acted as her cousin's deputy: 'After luncheon I went down to the House of Mercy to sit with the penitents for 2 hours (2.30 till 4.30) . . . I sat with them in the classroom while they worked.

[1] The accounts of two services, held on 2 March and 5 March 1879 have been joined so as to give a more complete picture of mission activities.

There were only 4 altogether; the girls took it in turns to read aloud, and I had to say a short prayer at each hour as the clock struck. It was very hot and having to put on a cap made me feel it more, and Rose had lent me a black shawl.'

Outside the penitentiary the sun was shining and girls were wearing fly-away bonnets on the backs of their heads. It was this fashion that prompted an anxious enquiry in the *Bedminster Parish Magazine* for July 1873: 'Jane enquires where she can get a Christian Bonnet. Did the Queen of Sheba ask a harder question of King Solomon? The editor has made enquiries and recommends a trial of Mrs Tamplin, Blandford House, Blandford St., Baker St.' It is doubtful if Mrs Tamplin appreciated this recommendation.

Later Minnie was to be closely concerned with the mother foundation at Clewer near Windsor. Although on a favoured stretch of the Thames Clewer was for many girls the stepping stone to gay life around Windsor Barracks or in London, and also a halting place for those who were returning home destitute. The predicament of these girls caused the rector of Clewer, Thomas Thelluson Carter (1808–1901), to establish in 1843 the House of Mercy, a penitentiary for prostitutes. The genesis of this institution was due to strangely diverse factors: the compassion of many Tractarian leaders, the Benthamite teaching that humans best thrive in the 'peace and calm' of a controlled atmosphere and the longing of many well-to-do women to have some outlet for their energies. The House of Mercy, now the Convent of St John, has been awarded a place among the notable abbeys of Europe. The great interest of the building, started in 1854, is the way in which the architect, Henry Woodyer, expressed the aims of the founders. The tower-dominated courtyard made constant surveillance possible, the high outer walls secured isolation from the outer world and the exuberant piety of the Anglican Revival is well illustrated by the fantastic brickwork of the large chapel, described as 'one of the greatest feats of virtuoso bricklaying in England.'[1]

The lives of girls who would have starved in the street were saved in the House of Mercy but whether they were given confidence to enter the world again with any prospects of happi-

[1] I. Richards, *Abbeys of Europe*, 1968, p. 169.

ness it is impossible to say. As most of the penitents were uneducated and uncouth and many savage, their only means of livelihood would have been domestic service with all its drudgery and temptations, or in the steam-filled laundries where the floors were awash with suds. As the century wore on and education became more diffused 'penitents of a higher grade' appeared and 'a separate department' was organised for them.[1] The Clewer experiment succeeded because the first Mother Superior, Harriet Monsell, was able to obtain the confidence of the penitents and the obedience of the Sisters, many of whom were little used to discipline, and because Carter's sympathies expanded as he grew older. His bishop had complained: 'Mr Carter is much upstairs', but in old age he came down to comprehend the predicament of those who had to sin to eat.

Minnie saw another aspect of Bristol life when she visited Rose's sister, Francina Morrell, at Stapleton Park. It was inevitable that one of the daughters of a family so connected with church affairs as were the Lanes of Badgemore should marry the local incumbent. In 1865 Francina fulfilled her destiny and married Thomas Baker Morrell, rector of Henley and rural dean. Morrell's arrival was eagerly awaited at Henley, not only because he was reputed 'to be zealous, energetic and possess a good fortune', but also because the officiating curate had not given satisfaction. Soon after Morrell's induction in July 1852 changes were apparent: 'The Rector has begun improvements. He gave out the Psalm this afternoon reading the whole verse. The specimen he had of Lever's performance this morning – 'Hunto the 'ills I lift my Heyes' was quite enough.'[2]

The Bishop, for Morrell was appointed Bishop Coadjutor of Edinburgh in 1863, was very sensitive about the dignity of his office and the correct pronunciation of English. When a Nonconformist preacher took the Sunday service at a hotel in Spezia, Morrell was outraged:

'We saw a notice up in the hotel that there would be Divine Service in the hotel at 11 o'clock. So we all settled

[1] W. H. Hutchings, *Life and Letters of Thomas Thelluson Carter*, 1903, p. 87.
[2] *St Mary's News*, June 1967. The quotation is from the diary of an old parishioner in the possession of Mr G. H. J. Tomalin of Henley, to whom I am indebted for much kind help in connection with St Mary's.

to go, but while we were wondering in which room it would be held, there came a little knock at the door, and the clergyman (as we fancied) looked in to say that it would be in the reading room. He did not know if we "'appened to know". Franzy put him down at once as a shoemaker, and said he could be no clergyman of our Church. We all went down at 11 o'clock, but when the Bishop looked into the room and saw the clergyman settling down with a Bible only before him and no surplice on, he could not stand it and retired. Franzy and I were sorry afterwards that we had not followed his example, for we had not our service at all but the man turned out an Anabaptist teacher. The Bishop was so angry when he heard. It certainly is very wrong not to say on the notice what the service will be. The Bishop took down the card and put all particulars down (I wonder what the man will think when he takes it down next Sunday?) The Bishop also noticed it in the visitor's book.'

Morrell's attitude was widely shared: 'It is the interest of Englishmen of every class and creed that the character and social standing of the clergy should not be lowered beyond the existing standard. Considering their position in the fabric of English society, it is desirable that, whatever else they are, they should be gentlemen'.[1]

John Ball had found an answer to this vexed question in the fourteenth century. The ecclesiologists held up this century as the great exemplar of ecclesiastical propriety, but they overlooked the fact that at this time most parish priests were working on their common-field strips alongside the other manorial tenants.

Neither Morrell nor his wife could feel quite at ease in Scotland; and after the bishop's retirement they thankfully moved south where both climate and doctrine were milder. Stapleton, three miles north of Bristol, admirably fulfilled their needs despite the fact that Hannah More and Victory Purdy, the renowned collier-evangelist, were born there and the freethinking Raja Rammohun Roy and the Chartist Robert Frost had died there.

In the early eighteenth century Stapleton was renowned for

[1] *Oxford Undergraduate Journal*, 21 November 1866, quoting from an article in the *Pall Mall Gazette* on the proposal to establish Keble College.

its mills. But, as Bristol advanced in consequence and wealth, many families moved away from the counter and quayside. Within the orbit of one of the seats of the Beaufort family and pleasantly situated on the Frome, Stapleton could claim to be an aristocratic and romantic retreat. The Morrells settled at Stapleton Park which, with its wooded grounds and model dairy, was not the least desirable of the residences beside the Frome. The old bishop was happy playing his harmonium in the oratory and he often presided over parish affairs as the incumbent refused to reside since he considered the rectory drains to be deficient. Although his wife had her own interests these as often gave her anxiety as pleasure. The entry in Minnie's diary for 10 August 1875 indicates the tenor of her cousin's days: 'Franzy has bothered herself over letters and servants and cows.'

In just over a year the Morrells were at it again: 'Franzy in trouble with her servants. Stubbs (the butler) and Mrs Freeman (the cook) both leaving'. Francina Morrell turned in vain from household problems to seek refreshment out of doors: her highly prized cows sickened in August 1875 from foot-and-mouth disease. By the end of the Napoleonic Wars the optimistic felt that man had conquered his environment; but the potato blight of 1848 and the outbreaks in the 1860s of rinderpest among the cattle of England and of scab among the sheep of New Zealand were reminders that victory had not yet been won. Francina had every reason to feel 'very unhappy about her beautiful cows; they have had the foot-and-mouth disease . . . Tulip is the only one who is pretty well, we drink her milk now' . . . 'The cow doctor has been and says we had better give up Tulip's milk, so we shall be minus milk and butter altogether now' . . . 'we have beaten up egg in our tea which is not a bad substitute.' Cattle diseases mainly affected the diet of the well-to-do; by the 1870s the dairy products on the labourer's bill of fare were restricted to imported hard cheeses.

That the decline of the spiritual and social influence of rural incumbents in the mid-nineteenth century was due to bread-and-butter causes was not suggested in the Wakefield discussions. Nevertheless, the meagreness of the agricultural labourer's diet was the chief factor which caused him to leave the village; and this exodus ended the old self-contained life of the rural community. New squires and new commercial undertakings came to the village; but with the departure of the labourers and artisans the vitality of the parish ebbed away. That this unit was 'too often the weakest point in the whole system of the Established Church'[1] was due not so much to the country parson mouldering on a shelf as to the parish disintegrating at his feet.

<hr />

[1] *Report of the Church Congress* 1886, p. 199.

CHAPTER FOUR

South Lambeth:
The New Whittingtons

> Dick Whittington . . . wanted to see London sadly, for he
> had heard the streets were paved with gold, and he was
> willing to get a bushel of it; but how great was his disap-
> pointment, poor boy!

To live and be known in the City was ceasing by the middle of
the eighteenth century to be the dream of embryo Whittingtons. Young men taking chances found it more advantageous to
establish themselves in the environs of London than under the
shadow of St Paul's. The arrival of these fortune seekers often
heralded far-reaching changes in the rural parishes dozing on
the Londoners' doorstep. When early in the 1740s young Mark
Beaufoy (1718–1782) left Bristol to start making English wines
and vinegar at Lambeth he founded a manufacturing dynasty
which was closely connected with the district for two centuries.
He also played a part in changing Lambeth from a rural parish
renowned for its mansions and gardens to a metropolitan area
notorious for its poverty, depravity and disorder. The Beaufoys
and their contemporaries had no difficulty in tabulating the
stages in which this metamorphosis was accomplished; but few
comprehended the dynamic urge to move which made it possible. By the 1850s an army of Whittingtons, drawn from every
class and every part of the kingdom was converging on Lambeth; and every man in this multitude had expectations of bet-
tering his condition in a setting which to the majority of the
newcomers was quite unfamiliar. The great expectations of the
immigrants were seldom realised. Some lost their possessions
soon after their arrival in the periodical inundations of the riverside areas, and others saw their high hopes fade away almost as
quickly. The theme of this chapter is the impact of this invasion

of the dispossessed on Lambeth; and on the Beaufoys, as individuals and as entrepreneurs.

The industrial colonisation of Lambeth began in the early eighteenth century when wharves and warehouses started to appear amidst the riverside osier beds. Fishermen were joined by stevedores and watermen whose settlements caused Pope to observe sedately, 'bad neighbourhood, I ween' (plate 18). Inland the atmosphere was more salubrious; though mansions like Norfolk House and Caron House had crumbled into ruins, the market gardens and pleasure grounds gave Lambeth an animated and rustic appearance. Only at the end of the eighteenth century was William Curtis (1746–1799) obliged to move his London Botanic Garden to Brompton from Lambeth so as to escape the bad roads, the drifts of smoke from London and the 'effluvia of surrounding ditches, at times highly offensive'. But it was the open sewers which made the Lambeth gardens grow and, despite the pollution of a century, many are still producing flowers at which the Tradescants, who lived near the present South Lambeth Road, would have taken a second look. Although Curtis deplored 'the rage for building which has been the means of extirpating so many plants',[1] the flowers of Lambeth held their own until the mid-nineteenth century when Alkanet still grew in Vauxhall and Solomon's Seal in the hedgerows of nearby Stockwell. Only in July 1972 were they going down, and with flying colours as a buddleia flowered in the roof of the half-demolished 56 South Lambeth Road and Oxford ragwort, persicaria and willow herb covered the cleared sites.

At the turn of the nineteenth century carnations, fruit trees, vegetables and vines still flourished between the potteries, distilleries and breweries of Lambeth. The renown of Battersea cabbages, Deptford asparagus and Maddock's auriculas at Walworth shows the leading part played by horticulturalists of the Surrey side. The exotics grown by the Tradescants and Curtis are recorded in botanical works; but an onion originated by a humbler Lambeth gardener still finds a place in every seedman's catalogue: James' Keeping Onion. The long-lived fame of James' onion has given an unduly plebeian aspect to horticulture in Lambeth which was also noted for

[1] W. H. Curtis, *William Curtis 1746–1799, Botanist and Entomologist*, 1941, see p. 84 for description of Lambeth and p. 95 for the dangers of development.

the splendour of its Black Hamburg grapes. Vine Lodge still stands in South Lambeth to recall the vinery in Langley Lane where as late as 1861 thirteen men, three women and two boys were employed. An old vine, possibly from this vinery, flourished until the Second World War on the premises of William Bloore and Son, timber merchants in the South Lambeth Road. Both the vine and William Bloore were exotics who took kindly to Lambeth. Bloore came from Birmingham in the mid-nineteenth century to make pianos, but finding the wood more attractive than the instrument, he founded a firm which is still in operation.

The tamed countryside of Lambeth where elms shaded the lanes winding through little fields and gardens to places of entertainment was exactly to the Londoner's taste. The possibility of combining the enjoyment of rustic pleasures and the pursuit of City undertakings induced 'numerous respectable families',[1] who included the spectacle-making Dollands and the money-making Ricardos, to settle in Lambeth. In the late eighteenth century John Bond, a City banker, fulfilled his own and his fellow citizens' dreams of country life by building a rustic estate at the junction of the present Wandsworth and South Lambeth Roads. Sedate brick terraces began to appear in the shadow of mansions like Montpelier House and Belgrave House; and the dwellings of market gardeners made way for the cottages and villas of the well-to-do. Among the last of these to disappear was Percy Villa, occupied by Lionel Brough. Acting in *Robinson Crusoe* at Covent Garden, Brough on 26 January 1877 paid young Mark Beaufoy, who was his neighbour, the compliment of a passing witticism.

When Lambeth became consciously rural the industrial serpent was entering Eden. The Doultons were adding lustre to the renown of the long-established potteries, Eleanor Coade was expanding the family stone works transplanted from Dorset, from the ashes of the Temple of Apollo had arisen the marine engineering works of Henry Maudslay (1771–1831) and Mark Beaufoy had brought new life to the decaying pleasure ground, Cuper's Garden, which he considered had become the emblem of the Haggard, the Seat of Desolation, and the Disgrace of our Neighbourhood.'[1]

[1] T. Allen, *The History and Antiquities of the Parish of Lambeth*, 1826, p. 398.

[2] Gwendolyn Beaufoy, *Leaves from a Beech Tree*, 1930, p. 145.

The young Quaker's sensibilities may have recoiled from the district, but wood from the 'snug alcoves' and other pleasure-ground buildings came in useful in constructing a manufactory which was to become one of the show places in the environs of London (plate 17). Industrial undertakings, provided that their situations and products were outlandish enough, appealed to the Romantic taste. This Thomas Pennant, the topographer, well understood when he described how from 'the genial banks of the Thames opposite our Capital' flowed 'by a wonderous magic . . . this ocean of sweets and sours'.[1]

The magic which caused English wines and vinegar to flow into cellars, ships' holds and kitchens was Mark Beaufoy's ability to understand the needs of his time. Despite his intelligence, however, he could not have embarked in his early twenties on the Lambeth venture had it not been for a handsome legacy, his marriage with an heiress and the goodwill of the distiller to whom he had been apprenticed in Bristol. With these aids, Beaufoy could take full advantage of the reversal in 1739 of Walpole's policy of trade before glory. The hostilities which caused many merchants and manufacturers to fail favoured the Lambeth enterprise and proved that virtue brought its own reward. Shocked, according to family tradition, by Hogarth's portrayal of the underworld ruled by the 'Stygian Liquor' Beaufoy had turned from gin distilling to the making of vinegar and wine. He secured Admiralty contracts for vinegar which, as his grandson was to point out, provided ships' stores with a fumigator, an antiseptic and a preservative.[2] Mark Beaufoy also ensured that, though wine imports were restricted, butlers should not be ashamed of their masters' cellars by directing 'the materials for the rich *Frontignac* to the more elegant tables; the *Madeira*, the *Calcarella* and the *Lisbon*, into every part of the Kingdom.'[3] Realising that his wines did need a bush Beaufoy increased his sales 'by planting pushing people in various parts of the Town'.[4] Their efforts were so successful that by the end of the eighteenth century Pennant estimated 'that

[1] T. Pennant, *Some Account of London*, 1813, p. 44.

[2] *Beaufoy's White Vinegar*, 6th ed., 1822, 28 pp.

[3] T. Pennant, op. cit., p. 43.

[4] G. Beaufoy, op. cit., p. 93.

half of the port, and five-sixths of the white wines consumed in our capital have been the produce of our home wine-presses.' Foremost amongst these were Beaufoy's.

The Old Quaker, as Mark Beaufoy was called by his descendants, was as good a father as he was an astute man of business as he refused to force his most able sons, Henry (1750–1795) and Mark (1764–1827), into the Lambeth concern; this was left under the control of the less gifted John (1761–1836) until the coming of age of Mark's eldest son, Henry Benjamin Hanbury Beaufoy (1786–1851). When Cuper's Garden was needed for the Surrey-side approach for the proposed Waterloo Bridge, John had to find a new site for the manufactory. Handsome compensation eased, but did not obviate, the difficulties in finding a site as convenient and attractive as Cuper's had been. In 1810 four acres were purchased on the Caron estate in South Lambeth for the construction of a dwelling house, manufactory and offices, and with easy access to the Thames beside which a wharf and mill were later established. In the vathouse of this concern, now belonging to British Vinegars Limited, are the remains of an unusually thick wall which may be the last vestige of the mighty edifice built by Noel de Caron[1] in a style befitting one who had been the friend of William of Orange, host to Queen Elizabeth I and Dutch ambassador to James I.

Before describing the new establishment, some attempt must be made to indicate the extent of South Lambeth. Like Eldorado, the name suggests great expectations rather than a clearly defined locality. South Lambeth, which once formed part of the manor of Vauxhall, consisted in 1871 of 346 acres served by the churches of St Barnabas, Guildford Road (established 1851), St Stephen, Albert Square (1861) and St Anne (1869) formerly the South Lambeth Chapel in the South Lambeth Road.[2] The area was bounded to the west by Nine Elms Lane, to the north by Harleyford Road and Kennington Oval, to the east by Clapham Road and to the south by Lansdowne Road (now Way). The slow emergence of South Lambeth with an official entity means that some documents, such

[1] The name is also spelt Carroun and Carron.

[2] Although this church often appears as St Ann's, the spelling used in the 1871 Census summary and at the present day has been adopted.

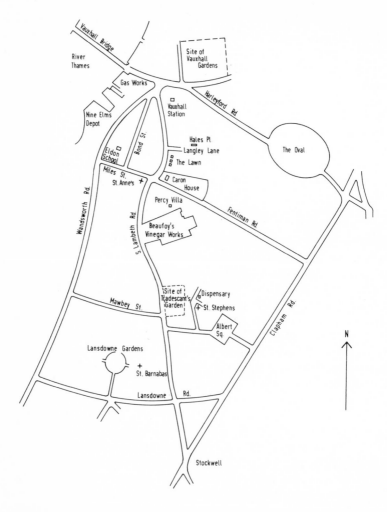

A map of South Lambeth (scale 4½ inches to 1 mile), showing the major streets and roads mentioned in the text. Based on Hugh McIntosh's map of 1886, by kind permission of the Greater London Council Map Collection.

as the reports of the Medical Officers of Health, covering the whole of Lambeth, must be used to indicate conditions in the southern area which included Vauxhall.

Much of the Beaufoy's vinegar yard in South Lambeth remains as it was originally planned in 1812 and is a fine example of the golden age of industrial architecture. The guiding principle in the arrangement of agricultural and industrial buildings in the late eighteenth and early nineteenth centuries was that profits depended on the master's eye. Industrialists laid out their undertakings so that they could see and hear the slightest variation in the routine of the workyard. When the rattle of carts, the clanging of the work bell and hammering in the cooperage ceased at Beaufoy's the silence was oppressive. On 5 June 1872 Minnie wrote: 'Bank Holiday to-day, the yard seems so dull and silent.' In the new vinegar yard the dwelling house, Caron Place, the vat and brew houses, the vaults and cooperage were planned as a harmonious whole. Vast and barrack-like industrial buildings, like those of Lowman, Barrett and Company in Bond Street (now Bondway) were the products of the 1880s when owners and managers feared that too close an association with the works might lower their social consequence. As the Beaufoys were proud of their concern rather than of the profits from it, they were content for the greater part of the nineteenth century to live in the yard. In the same way Belgrave House, belonging to Charles Francis, overlooked the wharves at Vauxhall where the cement, which had built the family fortunes, was loaded. The unrest and disorders after 1815 were particularly feared by men, like Francis, whose upward struggle had been a hard one. The only hope of these apprehensive citizens lay in Lord Eldon. In honour of the Lord Chancellor, whose last ditch was dug at Agincourt rather than Waterloo, Francis established in 1829 the Eldon School for needy boys; and Encombe Terrace was named after Eldon's seat in Dorset.

The Beaufoys, whose upward struggles had been eased by their faith and their connections with brewing which stretched back into the seventeenth century, had a more relaxed attitude towards possible social cataclysms. This confidence shows itself in the cheerful informality of the entrance to the South Lambeth vinegar and wine manufactory. Of the two small lodges which stood at the end of a tree-shaded drive one still remains bearing the Beaufoy arms above the loggia (plate 15), the top of which is appropriately decorated with moulded bunches of grapes.

The functional aspect of the vathouse, which was the chief building in the yard, is concealed by a handsome façade. The delicate white cupola above the clock in a wooden rusticated stage which surmounts the vathouse would not have looked out of place in the courtyard of a Bohemian hunting lodge (plate 16). From neighbouring streets this cupola can be seen, and never without a feeling of surprised pleasure, above the roofs and chimneys. The strike of the clock is silent as the nerves of the age, so tolerant of transistors, motor cycles and grinding gears, snap at the sound of church bells ringing and of a clock striking at night, the most moving of city sounds. South of the entrance only the shell of the three-storied brick dwelling house remains. On 10 May 1941 a bomb destroyed the splendour of the library and the principal living rooms. In this raid George Maurice, the last Beaufoy to manage the concern, was killed. One who lived overlooking the yard has observed that there was no quickening of the pace of work when Maurice Beaufoy passed by, as employees worked their hardest at all times for such a well-liked employer. To the rear of the dwelling lay the wine vaults and the cooperage which, in contrast with the silent vathouse, echoed with hammerings and the rattle of pebbles used to clean the casks. As craftsmen the coopers maintained their own little republic within the yard. Drinking was often heavy among these comparatively well-paid workers and rows not infrequent. On 7 June 1867 Minnie wrote:

> 'There is quite a commotion. One of the men (coopers) in the yard has nearly starved one of his children to death. He and his wife were both taken to prison yesterday. They are both let out on bail today; he came to his work here as usual. There was quite a crowd at the gates waiting to see this man come out; I expect he would have been half killed. In fact, he dared not venture out; but, however, managed to make his escape at about half-past three this afternoon when the crowd disappeared. I hear he has been discharged.'

Workmates and neighbours often protected children

against their parents. This is illustrated by the childhood adventure of one who has lived over seventy years in Lambeth. The money her father earned as a labourer was spent on drink though the shoes of his two daughters hardly covered their feet. Taking a chance, the youngest girl ran into the bar where her father had long been drinking and bawled out that her sister needed shoes. With a roar the man stumbled after the girls who raced home by back streets. When the father arrived, they were unconcernedly swinging round a lamp-post. Although drunk, the parent was not deceived and fell upon his daughters who were saved by neighbours hurrying to their rescue.

When the dwelling house, known as Caron·Place, and offices were completed, and the move from Cuper's achieved, John Beaufoy retired to enjoy the less harassing duties of lord of the manor at Upton Grey. The order of release had come for the uncle, and the nephew began his spell of hard labour.

Denied the outlet of the Meeting House Henry's zeal, like that of his father and Uncle John, found a vent in martial activities. While not going as far as his brother, Mark, who found 'the profession of killing without murder to be the most satisfactory, and the least mercenary, mode of attaining rank and fortune,' Henry at twenty-two wrote *Scoloppetaria or Considerations on the Nature and Use of Rifled Barrel Guns with Reference to their Forming the Basis of a Permanent System of National Defence agreeable to the Genius of the Country*.[1] His knowledge of ballistics, the interests he was known to share with his father and his observations during 'an aerial voyage' in a balloon secured Henry's election to the Royal Society in 1811.

All his life Henry Beaufoy remembered his 'mixed feelings of astonishment and delight' as he felt himself 'floating in the most delightful aeriform fluid', and also the new vision which he gained of the environs of London. From the air everyday sights had a poetic quality: the clouds of dust behind sheep being driven out of London, the bright and lively green of the pastures, the 'orange-yellow' roads and the 'peculiar brilliancy' of the stream running through Chelmsford. Although

[1] *The Gentleman's Magazine*, October 1799, considered: 'This valuable acquisition to the Military Library . . . is highly creditable to his talents, both as a Scholar and a Soldier'.

there was a constant smell of hydrogen gas and the rotary movement of the balloon impeded the accurate reading of barometrical heights, the voyage was considered a success. The balloonists opened a bottle of champagne which 'sparkled with more vivacity' than usual and drank the health of the Prince Regent, Sir Daniel Williams, and 'all friends at Hackney.'[1]

The last toast was a valedictory one as the happy home at Hackney was breaking up. Mark was soon to enlist, George had entered the Navy and their father was planning to carry out his astronomical observations at Bushey, near Stanmore. Henry, who was happiest in the family circle, had to come down to earth with that 'dislocating shock' he felt when the balloon landed, and settle in solitude at Caron Place. The sense of isolation was the more oppressive as the new vinegar yard was in a district noted for the liveliness of its entertainments. The pleasure grounds had been replaced by the transpontine theatres, the Coburg (later the Royal Victoria), the Surrey and Astley's Amphitheatre, renowned 'as the chief homes of the sensational drama and eccentric exhibitions.'[2] The fortunes of the Surrey and Coburg theatres fluctuated, but able managers ensured a more lasting popularity for Astley's. Who could resist 'the smallest ponies in Europe . . . almost fit to mingle in polished circles', or, when *Richard III* was performed on horseback, the affecting 'air of truth' with which the King's horse died? The riders were equally fascinating and by 1814 Henry Beaufoy had formed with one of the Columbines, Eliza Taylor, a connection which was to bring him lifelong happiness.

Beaufoy's scientific talents found an outlet in improving and increasing the production of vinegar and his benevolence in attempting to better the lot of those washed onto the Lambeth riverside by the tidal wave of industrialism. Incapable of

[1] T. Thomson, *Annals of Philosophy*, 1814, Vol. IV, pp. 282–91, Henry Beaufoy, Journal kept . . . during an aerial voyage with Mr James Sadler, sen., from Hackney, Middlesex to East Thorpe, Essex, five miles from Colchester, 29 August 1811. Sir Daniel Williams was a Colonel in the Tower Hamlets Militia, and also Chief Magistrate of Lambeth Street Post Office. I am indebted to Mr J. MacLemman of the Royal Society Library for this information.

[2] E. Walford, *London Old and New*, 1873, Vol. VI, p. 406.

half-hearted approaches Beaufoy was daily occupied eighteen hours with work in the yard, in his printing press, where his father's unpublished work was printed 'for gratuitous distribution', and in establishing a library and museum designated for 'some public purpose.'[1] Rejected statuary from this collection was scattered in the grounds of Caron Place, and Hercules found a resting place outside the acetate manufactory at Battersea.

Beaufoy devoted himself to the production of acetates needed by dyers and colourmen; and, above all, of malted vinegar, of acetic acid and of one of its diluted forms which he described in 1822 as a 'newly invented Acid (White Vinegar)'[2] because he believed they would benefit a society on the move.

White vinegar was invaluable 'to officers of the Navy and Army and Honourable East India Company's Service, to residents in the East and West Indies, Africa and the Colonies, to Planters and Medical Men . . . and every description of Persons going abroad, or undertaking long sea voyages, particularly in hot climates' as an antiseptic, a fumigator and a preservative. These properties of White Vinegar were equally valuable at home – 'in large public assemblies, courts of justice, jails etc' and also in pickling vegetables and preserving meat. 'Culinary Chemistry', however, was not popular with working wives who were seldom able to procure large quantities of meat or vegetables; and found it hard to follow Beaufoy's injunction that 'a *perfectly bright* brass, bell-metal or copper skillet' must be used. Those who worked in the yard or offices caught something of Beaufoy's enthusiasm, for prizes were awarded to workmen who suggested methods of increasing their output, and gratuities made to clerks of outstanding ability. These inducements to endeavour, however, were hardly needed as Henry inherited from his father, 'the dear Pip', a kind-heartedness to which few failed to respond. This family characteristic passed to his nephew and successor, Mark Hanbury Beaufoy (1854–1922), whose coming-of-age

[1] Information concerning Henry Beaufoy's activities has been obtained from his obituary in the *Proceedings of the Linnean Society*, Vol. II. 1848–1855 and from the *South London Times*, July 1851 and the *South London Journal* 15 October 1864.

[2] The Trade pamphlet, *Beaufoy's White Vinegar* first appeared in 1821; the sixth, and last, edition of 1822, has been used.

celebrations in 1875 were entirely arranged by the 150 employees in the works, and who was known in the family as 'dear Nunkie'.

Even the all-embracing benevolence of Henry Beaufoy could avail little against the destitution that threatened to overwhelm Vauxhall in the 1840s. Just as the Thames embankment could not contain exceptionally high tides, the possibility of dirt, disease and starvation could not stay the influx of those who sought a livelihood in the environs of London. Free from any regulations concerning drainage, construction or overcrowding, the builders had a field day, particularly around the London Gas Works (1833) and the railway terminus of the South-Western Railway Company (1838) at Vauxhall. A vain attempt was made to keep the new Lampton Worm, the railroad, outside the metropolis by establishing terminus stations at Nine Elms and Chalk Farm; but by 1848 the south-western railway was carried almost to the steps of Lambeth Palace. Even after Waterloo Station was opened, work-seekers continued to crowd into Nine Elms attracted by the railway goods yard and wharves. The steady influx of unskilled labour kept wages low, and drove out those who had sought a rural retreat at Vauxhall. The houses of the well-to-do were bought cheaply by speculators who let rooms to those seeking work in the district.

Soon hastily built courts and shed-like houses covered the gardens which had been the pride of the first settlers. By 1841 the district which had been a haven for the well-to-do had become the waiting place for the destitute. The 128 heads of families who had crowded into Bond Street and Miles Street were small craftsmen and labourers living from hand to mouth. The fact that the fifty-three householders giving their birthplace as Surrey were mainly unskilled workers suggests that the old established inhabitants of Lambeth and its environs were not benefiting from the new openings.[1]

Those who came from the country with a craft were most likely to succeed in Lambeth. The work of even rough hedge

[1] For Bond Street and Miles Street the 1841 census returns, made in pencil, are sometimes illegible and a clear distinction was not always made between householders and lodgers, so the figures can only be considered approximate.

carpenters satisfied the building speculators; and stone masons from Purbeck in Dorset found no lack of opportunities. The city had least to offer the agricultural labourer since only his strength was needed and none of his skills in ploughing, hedging and harvesting. So long as horse traffic remained there were openings or countrymen accustomed to horses. A harness-maker from Harpenden continued his work profitably until the First World War; two brothers from Cambridgeshire were equally successful. One, a fine upstanding man over six feet tall, became coachman to Edward VII; the other was in charge of the 196 horses in Tilling's bus yard, appropriately situated near the 'Bug and Flea' in Clapham Grove. On the whole unskilled workers, whether they were born in the country or Lambeth, seldom found steady employment. It was the labourer's wife who supported the family in slack times by taking in washing and simple piece-work and by going out to clean. At the end of the nineteenth century a wife by making paper bags at 6d a thousand was able to earn 6s to 7s a week. Her daughter remembers that she had to deliver the bags before going to school and was regularly caned for being late.

As a seemingly bottomless reservoir of unskilled labour, Lambeth attracted many undertakings the activities of which did not add to the amenities of the district. Fumes from bone boiling, 'a business of . . . a most filthy and disgusting nature',[1] from wax bleaching and from the gas works were added to the smoke from the potteries with which Lambeth had long been familiar. Twenty-five years was the average length of life in the parish in the 1850s and for many that seemed too long.

Caron Place lay amidst, yet apart from, the new developments in South Lambeth. As if by the turn of a kaleidoscope the old pattern of a few substantial houses and cottages set amidst fields and market gardens had reformed into one of far greater intricacy. South of Vauxhall, dominated by the Nine Elms Goods Depot and the gas works, new areas of gentility were appearing. The amount of stucco on the substantial houses in Albert Square proclaimed the opulence of the occupiers and warmed the heart of cement manufacturers; and the villas in Lansdowne Gardens had the appearance, so attrac-

---

[1] *The Lambeth and Southwark Advertiser*, 1 January 1855.

tive to the Veneerings, of being 'in a state of high varnish and polish'.[1] The industrial upsurge of the 1860s depended not only on the cheap labour in Vauxhall, but also on the capital provided by the Podsnaps of Albert Square and the speculative dealings of those who favoured the more showy Lansdowne Gardens (plate 19). The disparate districts of South Lambeth were linked by boarding-houses. These varied from the wharfside doss-houses to more select establishments patronised by young men from the country, particularly engineers and medical students. Mrs Lapidge, the widow of a naval captain and a friend of Anne Beaufoy's, kept such a house. Ellen Drummond considered it was 'not quite nice of her to have men lodgers with so many grown-up daughters. A lady lodger would pay as well and not get her talked about.' Whatever may have been the case with boarding-house keepers, lodgers were seldom talked about as they suffered even more acutely than other immigrants from a loss of identity. Small-part actors retained little of the Astley glitter when they crowded into lodgings, known as the Theatrical Barracks, in St George's Circus;[2] and the political refugees from Germany, a pocket-book maker, two soldiers, a gardener, a tailor, a stone mason and a waiter, lost their revolutionary glamour when harbouring in a Bond Street establishment. Despite their disadvantages, boarding-houses were often the starting points for young men, the sons of small shopkeepers, mechanics and foremen, who were determined to better themselves. John Bright spoke to these aspirants when he declared at the opening of the 1864 Industrial Exhibition at Lambeth: 'They might rely upon it that in our day it was not our statesmen and great men who had revolutionised Europe; it was our engineers, our mechanics, and our working men who, with their heart, and mind, and labour were devoted to the instruction of the world.'[3] But to instruct the world they needed to be educated themselves.

The desperate need for education of the submerged and those struggling upwards haunted Henry Beaufoy. He had ex-

[1] As a study of the new men on the crest of the industrial wave Dickens' *Our Mutual Friend,* in which the opulent Podsnaps and speculating Veneerings appear, is masterly.

[2] E. Walford, op. cit., Vol. VI, p. 401.

[3] Reported in the *Lambeth Observer and South London Times*, 5 March 1864.

perienced the intellectual exhilaration of the industrial expansion which had thrown so many families into the dark, and he

The Lambeth Ragged School

strove to lighten this obscurity. Encouraged by Eliza, who had found a small scullery maid struggling to mend a tattered hymn book used in evening classes held under a railway arch, Beaufoy sought to aid those who sought so desperately to learn. In memory of the 'unspeakable private worth' of his

dren', Beaufoy built and endowed the Ragged School for Boys and Girls in Doughty Street (now Newport Street). Only the south end remains of the schools built on the scale which Beaufoy felt could best express his wife's worth and fulfil the needs of children who had never known the comfort of large, well-lighted and, above all, well-warmed rooms.[1] This splendour inspired 'a Friend unable to attend' to break into verse:

> 'Success to the Mansion which *Beaufoy* has built
> And which Ashley has open'd to-day;
> For the children of sorrow, privation and guilt,
> Who around it in wretchedness lay.'

The same author was probably responsible for The Feast Day song, which may have gained something from the enthusiasm with which it was sung:

> 'Hurrah for our Annual Treat, in each returning year,
> In memory of the Founder, it should be very dear;
> How kind of him to us these Schools to build and raise;
> Here we are taught to read and write, and trained in
>   Wisdom's Ways.'

As well as establishing and endowing the Ragged Schools, Beaufoy made princely benefactions, amounting to £9,000, to the City of London School (plate 5). Although Beaufoy's connection with this foundation was fortuitous, it was a school after his own heart. An ancient benefaction was used in 1834 to break new educational ground. The study of literature, which included the Bible, held first place in the curriculum, no formal religious instruction was given, chemistry was taught and fees were moderate. Beaufoy's awards and scholarships indicate his philosophy of life. One scholarship, in memory of his father, was 'designed to encourage the study of mathemati-

[1] The south end of the Newport Street School, now used by the band of the London Fire Brigade, was visited by the kind permission of the Chief Officer of the London Fire Brigade. I am indebted to Mr R. J. Wood for lending the *Ragged School Union Magazine* for March and April 1851. The lines commemorating the opening appeared in the April issue and those sung at the school outing in the *Lambeth Gazette*, October 1853. According to J. Tanswell, *The History and Antiquities of Lambeth*, 1858, the cost of building and endowing the school for 800 children was estimated at £14,000.

cal science, with an especial reference to its practical application to the use and service of mankind': other prizes promoted
the study, which included acting, of Shakespeare and the writing of essays on topical themes. Beaufoy helped to create in the
City of London School an atmosphere in which 'it is safe to say
no boyish enthusiasm for literature or art has ever been resented by school-fellows as an insult to the community.'[1] Such a
background produced many Shakespearian scholars; but those
who in their youth fell under the spell of *The Fifth Form at St
Dominic's* will be glad that it also produced Talbot Baines Reed.

Henry Beaufoy died in 1851 and was buried in the churchyard of St Mary's, Lambeth, but his 'capacious tomb with
ornamented railings' cannot now be found. The present practice of emptying graveyards of tombstones means that the last
traces of many worth remembering are removed. In leaving
the memorials to the gardening Tradescants, Bligh of the
Bounty and Ducrow of Astley's the authorities probably felt
they had left a representative group of Lambeth inhabitants.

After Henry's death the vinegar and wine manufactory
passed to his brother. After forty-one years in the Navy, Captain George Beaufoy left a sphere hardly touched by time for
one which had been transformed in a few decades.

Quite adrift, the captain married Anne Harvey within six
months of his occupation of Caron Place. Beaufoy's bride had
been long known to him as the companion of a naval friend's
wife; and he had prepared her for a rôle which was as new to
her as to him by a year's education in France. This hallmark
of gentility and her own forceful ability enabled Anne Beaufoy
to steer Caron Place to the forefront of the social activities of
South Lambeth. The birth of Mark Hanbury in 1854 ensured
the Beaufoy succession; and the arrival of Margaretta (Rita)
five years later enabled her mother to feel that duty demanded
entertaining on a scale that would provide a fitting background for an heiress. Before his wife had got into her stride,
George Beaufoy died at Lyston in July 1864.

George Beaufoy had succeeded to the business at a difficult
time. The repeal of the Excise on vinegar had caused a fall in
prices; and Gladstone's Commercial Treaty in 1860 had facilitated the importation of French wines. This treaty certainly

[1] A. E. Douglas-Smith, *City of London School*, 2nd ed. 1965, p. 179.

strengthened Beaufoy's conviction that Whig radicalism was bringing the country to the dogs. But cheaper wines from France helped to popularise wines generally in England particularly in middle-class homes. The new customers who were buying wines were as likely to be attracted to British-made wines, such as the orange and ginger wines for which Beaufoy's was famous, as those bearing foreign and unintelligible names. The fall of vinegar prices in the 1860s was offset by adulteration[1] and by the increasing popularity of vinegar at home and around Grey's 'Anglo-Saxon hearthstones' overseas. Whether taken neat or in sauces, vinegar helped to conceal the flavour of tainted or alien foods; it also imparted some flavour to the monotonous diets of settlers in New Zealand and scavengers in London who, according to Mayhew, fancied 'a saucerful of red pickled cabbage, or dingy-looking pickled onions'.

After her husband's death the control of the business rested with Anne Beaufoy until Mark should come of age. As Mrs Beaufoy received up to £7000 a year from the profits of the business and also the property at Pays Bas in Battersea she was able to appoint an able manager, John Gooch, and embark on a social programme of formidable dimensions. Caron Place soon became a social attraction in a way that would have been impossible during the life of retiring George Beaufoy. When, as a compliment to his profession and name, the City of London School invited George Beaufoy to become a patron of the newly formed Beaufoy Rowing Club he refused. His widow had no such shrinkings. At the school sports in May 1875 'Aunt George gave away the prizes and made little encouraging speeches to the boys'. These would have been no formal exhortations for, though she may have overlooked the finer shades of feeling, Anne Beaufoy's wholehearted geniality awakened an immediate response from those around her. The Caron Place household would have endorsed Minnie's opinion when she wrote during her Aunt's absence: 'It seems so dull and strange without Aunt George.'

It was this gift of inspiring gaiety that made Anne Beaufoy's

[1] For a general account of the vinegar-brewing industry and of the adulteration practised by manufacturers, including the Beaufoys, see *Industrial Archaeology*, 1970, Vol. 7, No. 3, pp. 292-309, A. W. Slater, 'The Vinegar Brewing Industry.'

first social ventures so immediately successful. The Saturday afternoon parties for children stemmed from Rita's giving a dolls' party and inviting some friends. The grown-ups came to fetch the children and stayed to enjoy 'capital fun after tea, dancing and kiss-in-the-ring etc.' In the same way from the modest gatherings to sing hymns on Sunday evenings emerged the Beaufoy Glee Club and Madrigal Union: 'I believe Wednesday is to be our glee meeting night, we shall be quite swells in time.' But the gaiety of the schoolroom gatherings, of the first musical evenings, when Edward de Rudolph, later to found the Waifs and Strays Society, played 'beautifully on the flute', and of the croquet parties which, with candles on the hoops, lasted into the night was never recaptured. The noisy, jolly suppers gave place to evening dinners: 'We had dinner à la Russe – very swell'. This method of serving the dishes from the sideboard gave wealthy hostesses full scope to display their servants, crockery and cutlery.

Such formal assemblies were not to the taste of young people, and many of the older visitors perferred the more homespun ways: 'Admiral Cotton sat up in the little schoolroom with Minta Cookson and me this morning and told funny stories.' The old glee club developed into the Mayfair Minstrels. Even the fashionable audiences who came to hear these singers thawed in the warmth of Anne Beaufoy's geniality: 'Aunt George has been so busy all the morning arranging the flowers in the library. The house looks lovely. We were all dressed in good time . . . It was a delightful party and the music sounded uncommonly well. Mr Francesco Berger, the conductor, complimented me on my solo . . . Light refreshments and ices were going on, all the evening . . . There were no end of flirtations . . . After nearly everyone had left we went down and had a second supper' and, no doubt, the flirtations were well discussed and magnified.

When Anne Beaufoy was soaring into the sunlight of social success, George Puckle, Medical Officer of Health for Lambeth, was struggling to lessen the evils of over-rapid urban growth which could no longer be disregarded. The shaking up of public services in the 1830s had left them in a state of stunned inertia from which they were only revived in the 1870s. The tentative establishment of Boards of Health owed more to the cholera scare of 1830 and fears of revolution in 1848 than to any widely-felt conviction concerning the rightness of the measure. The vestries, elected by the ratepayers, still saw themselves as Hampdens opposing any infringements on their rights and any increase in the rates. They claimed, as Dickens observed, their 'independent right to have as much Typhus Fever' as they pleased.

In the year 1869–70 scarlet and other fevers (including typhus) accounted for 321 of the 919 deaths from epidemic diseases. Until 1856 water for South Lambeth was pumped from the stagnant Effra; and even after the water works moved to Thames Ditton householders who had wells considered themselves lucky. When typhoid struck the well-to-do household of Minnie's cousins at Clapham water had to be fetched from Caron Place: 'Poor little Anna wants to have some of Aunt George's well water. She says it's so nice and cold.' Destitute strangers, or families on the move, and the overcrowded courtyards were cited as the main causes of the smallpox epidemic which erupted in the hot, dry summer of 1870. This outbreak, described as 'one of the most alarming and expensive epidemics that have visited this country for over a century',[1] was estimated as accounting for almost a quarter of the total mortality in Lambeth 1871–2. All members of the household at Caron Place were vaccinated in February 1871.

Whether epidemics were raging or not, young children could hardly overcome the hazards of living. The total deaths in Lambeth for 1865–6 amounted to 4,109 of which 1,951 were of infants under five. Children were sacrificed to industrial progress at home no less than imperial expansion overseas. Puckle could report the death-traps, lightheartedly described as nuisances, but had no power to enforce the magistrates to order the emptying of cesspools or the provision of drains, ashpits and closets. In one instance the Lambeth magistrates did act with lightning speed. When 4,406 rotten fish were deposited before them for their inspection they ordered the instant destruction of the consignments.

George Puckle was also faced with the problem common to

[1] From the Report of the Medical Officer of Health for Lambeth, 1872. Information concerning public health has been taken from the *Proceedings of the Vestry of Lambeth*, established under the Metropolitan Local Management Act 1855 and 1856.

the Medical Officers of Health in all industrial parishes around the capital: the determination of parishioners to maintain rural ways of life. Old-established inhabitants wanted to live as they had done as children with a garden and pigsty at the door; while many immigrants from the country would not be denied the solace of keeping a pig, others wished to continue familiar crafts such as horse-breaking and cow-keeping. The undertaking of these activities when the pastures of Lambeth had shrunk to weedy and garbage-strewn patches was often a menace to public health. After the rinderpest outbreak of 1865 metropolitan cowsheds had to be licensed; and in Lambeth for the year 1868–9 there were ninety-six applications for cow-houses, six of which were made for the first time. Within living memory an old woman sold milk from a cow which she kept in Bishop's Park. The cowsheds could be visited but it would have been a brave inspector who tackled the stalwart milkwomen, mostly from Wales, many of whom George Sala declared he would be 'happy to back, and for no inconsiderable sum, to thrash Ben Gaunt.' They purchased their rounds, or milk walks, and kept their buckets and ladles as they pleased. Families, like the Beaufoys, who had the means and the space kept a house cow. Charles Pott, a vinegar brewer of Southwark whose concern was later absorbed into Beaufoy's, went in for cow-keeping in style. An Alderney calf was sent from the Midlands and arrived at the brewery in a cab.[1] So long as garbage lay about the streets it was impossible to check the keeping of pigs which had long been the poor man's scavengers. As in manorial days when pigs were 'presented' at court for roaming, there were periodical round-ups; in 1868–9 the streets were cleared of 166 pigs. These clearances seemed to snap the last links with the old way of life which could then be kept in mind only by tending caged birds and plants in pots. The demands of the new townsmen for goldfinches, linnets, bullfinches and larks were so great that their favourites were threatened with extinction.

Few birds could survive in the green open spaces, such as Kennington and Vauxhall Parks, which were preserved or created. They soon succumbed to the polluted atmosphere and to the assaults of boys. Charles Booth found Vauxhall

[1] W. B. Woodgate, *Reminiscences of an Old Sportsman*, 1909, p. 50.

Park, saved from building speculators by the efforts of Octavia Hill, the Kyrle Society and Mark Beaufoy (plate 6), badly kept; but it provided a green oasis for the people of Vauxhall and a setting for a monument of an eminent South Lambeth inhabitant, Henry Fawcett (1833–1884). This statue, according to Walter Besant, ennobled the park, although Fawcett appeared to be wondering if 'he ought to be dressed in some kind of Court costume – if he knew what – in order to receive the angel; or the angel might have assumed a frock coat in compliment to the statesman.'[1]

When Mark Beaufoy came of age in 1875 sweated labour, epidemic diseases, gin palaces and pawnshops were the fruits by which industrial civilisation was known. These manifestations were accepted as inevitable by many, but not by Beaufoy. When he crossed the water to Westminster as member for Kennington he did not forget the plight of his constituents. With Vauxhall Station and the Nine Elms Railway Depot on his doorstep, Mark well knew how over-worked were the railway servants, and how frequent were accidents as a consequence. Beaufoy supported not only a reduction in their hours but an eight-hour day in other industries. He pointed out that: 'Many working men must be dissatisfied with the present condition of things in England; on the one hand, we have hours of unusual length and low pay, and on the other hand, we have no work at all, and the only resource left – the workhouse.'[2]

Beaufoy was no platform reformer for he introduced the eight-hour day into his own works, and was able to report 'a larger output than before'. His advanced Liberal views and the enshrinement of Gladstone at Caron Place was not altogether to the taste of Beaufoy's relations (plate 6).

[1] W. Besant, *South London*, 1899, p. 113. The statue was removed, apparently unofficially, and only the head was saved by a schoolboy and taken to the Henry Fawcett School. This bust, with other South Lambeth relics, was shown at an excellent exhibition in October 1970 arranged by Mr Michael Gaunt, archivist for St Anne's church.

[2] *Hansard*, Vol. CCCXLI, 3rd series, 1890, p. 1113; for Beaufoy's support of reduction in working hours of railway servants see Vol. VIII, 4th series, 1893, p. 87. For general discussion on the question of working hours see *The Nineteenth Century*, Vol. XXVI, 1889, pp. 21–34, H. Cox, 'The Eight Hours Question.'

Mark Beaufoy made another break with family tradition when he moved his residence from Lambeth. Writing in March 1897, he described Caron Place as being 'completely transmogrified. My new manager, Cresswell, lives in the house and has my office. I keep mother's boudoir as a bedroom which I occupy when Mildred is at Coombe and the little library is my office! The family come up today, and I move to Park Crescent this afternoon.' Although vinegar brewers were at this time facing stiff competition from the manufacturers of cheap, unbrewed vinegar, Beaufoy had been able to build a baronial residence at Coombe, near Shaftesbury (plate 14). The beech-lined avenue, nearly a mile in length, showed something of the family panache; so did the imposing mansion which, though built from the rock on which it stood, dominated rather than blended with the surrounding terrain.

Outwardly South Lambeth showed little sign of the dead hand of depression which rested on trade and agriculture in the last decades of the nineteenth century. The vast warehousing and bottling establishment of Barrett and Company was extended and replaced some of the tenements in Bond Street, a condiment factory overshowed St Anne's and proudly proclaimed its aristocratic origins: Brand's Mayfair Works; and the growing consequence of the South Metropolitan Gas Company was the main cause of the great gas strike in January 1890. The appearance of new industrial undertakings and the expansion of existing ones were followed by fresh consignments of countrymen who heard of new openings mainly through railway workers. The newcomers were often resented since they were used to break strikes and their employment on long-term construction works tended to keep wages low. One of the measures suggested by Mark Beaufoy in an election manifesto was the provision of village allotments to save the cities from overcrowding. By this time, however, more than cabbage plots were needed to stop the hordes of countrymen seeking to better themselves in the towns. The depression did not deter men and women who, having known little else in the village, were determined to take their chance in the city. The chances for those without means or training were slender. Physical strength and determination enabled many families to stay the course and to consider their venture well justified; but only those who brought, as old Mark Beaufoy had done, outstanding abilities and some capital to the city were able to achieve eminence. The belief that Lambeth is the gateway to success still persists and the district continues to attract new faces and new races. The hopeful Whittingtons continue to arrive.

Vine Lodge

CHAPTER FIVE

St. Anne's, South Lambeth: Facing Two Ways

> The change that had come over the old place was quite
> marvellous, and now he thought the church was worthy
> of the district in which it stood. (Hear, hear). He was one
> who held that the churches should not be inferior to the
> residences in which they lived. (Applause.)
>
> Philip Cazenove speaking after the re-opening
> of the restored St Anne's on 19 October 1876.

Standing about a quarter of a mile south of the river, St
Anne's was placed between two worlds. Eastward stood the
imposing dwellings of the Lawn and Fentiman Road; to the
west and north were crowded tenement homes of railway workers, costers and scavengers. Of which district was the restored
St Anne's (plate 21) to prove worthy? Before this question can
be answered an attempt must be made to understand the religious needs of the South Lambeth parishioners. These included
the new poor who, through good times and bad steadily
trudged into the district, the established well-to-do like the
Beaufoys and the new rich who often made up with stucco what
they lacked in stability. Without facing two ways how was any
incumbent to meet the demands of the well-to-do who supplied,
first by pew-rents and then by voluntary offerings, the money
on which the church largely depended, and also the needs of the
poor? As railway servants, costers, factory hands and casual
workers outnumbered the well-to-do in the parish of St Anne's,
their needs will be considered first.

While the village mud remained on their boots those who
came to South Lambeth to rise but stayed too often to sink
may have made efforts to go to church. When drink, ill-health

and other misfortunes pulled the newcomers lower and lower
in the scale of employment, the lack of suitable clothes, of interest and of energy kept them at home on Sundays. New
arrivals steadily poured in to undertake the better paid work
until they, too, succumbed to city temptations and hazards.
These waves of misery, so steadily following one another,
almost broke Henry Beaufoy's heart and had an irresistible
attraction for Henry Mayhew (1812–1887). The son of a solicitor of utmost respectability, young Mayhew could not be
kept off the streets. In despair his father, who must have wondered why five of his seven sons should have such freakish
tastes, sent him to sea in an East Indiaman. Mayhew returned
with a single trophy: a tarantula spider pickled in rum. In his
London Labour and the London Poor (1851) he preserved for posterity the strange and often misshapen figures who lurked in the
London by-ways. Those in regular employment had little interest for Mayhew who described only the slipping or the
fallen. Although his picture of the London poor is one-sided, it
is nonetheless revealing, for Mayhew could catch every inflec-
tion in the voice of destitution. He bridged the gap between
the Romantics and the Gradgrinds dedicated to facts and
figures. Like a conjurer, Mayhew could draw from his hat
long streamers of statistics to prove that the London poor,
though resembling the phantoms of the damned envisaged by
Beckford and Fuseli, were real. If Mayhew's estimations of the
numbers of goldfinches and of primrose plants sold in London
are not convincing, his reporting of the views of the vendors
has the ring of truth. Dwellers in smoke-shrouded Vauxhall
could only distinguish the seasons by the contents of the costers' barrows; primrose plants made way for green peas and
apples for holly and mistletoe.

As the 1851 census returns show that 480 of these general
dealers out of a total of 1,157 living on the Surrey side dwelt in
Lambeth, their views on religion have some bearing on the
needs of the poor around St Anne's. The costers, mudlarks
and other scavengers often missed the drift of Mayhew's questioning on religious matters, but many of their answers
showed a relentless logic that proved hard to rebut.

The theology of the costers, like that of many more learned
men, centred on their own needs:

'Now they respect the City Missionaries, because they read to them . . . and because they visit the sick, and sometimes give oranges and such like to them and the children . . . London costers live very often in the same courts and streets as the poor Irish, and if the Irish are sick, be sure there comes to them the priest. . . . Many a man that's not a Catholic has rotted and died without any good person near him. Why, I lived a good while in Lambeth, and there wasn't one coster in a 100, I'm satisfied, knew so much as the rector's name – though Mr Dalton's a very good man. But the reason I was telling you of, sir, is that the costers reckon *that* religion's the best that gives most in charity. . . . I'm not a Catholic myself, but I believe every word of the Bible, and have the greatest belief that it's the Word of God because it teaches democracy.'

The ecumenical outlook of the coster was unusual in his age; he acknowledged the worth of the Evangelical city missionaries, the Roman Catholic priest, the erudite incumbent of St Mary's, Lambeth and the Christian Socialists. But his belief that the poor felt rejected by God and man alike was universally held: 'We are left to live and die like dogs and no one cares if we go to hell.'[1]

As the very poor felt themselves dispossessed of human rights, they did not venture into churches and chapels, where the well-to-do worshipped. On this point a street scavenger and R. W. Enraght, vicar of Bardesley near Birmingham (1879–1885), who was often assistant priest at St Anne's, were in agreement.[2] The scavenger declared: 'I never goes to any church or chapel. Sometimes I hasn't clothes as is fit, and I s'pose I couldn't be admitted into sich fine places in my working dress. I was once in a church; but felt queer, as one does in

[1] *Report of the Church Congress* 1890, p. 46, quoted by the chaplain of the Manchester Ship Canal.

[2] As brother-in-law of John Gooch, R. W. Enraght was a frequent visitor at Caron Place. He was an ardent ritualist and, when incumbent of Bardesley, was imprisoned for nearly two months under the Public Worship Regulation Act of 1874. His Sheffield sermon was printed as: *To the Poor the Gospel is preached.* A sermon advocating the right of the people to freedom of public worship, in the Church of the People, 1863, 18 pp.

them strange places, and never went again. They're fittest for
rich people.' This view was corroborated by Enraght: 'The
poor, I say, feel – they have only too good reason to feel – that if
they do find their way to the house of prayer . . . it will only be
to be looked coldly upon and disheartened . . . Or, worse still,
it will only be to be permitted, perhaps, to walk the full length of
the church aisle – the gazing stock, as they think, of the well
dressed people whom they see occupying the church'.

It is not surprising that a nine-year-old mudlark told
Mayhew: 'He didn't know what religion meant. God was
God . . . He had heard he was good but didn't know what
good he was to him.' The boy's elders shared his outlook. A
coster grew impatient with being questioned: 'No; I never
heard about this here creation you speaks about. In coorse
God Almighty made the world, and the poor brick-layers' labourers built the houses arterwards – that's *my* opinion . . . I
have heard a little about our Saviour – they seems to say he
was a goodish kind of man; but if he says as how a cove's to
forgive a feller as hits you, I should say he know'd nothing
about it . . . yes, I knows! – in the Lord's prayer they says
'Forgive us our trespasses as we forgive them as trespass agin
us.' It's a very good thing, in coorse, but no costers can't do
it.'

Another coster showed all the exclusiveness of the denomin-
ational groups around him: 'I don't know what the Pope is. Is
he any trade? It's nothing to me when he's no customer of
mine. I have nothing to say about nobody that ain't no
customers . . . O, yes, I've heard of God; he made heaven and
earth; I never heard of his making the sea; that's another
thing, and you can best learn about that at
Billingsgate . . . Jesus Christ? Yes, I've heard of him. Our
Redeemer? Well, I only wish I could redeem my Sunday togs
from my uncle's.

What of those whose Sunday clothes were immediately
available? Too often they were donned so that the worshippers
could set forth to mark ecclesiastical misdemeanours: 'A spirit
of gossiping and slander is spread throughout society. A religious school for scandal is opened in every town and village;
men employ themselves in the House of God in observing the
tones and gestures of their pastors, that they might report

something evil of them in next week's newspaper.'[1]

It was a misfortune for the Church of England that so many incumbents were engaged in disputes over ritual in the critical 1840s when the smoke from furnaces, gasworks, and factories began to obliterate the familiar landmarks particularly those of society, which hitherto had accepted, if not always observed, a belief in the common humanity of master and man. The Christian Socialists were aware of the problems of industrial society, but they hardly knew what solutions to offer. It was already too late to harness the tandem of Capital and Labour with co-operation; though this solution long continued to attract many church leaders. At the Church Congress of 1867, which met for the first time at an industrial centre, the Bishop of Oxford was still playing this safe card. He also recognised the needs of industrial cities by declaring: 'I say we do not want fine chapels filled with perfumed handkerchiefs, but we want great churches filled with working men (Loud Cheers).' By this time the cities were getting their large churches despite keen competition for sites;[2] but the scented handkerchiefs still predominated in the congregations.

When Mayhew questioned the mudlarks by Vauxhall Bridge, the South Lambeth Chapel, built in 1793, was still standing: an enigma to the young scavengers, a convenient landmark for artisans, and an object of derision to many well-to-do churchgoers who aspired to a more imposing edifice (plate 20). Neither the Evangelicals nor the Tractarians had any use for Georgian churches which appeared to both parties as frivolous and unsanctified. At best Hanoverian churches appeared barn-like edifices, lacking both the pointed arch and dimly-lit chancel which the Romantics had established as the correct ecclesiastical setting for those with awakened sensibilities. On 19 October 1876 the Bishop of Winchester consecrated

[1] *Life of Frederick Denison Maurice*, ed. F. Maurice, 1884, Vol. I, p. 344, from Maurice's unheeded appeal in 1843 to E. B. Pusey and Lord Ashley to unite in moderating the virulence of religious newspapers. On 21 September 1867 *Punch* noted they were still at each other's throats:

If *Record* and *Guardian*, like cats of Kilkenny,
To the tail eat each other, in proof of their zeal.

[2] Some indication of the effects of this competition is suggested by a cutting from an unnamed and undated newspaper in H.S.T's diary for 1878: 1850 20 acres of land bordering on Wandsworth Common sold for £600; 1877 14½ acres of land bordering on Wandsworth Common sold for £14,500.

the new chancel of the restored St Anne's which took place of 'a church which, in the past, was in some respects less pretentious than a modern barn, but which, now that it has been in the hands of the builders, and they have carried out the design of the architect, will be a credit to those who originated the work of restoration . . . The best thing that can be said of the church, as it now appears, is that it is an unlike the old church as it is possible for it to be. The old church was formerly known as the South Lambeth Chapel. It was built about the end of the last century, and was a proprietary chapel.'

The general disapproval of eighteenth-century church activities extended to the proprietors whose rights had to be bought out so the site could be conveyed to the Ecclesiastical Commissioners. Of the proprietors of the South Lambeth Chapel it was said, 'some of them were dead, some insolvent, some had left for their country's good – (laughter) – and many could not be found. For three years a lawyers' bill was being got up, and without exaggeration it was when finished long enough to stretch across the room. (Laughter).'[1]

The sweeping away of the proprietors, many of whom had subscribed regularly to their chapel, did not ease for the incumbents of St Anne's the burden of meeting the needs of an increasing number of parishioners with inadequate funds. The ways in which this hard task was undertaken are suggested in the diaries of Minnie Thornhill, who worshipped for thirteen years at St Anne's and taught in the Sunday School for eleven, and in the memoranda book of W. A. Harrison, vicar of South Lambeth 1867–1891. These accounts show the day-to-day advances and setbacks of the parish in the second half of the nineteenth century which was spanned by the pastorates of three incumbents: Charles Pitman Shepherd, minister 1857–1867, William Anthony Harrison and William Alexander Morris, vicar 1891–1903. Few men keep in step with their times; but the careers of these parsons indicate the different attitudes which could be adopted towards a pastorate in a South London parish. A social man could enjoy himself, a conscientious one achieve a large measure of success and a feeling man could die

[1] The quotations from the speeches made at the reception in Caron Place after the re-opening of St Anne's are taken from the report in the *South London News*, 20 October 1876.

under the burden of endeavouring to restore their self-respect to those whose orbit was the gas-works, the public house and the tenement.

When Minnie and Ellen Thornhill, still bewildered by the death of Dearest, arrived at Caron Place they found the minister of the South Lambeth chapel, Charles Shepherd, reading aloud *Childe Harold*. The employment and choice of reading matter throw some light on Shepherd's disposition. He was a young man of sensibility who found his greatest happiness in social intercourse. He had in full measure that wit which he once described in the course of a sermon as 'a cause of social and even intellectual enjoyment'. Such a man, personable and entertaining, was indispensable to Anne Beaufoy as she emerged from the seclusion of widowhood to storm the social heights of South Lambeth. For the years 1866–1868 the diaries and Minnie's correspondence with her cousins illuminate Shepherd's activities as a master of ceremonies at Caron Place and as minister at the chapel.

Shepherd grew up at Milborne Port in Dorset, and left Sherborne School destined for academic honours. His well-wishers were not disappointed; he obtained the Hulsean prize and a good degree at Cambridge. Shepherd then entered the unsettled period which so often succeeds a successful academic career. He was chaplain at a Derbyshire school, then headmaster of the Grammar School at Sudbury in the same county before he reached the goal of ambitious young clergy: a curacy in London. From Westminster he obtained the living of South Lambeth in 1857; and early in the 1860s Minnie's Lyston diaries show that he was also acting as tutor to young Mark Beaufoy. Having secured the services of this invaluable young man, Aunt George made full use of him. Minnie not infrequently noted that he 'took Marky to Marsh's to have his hair cut'. More in harmony with his office Shepherd also accompanied Mark for his confirmation at St James', Piccadilly. The choice of this church rather than St Mary's, Lambeth suggests that Shepherd had some connection with the forward-looking incumbent, J. E. Kempe.

As he was both quick-witted and conciliatory Shepherd may have been as invaluable at Kempe's discussion groups as he was at Caron Place. Here the household was not infrequently ruffled by Aunt George's arbritary and impetuous decisions. The minister attended the tea parties Rita gave for her dolls; and played croquet, chess and billiards with her seniors. These everyday services were performed with a good will and tact which made Shepherd constantly in demand; but he particularly shone on festive occasions. As the young Thornhills were either at Radley or in New Zealand, Shepherd escorted parties to the opera, the boat race, the Crystal Palace, where Toole was 'very amusing' but the chimpanzee was 'horrid', and the Eton and Harrow match. When the ladies were bored by the cricket he took them in turn for strolls: 'Mr Shepherd and Miss Mercier were gone about an hour and a half.'

The position of Anne Mercier at Caron Place was similar to Shepherd's. Officially she taught Rita, but was retained for her good looks, social aplomb and accomplishments. Alike in temperament and in their positions as dependents Anne and Shepherd became attached; but he was married. His wife was a sad figure who crept into Caron Place on undress occasions; she suffered from attacks of insanity. In 1868, when Shepherd had obtained the living of St Katherine Cree, Mark failed in his initial attempt to get into Eton. Although intelligent and 'such a good boy at his lessons', Mark was unnerved by examinations and later entered Cambridge having failed to get into Oxford. Perhaps Ellen's description of Shepherd as being 'forbidden the house' after his pupil's failure was overdramatic; but he was shunned to the extent that when he took evening duty at the chapel Minnie 'went with Sarah, the maid, to St Peter's'. Unfortunately Shepherd continued to reside in his old parish, so he was largely excluded from the South Lambeth social circle. Aunt George now dominated this circle, but she could not afford to disregard gossip. Kind friends were not lacking to tell her that Anne Mercier had visited Shepherd at Eastbourne, where he had gone with a serious complaint which caused his death in February 1870. Almost automatically Miss Mercier, too, was forbidden the house. From India Ellen Drummond wrote: 'What a horrible affair this is about Miss Mercier. When you first mentioned that she had left, I couldn't think of any reason but that Rita must have got beyond her teaching; particularly as you had mentioned Mr Shepherd's death before. I cannot tell you how sorry I was to hear about it, as I fear from your last letter she must have regularly gone to the bad, and what will become of her now?'

Shepherd's contacts with his poor parishioners can only have been fleeting; but his tact and pleasant manners may have made him more welcome than an earnest pastor with the knack of appearing on the doorstep at the wrong moment. When W. A. Harrison accompanied Minnie Thornhill on a visit to the mother of a Sunday School pupil, the time was not propitious for she 'seemed half ashamed for her appearance and shielded herself behind the door'. The unfortunate working wives could seldom put a foot right. If in the morning they appeared blackhanded they were castigated as 'slatterns and dowdies', and if they spruced themselves up early to stand at the doorway they were 'gossips . . . thinking more of their neighbours' sins than of their husbands' dinners.'[1] Although his parish visits must have been infrequent, Shepherd had grasped some of the social implications of the Industrial Revolution; this is clearly shown in extracts from his sermon on *Sins of the Tongue, Lying and other Fraud*: 'There are companies of men, – whole streets, – whole cities of them, – who . . . talk of nothing else but covetousness, – morning, noon and night . . . consider the enormous and all but universal fraud of adulteration . . . in which fraud such large numbers seem to be involved that it assumes the proportion of a national crime . . . They are accustomed to think of the Gospel as a grand abstract science in which it is good to be orthodox, but they like not to meet Christ in the streets'.[2]

Shepherd could recognise the manifestations of industrialism, but he could not feel at home with the offspring of the new society. When a Sunday School outing took place on 14 June 1867 Minnie wrote: 'We met all the children at Vauxhall. They were all packed in with us amongst them. Mr Shepherd and Mark after they had seen us all packed in second or third class compartments went higher up and jumped into a first

[1] *Report of the Church Congress 1890*, p. 511, the authority on working wives was S. Reynolds Hole, Dean of Rochester, who was more at home with gardening than domestic economy.

[2] C. P. Shepherd, *Sins of the Tongue, Lying and other Fraud*. a sermon preached at South Lambeth Chapel, published by request, 1858, 12 pp.

class, pretty cool, I thought . . . all the children were marched
two by two into Richmond Park. They did just rush about
when they were first let loose, and went and bought a lot of
nasty ginger beer and rubbish. We played games with the girls
and Mr Shepherd and Mark cricket with the boys.'

When W. A. Harrison (plate 23) took over the living of South
Lambeth in 1867, the chapel soon became 'certainly quite a different place. All the seats have been turned, the pulpit and
reading desk, or rather lectern, are now near the altar. We have
choir stalls, a good many gentlemen have joined the
choir . . . there are collections both morning and evening.'

As Aunt George's social prestige was rising with that of the
chapel, it was immaterial to her that the new vicar was a
serious man with a large nose and a staid manner. As a pert
girl in her teens Rita wrote: 'Mr Harrison came last Wednesday and brought his sitting breeches in his pocket which he
put on coming into the house, to judge from appearances for
he stayed nearly three hours.'

Harrison may have had the common failing of not knowing
when to go, but he well comprehended how to make a good
start. Before drawing up his plans for restoring the chapel and
making it a weekday, as well as a Sunday, reality in the
parish, Harrison surveyed his assets. The chief of these was
the number of young people within the orbit of the church.
There were 198 boys on the books of the Eldon School which,
even after the management was undertaken by a board, was
the chief source of recruits for the Sunday School. The seven
classes for boys were managed by the leading families, such as
the Russells and Lapidges, of the parish; and the six girls'
classes came under the same control. Superintendents of the
Sunday Schools probably had more trouble with their sixteen
teachers than their 120 scholars.

The church had 620 free sittings so that an incumbent
without private means would have been in a bad way had not
the Ecclesiastical Commissioners contributed a yearly £200
towards the income of the benefice. During the years 1876
–1881 the average yearly income from fees was £16 12s 4d and
from offertory collections £66 19s 9d. From the total income of
the benefice, £283 12s 3d, the curate's yearly salary of £120 had
to be found. Even though Harrison had a private income

ambitious schemes entailed constant efforts to raise funds. Harrison was no new broom, he started and continued an indefatigable parish worker. He not only restored and enlarged the chapel, renamed St Anne's, possibly as a compliment to Anne Beaufoy who had 'acted . . . with marked liberality' towards its restoration; he distributed soup, blankets and school prizes, started elocution and cricket clubs, held frequent services and investigated the drainage of tenements off the Nine Elms Road. He visited constantly both eastward and westward, taking his 'sitting breeches' to Caron Place and also to Neptune Street, in 'a dreadfully dirty, nasty part of South Lambeth'. The appointments for 1867 and 1868 in Harrison's memoranda book show that his only dissipations were visits to St Alban's, Holborn and to the British Museum, that 'Palace of Chasten'd fun', with his children. Though the Harrisons did give a juvenile party, it was a serious household where social pleasures were rationed. When Minnie went with Aunt George to a 'most enjoyable ball' she stayed until the last dance, but 'Eleanor Harrison came with Mrs Harrison and was taken away at 10 o'clock, poor girl'. Sons left parsonages to roam the world, but biddable daughters were often conscripted for life service in the parish. The tone set by these clerical deputies was sometimes inimical to youthful exuberance. The recreational fare of the girls after Sunday School was listening to 'a good mild little story.' This cannot have been easy to find as in the mid-nineteenth century the best sellers among girls' books were far from mild. The first in the field, *The Wide, Wide World* was, despite strong evangelical overtones, a worldly book. The vicissitudes from which the heroine emerged triumphantly included the rough-and-tumble of farm life in New England, assault on the highway and the dissipations of wealthy homes; *Jessica's First Prayer* was less sensational, but *Stepping Heavenward*, which was surprisingly esteemed by Francis Kilvert, again provided stronger fare from America with the vicissitudes of a family which would have felt at home at Cold Comfort Farm. It was not until later that the girls received what Harrison tried to provide for the boys: the means whereby their imaginations were stirred and their capabilities stretched.

Harrison's love of Shakespeare may explain his imaginative

development of the boys' interests. With a strong-willed and able superintendent, Edward Rudolf, Harrison re-animated the Sunday School; and, to retain the interest of the leaving boys, established an elocution class. Perhaps this was his most important contribution to the welfare of South Lambeth. Incorrect and illspoken speech, such as 'Hunto the 'ills I lift my Heyes', was the greatest obstacle which prevented working-class boys from rising in the world. After they had quarrelled as Brutus and Cassius, stirred with the times as King John and refought Bulwer Lytton's 'Battle of Hastings', the boys did begin to speak with confidence. Like Mayhew's street reciter, who declared: 'When I act Shakespare I cannot restrain myself', they were swept outside their hesitations and fears of appearing foolish. Mrs Harrison was not so successful with her ladies' Literary Shakespeare Society. After the first meeting, when Minnie took the part of Portia in *The Merchant of Venice*: 'Alice Baillie says her mother will not let her read next time, so we shall have more bother.' Mrs Baillie either did not think Shakespeare suitable reading for girls or was aggrieved that her daughter had not been assigned the chief part.

The most active boys in the elocution class were Frederick Douglas, the son of a labourer living off Bond Street, and Alan Cunningham whose home on the Albert Embankment was equally humble. They had both graduated from Minnie's class at Sunday School (plate 25). Rather reluctantly Minnie started to teach in Sunday School on 15 March 1868: 'I got on pretty well with them all things considering.' The novelty of having a new teacher soon wore off and her pupils became 'so naughty' that she 'could hardly manage them at all.' But time taught Minnie how to manage her barbarians: 'I took them each an orange and they were awfully good.' Nevertheless relapses were frequent; when Minnie was away a reliable boy left in charge of the class gave himself attendance marks without bothering to put in an appearance.

When the class settled down after the initial comings and goings two nine-year-olds, Frederick Douglas and Alan Cunningham, stayed with Minnie for ten years and remained her lifelong friends. Pupils drifted away when their parents moved, when they lost interest, or because they fell ill. Poor health was general among the boys and Minnie was called upon for tickets for the dispensary the foundation stone of which had been laid on 12 July 1866 by General Lawrence (plate 22). Though fast becoming derelict the dispensary still stands and has a more ecclesiastical appearance than the new St Stephen's church opposite it. Among other local doctors Edward Wright gave his services at the dispensary. When Cunningham appeared looking 'so pale' Wright forgot he was not prescribing for one of his Caron Place patients: 'He has a fever about him, little overworked and must have perfect rest.' The complaint of Harrison, another Sunday School scholar, was diagnosed as 'only his growing'. Soon after Harrison was 'seriously ill', but survived to ask Minnie to act as godmother to his first child. Redman was not so lucky; when she visited his home Minnie found him 'so weak with hardly strength to cough.'

Sick boys and those in scrapes found a true friend in Minnie, but Harrison's new Sunday School superintendent, Edward Rudolph, considered she was 'too good-natured with them'. Rudolph, the founder of the Waifs and Strays Homes, first appeared at Caron Place when Aunt George threw her net widely for talent. In the spring of 1867 a young civil servant, Edward de Mountjoie Rudolph brought his flute to a musical evening.[1] He lived with his brother, Robert, in Meadow Road. The Rudolphs were typical of their age when earnest young laymen came to the fore in church and social activities and caused an irascible member of 'the old brigade' to refer slightingly to the proliferation of churches and 'the goody-goody ways that make up our present monotonous existence.'[2] The dash which the old soldier missed had not disappeared but been diverted into other channels. Edward Rudolph had the energy and power of self-assertion which could have made him prominent in 'the rackety times'; but he directed them into social work, and in 1871 became superintendent of the Sunday Schools in South Lambeth. Both teachers and scholars needed, though they sometimes resented, the control which Rudolph was well able to exert. He had both energy

[1] The Mr Rudolph mentioned frequently in H. S. T's diaries was generally Edward; though his brother, Robert, also played a prominent part in the South Lambeth Sunday School and in his brother's later activities connected with the Homes for Waifs and Strays.

[2] One of the Old Brigade, *London in the Sixties*, 1st ed. 1908, 1914 ed. p. 1.

and organising ability: 'Mr Rudolph certainly does take wonderful pains to advance the good of the School; he has got up a library for the boys, and a club.'

He also revived two activities for which the district had once been notable: acting in pantomime and gardening. In Rudolph's production of *Bluebeard* a number of Minnie's boys let off steam, and many of them entered plants at the Poor People's Flower Shows at Lambeth Palace. On 17 July 1876 Lord Shaftesbury presented Walter Rogers with 1s 6d for a geranium which Minnie had bought for him for 6d in the Kennington Road. Three years earlier Mrs Douglas had won a prize for her window box. Her jubilation was possibly short-lived as women often parted with their husband's clothing so as to have 'a good window',[1] and Mrs Douglas may have had good reason to echo the refrain of Dean Hole's 'The Song of the Exhibitor':

> I'm a poor, used-up exhibitor,
> Knocked out of present time.

Rudolph could love the waifs and strays, 2,943 of whom had been found homes in the first ten years of his venture; but he could not always understand the anxieties of boys who from their early teens were haunted by fears of not finding work. The vicar could easily find a situation for Colville, 'a very nice, good boy' with an attractive appearance, as a page in the Wyndham Club. But when he grew out of his uniform, Colville had only the prospect of becoming a porter or general cleaner. Unless they were Carnegies or Josiah Bounderbys, boys whose parents were too poor to apprentice them to a trade, found it very hard to rise above a grasshopper career of moving from one unskilled job to another.

Minnie's life in Caron Place was not always easy, so she could understand the anxieties of her boys and was concerned about their prospects when they left school. The boys returned her affection; in the middle of a lesson one exclaimed: 'Oh, teacher, you are a blue-eyed beauty!' But the temptation to take advantage of her kindness was often irresistible: 'Shaw, Edwards and Bimson were terrible this afternoon after school.

[1] H. Mayhew, *London Labour and the London Poor*, 1851, Vol. I, p. 139.

They would not leave the school. I could do nothing; they threw things about and read Mr Rudolph's letter.'

Edwards' mother was anxious to keep her boy off the streets, but Bimson's father was an elderly Liverpudlian, worn out trying to make ends meet with his carpenter's wages. Shaw was growing up in the hard-drinking area around the Nine Elms depot where his father worked. As he grew older Shaw felt the strain of conflicting standards at home and at school: 'Shaw is in a very tiresome mood just now; he would not have the mittens I made for him.' Later he succumbed to the pressure of his environment: 'Shaw came to school hardly knowing what he was doing and very excited. He has been drinking and it seems it is not for the first time. I kept him back and talked to him.' Shaw's difficulties in finding work made it hard for him to keep his promise to reform. Also, boys who did not frequent public houses with the men felt they cut poor and 'preaching' figures.

Even the exemplary Alan Cunningham, who took a class in Sunday School, drifted from being a telegraph boy into Beaufoy's yard, and from there to 'a place on the Great Eastern at 25s. a week' before he could tell Minnie that 'through Mr Rudolf's kindness and a splendid testimonial from Mr Harrison he had a good situation at the Civil Service Stores as a porter and occasional packer, with a good chance of rising.' The chance was never taken as before the year was out Cunningham had become engaged and found employment as a storeman at the Woolwich Infirmary at 12s a week, with board and lodging found. Cunningham did not want to be left behind his friend, Frederick Douglas, who 'was a great favourite with the girls.' On a Sunday School outing: 'Douglas was inside coming back between Bertha Ford and Lizzy Hiscock. I had to tell him to keep his hands to himself once or twice.' The cloven hoof often appeared during outings. On an excursion to Petersham in July 1876: 'My naughty boys could not resist going into a public house . . . Rogers was very tiresome and finished by having a fight with Bist and getting a knock on his nose which made it bleed. Shaw was rather unkind to march off, but he was very good and walked with me to the station.'

A month earlier the boys had presented Minnie with a handsome ornamental brass inkstand accompanied by a letter which clearly showed Rudolph's guiding hand: 'At times you may feel discouraged at the little advance we make in our spiritual life, but we pray God that the seed which is now being sown may at last bring forth that fruit which you so much desire, and for which you labour so earnestly.'

The labour was not in vain. Though young people drawn into the orbit of St Anne's may have grumbled at being rounded up for classes and for meetings, they began to lose the stigma of rejection that had marked their parents' lives. Although only a small proportion of Lambeth children came under the influence of men like Harrison, Rudolph and T. B. Stephenson, the Methodist minister who founded the National Children's Homes, this leaven had its effect. By the 1870s many of those who had earlier come to London to work had few hopes this side of the grave. Unfettered by memories their children, like sparrows, were prepared to pick up whatever the city had to offer. The Ragged School in Newport Street, the Eldon School and the Sunday Schools had given them a confidence unknown to their parents and had sharpened their wits.

Unlike Shepherd, who had faced consistently eastward, Harrison kept the interests of both Neptune Street and of the Fentiman Road in mind. As Minnie noted, gentlemen sang in the choir but so did Sunday School boys who keenly competed for places: 'James Weeks wants to be in the choir but it is full now.' By the time he left South Lambeth Harrison had widened the horizons of the boys and girls who attended the Sunday Schools; his successor was to help the men to stand upon their feet. William Alexander Morris (plate 24), vicar of St Anne's 1891–1903, did not have to face two ways as his heart was large enough to hold all his parishioners: 'He seemed to have the freedom of every class'.[1]

When Morris came to South Lambeth the Church of England had, at last, taken a headlong plunge into industrial problems. By 1890 the representative of the Pattern Makers Association was assuring the Church Congress that the Church must hail the new unionism (although not perfect) 'as a distinct step upward and onward to millenial com-

[1] N. Dearmer, *The Life of Percy Dearmer*, 1940, p. 70, quoting from Dearmer's article on W. A. Morris in *Commonwealth*, March 1904.

pleteness'.[1] While many may have found this oratorical flight hard to swallow, the majority of clergymen agreed that something should be done to 'regulate those remorseless laws of competition'. Morris had no doubt about this; and his curate, Percy Dearmer (1867–1936), never wearied of stressing that Christianity '*is* Socialism' and, he conceded, 'a good deal more.'[2] Already in the 1840s F. D. Maurice had striven to show that 'human relations' and not 'land, goods, money, labour' were the basis of society.[3] Lack of experience hampered the early efforts of co-operative associations to establish the dignity of labour; also harder-headed leaders than Maurice and his sympathisers were needed. The times produced the men. Labour leaders like John Burns, Will Thorne and Ben Tillett combined the Christian belief that man is not merely a money-making machine with the drive and tactical skill of the industrial captains and with the nineteenth-century consumer's determination to strike a good bargain. By the 1890s labour rockets kept illuminating the European skies. A skilled pyrotechnist himself, William II of Germany proclaimed his intention of leading an international crusade to redress the working man's wrongs; while the public gardens of South London were once more filled with excited crowds. Sunday after Sunday they watched the fiery displays of new unions, particularly among women. These went up one after another as the shirt-makers, the confectioners, the laundresses, the umbrella and parasol finishers, the cigar and the brush makers, and the match-girls sought to better their working conditions. Among these short-lived scintillations, the union activities of the gas workers and the coal porters glowed with a steady and persistent light. These were the men among whom Morris lived and by whom he was accepted as 'the Gas-Workers' Parson'.[4]

Morris came from Liverpool, a city where the manifestations of first the slave trade and then of Irish destitution had fostered tender consciences among feeling men. William Morris

[1] *Report of the Church Congress, 1890*, pp. 114–137, discussions on the Church's Attitude towards Strikes and Wages Disputes.

[2] Fabian Tract 133, P. Dearmer, *Socialism and Christianity*, 1907, 23 pp.

[3] F. Maurice, op. cit., II, p. 114.

[4] *The Guardian*, 10 February 1904, in obituary of W. A. Morris.

left Oxford determined to understand from within the misery which he had hitherto only viewed from the bastions of a comfortable home. In 1881 he was ordained to the curacy of St Peter's, Vauxhall. This church shared with St Anne's the original sin of having been a proprietary and Georgian chapel. Built on a good industrial site by the river, St Peter's was first incorporated in Price's candle factory and then engulfed by the gas works before it was resuscitated in 1859 as a 'pioneer church' in an attempt to heal the running sore of violence and crime on the South Bank.

When Morris arrived the gas works had travelled a long way since their establishment in 1833. The Company of the South Metropolitan Gasworks had secured the control of six undertakings on the South Bank, including Vauxhall; although the Company's gas had not always been above criticism,[1] the management had moved from strength. When the great strike started in December 1889 the chairman was George Livesey, whom the *Guardian* found 'arbitary,'[2] and whom Cardinal Manning addressed in more down-to-earth terms at a Conciliation Board: 'I have heard of you, sir, and now I have seen you, and I will tell you that it is your obstinacy that is causing all this trouble. You are doing a most wicked thing in bringing in these new men to take the place of the men who are leaving. Public opinion is against you, and in two or three weeks you must be defeated.'

If the Cardinal's prognosis was wrong, his evaluation of Livesey's character was correct. It must be said in his favour, however, that Livesey gave the plot of land on which the first public library in the Borough of Camberwell was built.[3]

As he served in a church standing in the midst of Vauxhall gasworks and lived in a club which he had founded for its workers, Morris could claim some understanding of the great gas dispute of 1889–1890. The workers chiefly concerned were the stokers and the porters who unloaded and brought in the coal which kept the furnaces burning day and night. The

---

[1] *Report of the Medical Officer of Health*, 1865.

[2] Accounts of the strike of the gasworkers have been taken from the *Guardian* where events were covered in the issues between 11 December 1889 and 12 February 1890.

[3] *The Times*, 7 February 1964.

Company had accepted eight-hour shifts, but the work was heavy, monotonous and unhealthy. Men left the blaze of the furnaces for mean, unheated homes and for riverside streets often blanketed with fog. Londoners accepted fogs as an inevitable facet of English weather; in her diaries Minnie merely noted the number of daylight hours when the gas had to be kept burning. To foreigners the phenomenon had a vicious entity of its own making 'the human beast . . . inflamed: it wants something strong, animal-like, fighting, excess, greed, the flush brandy gives, passion: London exhales violence and crime on a winter's night.'[1]

No Londoner could ignore the winter's night tales of 1889; from every public house and street corner came whiffs of gin and discontent. Sensing that the gasworkers were unlikely to remain unaffected by the country-wide unrest, George Livesey put forward a profit-sharing plan. The basis of this scheme was that every employee of the South Metropolitan Gas Company who had signed a year's contract, was to receive a bonus of 1 per cent on their year's wages. This 'nest-egg' was to accumulate for workers who remained with the Company for three or five years. In small concerns profit sharing might have worked; but the days when Dick Whittington's fortunes were made by an honest master had gone. The heavy barricading of the Company's chief works in the Old Kent Road and the provision of stores and of 'large sheds of corrugated iron' to house men recruited from the country show that Livesey had little expectation of his offer being accepted. On the South Bank sad sights could be hourly seen, but none were so heart-rending as 'the police-protected processions from the agricultural districts to the seat of war.' Livesey had reason to be grateful to the police who escorted his new recruits to the gasworks where the distribution of free beer encouraged them to think the city lights had not twinkled in vain. When presented with £1,700 by his grateful Company Livesey gave £600 to the Metropolitan Police Funds. After many threats and attempted settlements the gas stokers' and coal porters' unions came out early in December 1889, but about 1000 men accepted the profit-sharing scheme. The strikers' places were filled by the

[1] Eça de Queroz, *Letters from England*, trans. 1970, p. 29; the letters, written by a Portuguese consul for Brazilian readers, cover the 1880s.

steadily arriving recruits from the country, so Livesey could pose as a public benefactor by providing jobs for honest men and light to save South London from darkness and from violence.

In February the unions accepted the terms offered by Livesey who agreed to revert to eight-hour shifts and to take back the strikers as vacancies arose. During the weary and hungry months of the strike, Morris had been constantly beside the men; when he visited their anxious families he brought warmth to cold homes. Large and physically strong 'with a tremendous voice, a bushy black beard and remarkable eyes', Morris so filled the little rooms that there was no room for despondency. The very presence of this visitor who was 'unwearingly kind, both bluff and gentle' gave courage to the faint-hearted and restrained the violence of those inflamed by fog, drink and a sense of injustice. The men could only explain their devotion by saying he was 'so unlike a parson'. But Morris 'was loved by the men of South London – loved, trusted and understood' because he did not fear to meet Christ in the streets. Today an old parishioner of South Lambeth remembers how courteously Morris greeted each girl as she arrived at meetings of the Guild of Perseverance. By the respect he accorded every one of his parishioners, Morris helped them to lay aside their feelings of inferiority and also their inclinations to overlook the rights of others.

When Morris was vicar of South Lambeth, the second resurgence of the Church of England during the nineteenth century was in full swing. 'Advanced' ritual had come to stay, and many who favoured it were in full cry after social reform. The *Guardian* inquired, almost plaintively: 'But if Marx's theoretical basis is rejected what has been substituted for it?'[1] Percy Dearmer, Morris's first curate at South Lambeth, was getting into his stride and Stewart Headlam had founded the Guild of St Matthew which endeavoured to align the Church of England with the forces of social reform. A treasurer of this Guild was Joe Clayton, one of Morris's gasworkers.

Until he married in 1892, Morris shared the vicarage with Percy Dearmer. Despite the fumes from Brand's factory and

[1] *The Guardian*, 24 September 1890, in review of G. B. Shaw's *Fabian Essays in Socialism*.

the noise from the boys' club in the garden, Dearmer found the vicarage 'a very jolly place'. If by 'jolly' he meant the centre of ceaseless activities, Dearmer was right. In January 1892 he wrote:

> 'We are running the Progressives [candidates in the London County Council elections] from the vicarage here. I was on the platform at the meeting at Beaufoy's yard, at which Morris and Will Thorne and the candidates and John Burns spoke . . . it was rather long and cold but interesting enough; Beaufoy spoke . . . after tea we arranged the vases and candles on the three shelves [above the altar] with great success: it looks very beautiful. I put one of my de Morgan vases on the middle shelf as I thought a blue note was wanted there.'[1]

On his arrival at South Lambeth Dearmer found St Anne's 'really quite nice, so plain and devoid of meretricious ornament . . . there is splendid room for frescoes and mosaics' (plate 21). This was hardly praise that would have satisfied William Harrison or Anne Beaufoy.. The curate was soon to regard their efforts as coldly as they had regarded those of the chapel proprietors: 'I really can't stand the church as it is; it is impossible to say one's prayers in it. We are to have a Morris tapestry baldachino (£20 – £10 to cover frontal risings) and some delicately simple Morris frontals; the whole will be under the direction of Selwyn Image'.[2]

Dearmer's devotion to Morris and wholehearted religious enthusiasm could not reconcile him to some aspects of South Lambeth life. When he wrote his mission hymn, Dearmer felt the attraction of boys in distant lands:

> 'Where children wade the rice-fields
> And watch the camel trains.'

But in South Lambeth he wondered if he would 'ever get on with the boys: I don't seem to take to them very strongly; their attempts to be funny and their horse play bore me at present.'

In 1894 Morris lost his gifted curate whose ever-expanding interests, which were to cover the Russian Church, hymn writing, ritual, cathedrals, socialism and, surprisingly, the *Fellowship of Silence*, necessitated a part-time curacy. Morris had

---

[1] N. Dearmer, op. cit., p. 83. The Progressive candidates for Kennington were the Hon. R. G. Grosvenor and W. Stockbridge.

[2] N. Dearmer, op. cit., see p. 67 for Dearmer's qualified approval of St Anne's and p. 79 for his dissillusionment.

hardly a decade of activity before him. Ill-health forced the man who had been tireless to rest. A friend who met Morris after his retirement found: 'His once powerful frame now worn to a shadow by a terrible disease, almost blind . . . He was perfectly happy, and dwelt on the never-failing love of his people, and his equal affection for them. He would, he said, of all things, rather go back to labour among them, if he had to choose than be preferred to the highest dignity in the Church.'[1]

Morris died at Torquay on 2 February 1904.

Had he lived to be an old man, Mayhew's coster with the ecumenical outlook could have attended the funeral of Morris whose ministry had perhaps fulfilled the costers' exacting demands for the best religion. Of the 'enormous crowds of poor and well-to-do men, women and children' who attended the funeral in South Lambeth none was too indigent to wear some sign of mourning. St Anne's was soon overfilled, and crowds were hammering at the barred doors for admittance. Not since the benevolent potentate, Noel de Caron, had been carried to his grave over three centuries earlier had such a funeral turn-out been seen in Lambeth. The whole of the South Bank claimed as their friend 'the Gas-Worker's Parson'.

Morris would have been the first man to acknowledge his debt to his predecessors. The effects of early industrialism, like those of pollution of the environment, were slow in impinging on the public consciousness. When Mayhew described the activities of a coster who took to catching rats and killing them with his teeth 'like a dog', most people turned away with Mr Podsnap: 'I don't want to know about it; I don't choose to discuss it; I don't admit it!' As minister of South Lambeth, Shepherd had not refused to acknowledge the implications of the Industrial Revolution. He saw the adulterated goods in every shop window and watched tenements spreading over the fields and the gardens of Lambeth; but, like many churchmen in the 1850s and early 1860s, he hardly knew where to make a start. As a body the Church first put a toe in the steaming cauldron of industrialism at the Wolverhampton Congress of 1867. In succeeding years many churchmen attacked the problem with all the ferocity of the rat-catching coster.

Shepherd may have grasped the implications of the new

---

[1] *The Guardian*, 17 February 1904, appreciation by G. H. F. Nye.

forces at work in South Lambeth more readily than his successor, but he lacked Harrison's singleness of purpose. This resolution was Harrison's strength; his triumph was that, like Henry Beaufoy, he gave those growing up in the narrow confines of court and alleyway the chance to escape into a wider world of faith, of imagination and of gaiety. Harrison's penny readings now seem milk-and-water affairs, but they offered an alternative to the penny gaffs, where Mayhew saw performances 'which were forcing into the brains of the childish audience before them thoughts that must embitter a lifetime, and descend from father to child like some bodily infirmity.'

A measure of Harrison's success was the skill with which he utilised the abilities of his helpers. By their drive and organising powers the Rudolph brothers revived the Sunday Schools, but their direction sometimes seemed autocratic. Minnie complained: 'My boy Cunningham has been so naughty that Mr Rudolph has turned him out.' Teachers found, however, that the stricter discipline removed many of their anxieties. Edward Rudolph kept the boys in order, but Minnie gained their confidence. Her scholars ran true to form when she gave a farewell tea to them and some of their mothers on 12 July 1879: 'It went off fairly well . . . Cunningham spoke very nicely and Douglas most sweetly – dear boys – Poor Shaw was not sober. We had a cab back at 10.30 p.m.'.

The remaining structure of the eighteenth-century chapel, which so offended the taste of the 1870s, and the restored church which made Dearmer shudder, have disappeared. Most of St Anne's was destroyed by enemy action in May 1941. But the building had not been in vain; today St Anne's, reconstructed above the earlier foundations, has that atmosphere of good fellowship which is associated with an upper room.

CHAPTER SIX

'Dear Old August'

Yes: here is dear old August come upon us, with its ripe harvests and riper holidays; and let us welcome it with grateful hearts. You and I, dear reader, let us hope, have done seven months' good work this year; and shall we not be prepared to do some more good work, by and by, when we have played a little?

J. W. Kaye, *Essays of an Optimist*, 1870

No one considering Kaye's massive volumes on the Afghan and Sepoy wars and his work in the India Office could question his right to a holiday. But seven months' work was not always a prelude to his readers' holidays. Anne Beaufoy escaped in August to recover from the strain of the London season; but, agreeing with Kaye's dictum that 'holidays are a substantive part of the whole duty of man', she did her duty not only in August and September, but also in May, November and December.

This almanack governed the holiday comings and goings of the wealthy; but the less affluent were following closely on their heels. In 1842 *Punch* described August as the time when 'Tooley Street removes to Ramsgate, and Belgrave Square retires to Brighton'. The uninhibited frolics at Ramsgate where ladies went bathing 'with no more thought than if they were mermaids'[1] continued to hold the affections of Tooley Street on the South Bank; but the day-excursion fares to Brighton forced Belgravia to move further afield: to Wales, the Lake District and Scotland. The pattern of holiday making as it evolved in the mid-nineteenth century is worth considering in detail as one of the most striking manifestations of indus-

[1] D. Jerrold, *The Barber's Chair*, 1874, 1890 ed., p. 46, quoting from *The Times*.

trial society. The movement of men into the cities to make money in order to return periodically to the country for recreation contributed towards the creation of the hybrid town-and-country world which was established a century later.

When the far-ranging peregrinations of Belgravia started, public holidays were almost non-existent. Those who worked hardest, like Sir John Kaye, supported most whole-heartedly their establishment. To the inevitable assertion that workers already enjoyed fifty-two holidays in the year, Kaye had the courage to answer: 'Who can really enjoy Sunday when the ghastly image of Monday peers over its quiet shoulder?' Sir John Lubbock, another hard worker, ensured in 1871 that at least three Sundays in the year should not be so bedevilled. This concession came at a time when nearly all the traditional holidays had disappeared in the towns and countryside. The few that had lingered on, like the Whit Monday Revels at Bedminster, were censured as being the 'scenes of rude festivity, and . . . low debauchery'. The fact that such criticisms were often justified had created a widespread aversion to holidays, for moral and economic reasons. In the early nineteenth century Hannah More voiced the feeling of her times when she wrote, 'it is the bright day brings the adder forth. The sunshine of summer, with sweethearts, apples and nuts, are as dangerous to the preservation of Shipham virtue as all the pleasures of Ranelagh can be to the fine gentlemen and ladies of London.'[1] That holidays from collieries, factories and farms were taken unofficially, and often in a spirit of defiance, could turn wakes and fairs into scenes of drunkenness and brutality. A fresh breeze blew through popular entertainment after the passing of the Bank Holiday Act in 1871; within a decade the public houses had many rivals in the field of entertainment. This is well illustrated by the activities of the Easter holiday described in the *Peterborough Advertiser* of 23 April 1881. Neither the gloomy discourse of the Bishop on Easter Sunday nor the almost inevitable cold snap on Easter Monday checked the holiday makers. They raided the boats on the Nene, filled the excursion trains to Skegness, where the wind was blowing at hurricane force, and appeared 'in various cycling uniforms' on

[1] Hannah More, *Mendip Annals*, ed. A. Roberts, 2nd ed., 1859, p. 103.

the roads. The less hardy filled the Rink where they skated to the strains of the Great Northern Band. The Quoit Club opened, the Peterborough Co-operative held its soirée and, on Good Friday, the pupils of the Wesleyan Sunday School had their annual tea. Often holding aloof from public merrymaking, many Wesleyans released their bottled-up spirits on Good Friday, which was also 'a day of great joy' in East London. Emigrants took this custom overseas so that a Good Friday picnic in Australia was described as a time when 'kissing, playing and foolishness were the sum and substance of the matter.'[1]

If the inhabitants of Peterborough almost emptied the city on a Bank Holiday, how much more anxious were the dwellers in the industrial cities to escape. An outlet for Londoners on the south coast had already been established by the well-to-do, and the concession of Bank Holidays came at a time when, as Kaye pointed out, 'the toil-worn artisan may transport himself . . . to the fresh, breezy coast of Brighton, for half-a-crown, and be carried home again for nothing . . . there is nothing pleasanter than a sight of a railway-train freighted with excursionists all outward-bound, all radiant with the expectation of a day's pleasure.' It was the arrival of these August excursionists that created the winter season at Brighton, and sent the well-to-do further afield in the summer.

The more distant excursions of the well-to-do necessitated longer holidays, and soon the crown of the year for those who could afford it was the holiday lasting through August and September. This excursion often stretched into October and merged into the winter holiday, as when Aunt George moved at the end of October from the Teign valley into Torquay. Despite the rival attractions of Torquay, Ventnor and Bournemouth, Brighton held its own as a winter resort; and no account of holidays in the mid-nineteenth century would be complete without some reference to its attractions during November and December. Also the expansion of Brighton provided the blue-print for the development of other seaside resorts aspiring to a winter season.

[1] *Diaries of Sara Midgley and Richard Skilbeck*, the story of Australian settlers, 1851–1864, ed. A. McCorkell, 1967, p. 158. The Good Friday activities in London were described in W. Besant's *East London*, 1901, p. 291.

Brighthelmstone was the first of the south-coast villages to be invested by the pleasure seekers, who gave their prize the less uncouth name of Brighton. By the second half of the nineteenth century there was little left of the freakish gaiety that had established the fashionable resort. The strand where courtiers had endeavoured to smile at the Prince's oft-heard jokes was taken over by the ubiquitous popularisers of natural history. They were concerned that the 'unreflective wanderer by the seashore' should pause to consider the 'water-worn pebbles as evidences of changes which are continually yet almost imperceptibly going on in this earth which we inhabit.'[1] But the Prince Regent went to Brighton to forget the moving hand of Time.

That Brighton arose from the ashes of Brighthelmstone was due to the wayward and convivial temperament of the Prince Regent: that the popularity of the resort did not wane with that of George IV was due to the doctors. The medical men, whose path was blazed by Dr Russell of Lewes, had no difficulty in taking over from the First Gentleman the patronage of Brighton. The search for health became as engrossing to the fashionable world as the pursuit of pleasure; and by the 1840s many doctors, like Sir James Clark and Augustus Granville, felt that climatic conditions were the guiding factors in the quest for fugitive vigour. Clark put Ventnor on the map of the health seekers and Granville undertook the pleasing task of investigating the possibilities of the spas and bathing places of England. Hotel and lodging-house keepers must have dreaded the advent of the active doctor consulting his thermometer, smelling the drains and criticising the accommodation and the environs. In Brighton he found the lodgings often expensive and not always sanitary, and that 'nothing can be more dismal-looking, barren and discouraging than the general aspect of the immediate surrounding country'.[2] By the 1870s hotels and lodging-houses had increased in number but not always in cleanliness. At Mr King's private hotel in Oriental Terrace Minnie found: 'The great drawback to this house is

[1] Mary Merrifield, *A Sketch of the Natural History of Brighton and its Vicinity*, 1884, pp. 25–6.

[2] A. B. Granville, *The Spas and Principal Bathing Places of England*, 1841, Vol. II, p. 580.

the number of black-beetles. I found one in my bed and another in the fireplace, so I jumped on a chair to finish my toilet. It is horrid.'

Minnie's reactions to the black-beetles are not surprising; even that fearless investigator, Beatrix Potter, found at Torquay, 'it is possible to have too much Natural History in a bed.'[1] The Turkish saying that 'an Englishman will burn a bed to catch a flea' suggests the English traveller abroad adopted an over-finical attitude that was hardly justified. Until the turn of the present century there was no lack of insect pests in even well-kept English homes and hotels, including the Imperial at Torquay.

Neither Granville's adverse comments nor the redundance of cockroaches could check the development of Brighton which, with other south-coast resorts, continued to expand steadily in the mid-nineteenth century. It is significant that at this time the term 'jerry building' came into common usage. Many of the new houses, commonly designated villas, had stylish finishings in the way of gables, ornamented barge-boards, and balconies sprouting with ironwork, but were 'neither wind, rain or cold proof.'[2] As the resorts spread new churches appeared. Many of these, like Holy Trinity at Ventnor and Christchurch at St Leonards, had bleak and admonishing spires raised like reproving fingers over the streets of new houses built for the pleasures of a season. Despite the cold and uninviting interiors which often characterised Victorian Gothic, these churches were filled on Sundays. When Minnie Thornhill and Anne Mercier went to St Andrew's, Brighton, on 25 November 1866, they 'were obliged to come out as there were no seats for us . . . we went to St Paul's (it was dreadfully crowded). We had to stand for some time. Lots of others were standing too; then they brought chairs. We could hardly hear a word.'

Each resort imposed its own routine on the pleasure, or health, seekers. But some activities were common to them all: attendance at church on Sundays, joining the lending library,

---

[1] Beatrix Potter, *Journal*, transcribed by Leslie Linder, 1966, entry made at Torquay, 14 March 1893, p. 307.

[2] *Once a Week*, 6 August 1859, pp. 117–119, this description appears in a good account of jerry building entitled 'Sebastopol Villa'.

walking or driving along a prescribed route and visiting nota-
ble pastry cooks, such as Mutton's at Brighton or Self's at
Newport, the starting point for excursions to Carisbrooke
Castle.

On the whole the winter routine imposed at Brighton in the
1860s was decidedly slow compared with the summer dissipations which R. S. Surtees described a decade earlier in *Plain or
Ringlets?* In November 1866 Minnie noted: 'It seems the swell
thing here to walk in the morning and to drive up and down in
the afternoon. When it is fine the streets are crowded and
strings of carriages drive up and down. In fact it is Hyde Park,
"the ladies' mile", by the sea . . . Aunt George and Louey
Lean did the swell up and down in the carriage.'

Innovations came slowly to health and pleasure resorts
where visitors were more anxious to forget the outside world
than to keep up with its changes. Two decades later the 'swell
thing' remained unchanged at Brighton: 'fashion decrees that
to walk in the morning and to drive in the afternoon is the correct thing to do . . . the morning stroll, the afternoon drive, the
evening dinner party or dance, theatre or concert, making up
a pleasant day'.[1] The dinner parties could be as slow as the
crawling drives along the King's Road: 'Mr Hope (the only
young man) took in Miss——, (*sic*) an elderly, plain lady. The
Misses Long and I had to fish for ourselves. Aunt George was
a great swell in her velvet and diamonds and pearls. I wore my
white dress I had for Miss Brook's wedding . . . We were
home very early; I was in bed at my usual time, soon after 12.'

For men the pace was not much faster. When Charles Shepherd joined the Beaufoy party at Brighton for a three-day
respite from his parochial labours, his activities included 'a
turn after tea', marred by the lack of moonlight, listening to a
concert given by the Marine Artillery Band at the Town Hall
and a swim at Brill's. By building a 'hemispherical dome'
above his circular swimming pool and keeping his establishment clean Charles Brill was able to provide his clients with
both novelty and hygiene. By the 1840s he had outdistanced
his rival, Sake Mahommed, although this old sepoy offered his
patrons a special 'method of schampooing', oriental oils and
his reminiscences of 'all the battles on the Banks of the Ganges

[1] *The Lady's World*, 1887, p. 64.

and Brahmaputra.'[1]

Despite her anxiety 'to do the swell', Aunt George had a genuine capacity for fun and welcomed visits from her South Lambeth friends who were indifferent to the rigid prescriptions of the Brighton season. She took a large party to the Pier where they 'all walked in a long string two by two . . . Captain Russell and Lewis Mortimer behaved very badly this afternoon – so wild.' The next day Aunt George took her revenge and 'had a bonfire and burned the captain's old hat – such fun. He could not make out what the little joke was.'

Perhaps Anne Beaufoy would have been happier with the summer excursionists to Brighton for whom new entertainments were appearing in the 1870s. Chief among these was the aquarium where the octopuses were often 'most kind, flourishing all over the tank for one keeper.' The passing of the Bank Holiday Act encouraged entertainments, such as aquaria, comic musical performances and peepshows, which could be enjoyed by those with only a few hours to spare. It was the proliferation of these diversions which caused popular resorts to spread into the surrounding countryside.

By the 1870s seaside resorts such as Brighton, Shanklin and Torquay were considered fashionable in winter, but vulgar in summer. When Minnie visited Shanklin in September 1876 'it was a regular Ramsgate; men and women bathing, children without shoes or stockings paddling in the water and making sand castles, people working, etc. We met Mrs Stammers, the housekeeper at Caron Place, and Sheaf, the gardener, to our surprise – they are both away for their holiday.'

By this time those in the higher echelons of domestic service were often allowed a week's holiday. Occasionally their wants met with marked consideration: to ensure that her devoted cook, who was unwilling to leave her mistress, had a holiday Grandmother Siddons herself accompanied her to Ramsgate. But undermaids and general servants were only entitled to the three statutory Mondays in the year. These breaks provided the young with an outlet for high spirits and the old with a breathing space but they were too short to allow recreation in the true sense. For the re-animation of old interests and the discovery of new ones a longer pause was needed.

[1] A. B. Granville, op. cit., Vol. II. p. 563

The Victorians were indefatigable in 'seeing the celebrated things that *ought* to be seen in different places' and in collecting ferns, rocks and, above all, seashore miscellany. The enthusiasm for the shore which sent holiday-makers collecting with the same feeling of awe as Wordsworth's shell-gatherer was primarily due to the writings of Philip Gosse. A naturalist whose knowledge was respected by his fellow scientists and who could communicate to the public his wonder at the vivid and mysterious life of rock pools was sure of a large following of amateur naturalists. But Gosse lived to realise that his *History of the British Sea-Anemones and Corals* helped to destroy 'the ring of living beauty drawn about out shores'.[1] In a short time the grubbers and the collectors had 'ravaged every corner of them.' Writers, like Philip Gosse, Francis Buckland and F. O. Morris supplied the inspiration, and manufacturers were not far behind in providing the apparatus for collecting. In the Great Exhibition of 1851 appeared the improved microscopes, aquaria and botanical cases, which helped to make collecting fashionable. Microscopes took their place on drawing-room tables and ladies clamoured for the green slime of ponds 'in which the *dear* animacules and infusoria, about which Mr Gosse writes so charmingly' were to be found. Concerning the colourless extremities and power of changing its appearance of *Euglena sanguinea* Gosse wrote: 'Whether this ability to prove an alias to be at all dependent on the remarkable *clear-headedness* of the subject, I leave for those who are skilled in metaphysics to determine.[2]

In his *History of British Butterflies*, Francis Morris, incumbent of Nunburnholme, exhorted his readers to study entomology in a humble and reverent spirit, but he concluded with the wish, 'may you never "go out" without catching a Purple Emperor, or a Scarce Swallow-tail, a Large Blue, or a Pale Clouded Yellow, a White Admiral, or a Camberwell Beauty, and if these pages shall have assisted you in the chase – "Plaudite" '.[3]

[1] Edmund Gosse, *Father and Son*, 1907, p. 140.

[2] P. Gosse, *Evenings at the Microscope . . .* , 1877 ed., p. 398, the reference to Gosse's charming writings appears in *Once a Week*, 6 August, 1859, pp. 117–119 Albany Fonblanque, junr., 'Sebastopol Villa.'

[3] F. O. Morris, *A History of British Butterflies,* 1st ed.,1852, 6th ed., 1891, p.184.

In this spirit of seeing is collecting many travellers set out on their summer holidays; but the wonders they sought were fugitive. The out-spreading villas on the cliff tops as well as the collectors were driving out the Large Blues; while on the shores not only the serious collectors but the increasing number of visitors rifled the rock pools with 'the rough paw of well-meaning, idle-minded curiosity.' Nevertheless the Britain through which Aunt George and her entourage travelled in the 1860s and 1870s still held many unspoiled natural beauties, and a flora and fauna that would delight the naturalist today.

One of the great advantages of the enthusiasm for natural history was that it could be shared by the man-in-the-street, and was often his key to a fuller life. Philip Gosse believed that by his youthful studies of wild life on the banks of the Stour and reading Byron's 'Lara' he 'acquired a new sense.' This combination of observation and imagination enabled Hugh Miller, the stone-mason, to take his place among the leading geologists of the age, and James Widger to jump over the drapery counter to discover a forgotten Devon. From his findings in the Torbryan caves Widger could envisage how 'the lion would be standing at the mouth of the cave, stretching himself and yawning, having just been roused from his slumbers within by the croak of the night bird as a signal that the day is far spent, and the ruminants ever on the alert, trembling at the sound of the terrible roar.'[1]

As regards 'the celebrated things that *ought* to be seen in the different places' of Britain opinions differed. Foreigners, like Taine and Turgenev, hastened to see the marvels of the Industrial Revolution at Liverpool and Manchester. The ever-pounding machines in the cotton mills and the Manchester fog oppressed the Frenchman who 'felt for a moment all the fearful weight with which this climate and this industrial system press down upon men.'[2] Taine was conscious of the brutalising effect of machines on operatives, but Turgenev felt they generated a power which could create a race of supermen. He tried, not altogether successfully, to express this idea when

[1] Quoted in Hilda H. Walker and Antony J. Sutcliffe, *James Widger, 1823 –1892 and the Torbryan Caves*, 1968. Reprinted from Vol. 99 of the Transactions of the Devonshire Society.

[2] H. Taine, *Notes of England 1860–1870*, Trs. E. Hyams, 1957, p. 220.

he created the worker-hero, Solomin, in *Virgin Soil*. British tourists, however, eschewed the docks, cotton mills and coal mines which had been the bridges that carried so many of them from small-town insignificance to the consequence of opulent pleasure seekers. With money drawn, directly or indirectly, from industrial progress, such tourists hurried to the countryside to rediscover Nature.

The early-morning ecstasy with which the enthusiasts of the late eighteenth century approached castles and crags had faded. The Romantics drew near to the hills with veneration; most mid-Victorians scanned them appraisingly. They provided fresh air and exercise, the lack of which was increasingly deplored by town dwellers, and secluded retreats where young men on reading parties could be kept out of mischief. But such retreats, whether in the mountains or by the sea, were not always so sequestered as parents hoped. There were many students who could have echoed the reminiscences of a student at Scarborough in the mid-nineteenth century:

> 'I came "to read for honours" (so, in letters home, 'twas said),
> And took to flirting on the Spa, and playing *Poule*, instead.'

When, in August 1867, Aunt George escorted by John Gooch, Louey Lean, Clara the maid and Thomas the footman, took her children and Minnie to Wales, she had all the pleasurable anticipation of entering an unknown country, of communing with nature and of extending her knowledge of antiquities. The second Saxon invasion which started in the 1850s, was welcomed by the shopkeeping interest, but has been condemned by the nationalists as corrupting the natural and unselfconscious development of Welsh life.[1] Perhaps the English tourist was too eager to equate the tall beaver hat with the Welsh way of life, and overstressed the wildness of Wales. Hardly a Saxon crossed the border who could not have found, had he dared look, scenes of greater desolation at home.

When the train for Llangollen left Birmingham, 'such a funny place, it looks so smoky and black', the Beaufoy party were carried into 'the coal country for the sky looks quite

[1] *Folk Life*, 1964, Vol. II, pp. 45–57, E. G. Payne, 'Welsh Peasant Costume'.

black. We are in the middle of the coal works; it looks so wretched. There is nothing to be seen but tall chimneys smoking and most of them looking as if they were on fire. All the coal is going about; I never saw anything look so desolate. We have been obliged to draw up the carriage windows.'

Desolate indeed the district was. It was the boast of the chain makers of Lye Waste, on the outskirts of the Black Country, that coroners' inquests on infanticide were unknown among them. Living in scattered hovels, most of the chain makers kept pigs. If, as was not unlikely, 'there chanced to be a superfluous baby, the family pig was kept on short commons for a day or two. Then the infant (somehow) fell into the sty . . . in half an hour no coroner could have found any remains to sit upon.'[1]

Deposited 'with dragon speed and dragon noise' at Llangollen, as was George Borrow in 1854, the Beaufoy party realised that the travellers' tales had not been exaggerated. Immediately to hand were mountains, a river flowing between wooded banks and an ancient fortress. Borrow had listened to a Welsh harpist, but by the 1860s the Saxon rot was setting in and singers at Llanrwst were imitating the Christy Minstrels. Llangollen itself, 'a small town... of white houses with slate roofs', had charms only for antiquarians and controversialists like Borrow who was bent on showing local place-name authorities and Dissenters the error of their ways. But the Welsh were well able to turn the tables on pragmatic Saxons as John Gooch found when he had to endure 'a long jawbation about politics' from the custodian of Valle Crucis Abbey.

On the whole, none of the Caron Place party were enthusiastic about ancient buildings unless they were inhabited and well kept like Chirk Castle: 'It is a jolly place, I never saw a castle in such good repair.' The Thornhills, for Minnie's cousin, William, had joined the party, preferred natural beauties to antiquities. The charm of a visit to the fortifications of Dinas Bran was 'running down the hill at an awful pace. The path winds so much that you can run very fast without falling.' At Bala, fishing on the lake was popular but not the

---

[1] W. B. Woodgate, *Reminiscences of an Old Sportsman*, 1909, p. 40, Woodgate and George Thornhill rowed together in the Radley boat against Eton at Henley on 26 June 1858.

church service conducted by 'a little fat Welshman' assisted by 'a little round-faced curate'. Only Louey Lean, a Nonconformist, was satisfied with Sundays in Wales, especially in markedly Methodist districts like Tan-y-Bwlch. It was in hostelries here that George Borrow and Anne Beaufoy ran true to form. At a small inn George Borrow entered into a dispute with a Calvinist whose sombre pride in his certain perdition caused Borrow to exclaim: 'There is no doubt that the idea of damnation is anything but disagreeable to some people; it gives them a kind of gloomy consequence in their own eyes.' In a larger establishment, the Oakley Arms, Aunt George, finding the accommodation reserved for her party (which now included Richard Enraght and his wife) 'pokey', made such a stir that the Public Coffee, or Dining, Room was comandeered for her use. Minnie rightly observed. 'I don't think the Coffee Room visitors like it much; the little room we had is made into the Coffee Room'. But, as Borrow told a Welshman, 'at carnal things, you know, none so clebber as the Saxons'.

By 1854 'a very magnificent edifice' had been built at Capel Curig to accommodate visitors anxious to ascend Snowdon. As often happens, this almost obligatory climax to a holiday in North Wales was less pleasurable than everyday activities like nutting in the lanes around the village. The ascent was made on 13 September:

> 'It was a very nice fine morning so we all bundled up and had breakfast soon after eight . . . We went off in grand style, a wagonette and four horses and postilions. We got to Llanberis a little before eleven, had lunch and then started. We had seven ponies . . . Will walked almost all the way up; Aunt George and Mr Gooch did not come all the way up; Aunt George got frightened as the saddle was not quite comfortable, so they walked quietly down again and sent on their ponies for us . . . our ponies knew the way quite well and were very anxious to go up quickly. . . . We could see no view at all when we got to the top. The summit was overset with clouds and there was a nasty drizzling rain. It was beautifully fine until we got about half way up the mountain and then we seemed to get into the clouds (it was then that Aunt George and Mr Gooch turned back) . . . We had a most lovely view coming down; the clouds suddenly rolled away and then

we saw all the valley in the sunshine. We could see the Menai Bridge, another time we saw the Llanberis lakes and the stone quarries. I had Aunt George's pony part of the way coming down. I had a jolly canter; it was a beauty. We then had dinner and came home by moonlight; it was very jolly.'

Bangor was the point of departure for many visitors who travelled by steamer to Liverpool, and were then whisked to London by the Irish Mail 'at the rate of about 60 miles an hour'. The Beaufoys stayed long enough in Liverpool to admire the Town Hall and pay their respects to one of the wonders of the industrial age, the *Great Eastern*. Brunel's steamship aroused great acclaim and also the wonder as to how this engineering triumph of the age could be used. The schoolboy who wrote, 'the names of Wellington and Napoleon are indeed glorious, but the names of Canning, Glass and Anderson are equally, if not more so'[1] was over-optimistic. Once the Atlantic Cable was successfully laid in 1866 the engineers concerned with the undertaking were soon forgotten.

Although she felt dizzy on mountains and sick on lakes, Aunt George persisted in her pursuit of the picturesque. By the 1860s her tastes, and those of thousands like her, were being met by lodging-house keepers and publicists who soon learned to put a price on natural beauty. The melancholy cry of 'going-going-gone' that echoed through Rydal Mount in the summer of 1859 not only disposed of Wordsworth's books and pictures but of the seclusion of the district. The increasing numbers of visitors made it almost impossible to walk, as Dorothy Wordsworth had done, 'quietly along the side of Rydal Lake with quiet thoughts', and encouraged innkeepers to adjust their prices to include the views. Guides began to pursue visitors and to put out 'their hands for a shilling, in consequence of the scenery.'[2]

Among the visitors who sought the disappearing refreshment of solitude was Anne Beaufoy. She rented a small house at Grasmere where her brother-in-law, Mark Beaufoy (1793–1854), had settled and died. Beaufoy's career well illus-

[1] Essay written by E. W. Kerr at the Royal School, Dungannon, 21 August 1866.

[2] *Once a Week*, 6 August 1859, pp. 107–9, Thomas Blackburne, 'A Talk about Rydal Mount'.

trates the fate of the many ardent and sensitive souls who lost
their optimism and their fortunes in the frenzy of speculation
that swept the uneasy continent after 1815. Mark Beaufoy
seemed destined to share all the glories of his age; he inherited
his father's enthusiastic interest in the natural world, fought at
Waterloo, sailed with the adventurers to Mexico and sought
with the Romantics the unsullied civilisation of the prairies. In
Mexico he made meteorolgical observations, studied the antiquities of Otumbo and Cholula and walked in a religious procession 'bearing a burning taper under a burning sun'; but he
did not make money. He lost the £4,860 he had invested in the
Tlalpuxahua silver mines and gave up his manager's salary of
£800 a year as he 'was not allowed to fulfill the duties it entailed'. Having lost all his money in the new republic of Mexico,
Beaufoy sought to restore his ideals by a visit to the older republic of North America. He was shocked by the uncouth table
manners, the spitting, mob violence and by America's 'living
ruins', the Red Indians;[1] but he had his moments of elation.
Beaufoy never felt so proud of being an Englishman as when he
enjoyed in the United States the 'sight of a well-fed, well-
clothed, industrious people, without beggary, or fears of having
too large a family. . . . Where are the colonies of the Egyptians,
the Phoenicians, of Greece and of Rome? If Britain shall follow
the law of nations, and, like all other powerful dominions, sink
into insignificance and ruin, she will still live in a portion of
America as large as half Europe. Probably she will appear also
in the vast settlements of New Holland, which will no doubt,
likewise free themselves from the tutelage of a government situated on the other side of the globe.' His failure in Mexico and
his faith in the United States were both effaced by sorrow; in
1827 the two beings whom Beaufoy most loved, his father and
his betrothed, died. Consciousness of his reserve made his grief
all the more intolerable: 'I don't know how it is; I certainly feel
things very often most intensely, and yet I have not the mode of
showing my affection.'[2]

[1] Quotations of Mark Beaufoy's impressions of Mexico and the United
States are from his *Mexican Illustrations* . . . 1828, p. 142 and *Tour through Parts of
the United States and Canada*, 1828, pp. 137–8.

[2] Quotations concerning Beaufoy's business activities and state of mind
are from letters quoted in G. Beaufoy, *Leaves from a Beech Tree*, 1930, p. 238
and p. 231.

Mark Beaufoy took his sorrows to Bowness on Lake Win-
dermere, and remained their bondman for the rest of his life.
In St Martin's churchyard are buried two men whose fates
were exactly reversed. The destiny of Rasselas Belfield, the
slave, is told on his tombstone:

> 'A slave by birth; I left my native land,
> And found my freedom on Britannia's strand
> Blest Isle! Thou Glory of the Wise and Free!
> Thy touch alone unbinds the chains of slavery.'

Mark Beaufoy's cottage at Bowness, which Aunt George's
party visited in 1868 and 1872, was his prison. His memorial in
the church records the only phase in his career which he could
recall without regret:

> Captain Mark Beaufoy
> formerly
> of the Coldstream Guards
> with which regiment he served
> at the battle of Waterloo.
> He died at Windermere
> May 31 1854
> Aged 60 years

Nothing could have been further removed from the melancholy seclusion of Mark Beaufoy's cottage than Eller Close,
the house which Aunt George rented at Grasmere (plate
26). This compact stone building still stands facing the Swan
and beside the main road between Kendal and Keswick. On 2
October 1872 'the coach upset just in front of Eller Close this
morning; all the people were thrown over in the hedge, but no
one was hurt'. Although Eller Close was overshadowed by
Helm Crag, Aunt George felt more at home in the Lake District
than she had done in Wales. She was no longer at the mercy of
wayward Welsh ponies but was 'quite happy with coachman
and the steady old greys' which had been sent on ahead of the
train party. Her enthusiasm for the less accessible beauties of
nature had waned; while the younger ones scrambled up Dun-
geon Ghyll she 'sat on a stone and read the paper'. Mark alone
ventured to climb Helvellyn and, unencumbered by his relatives, he made the ascent at night. His high spirits and sweet
temper made Mark a favourite; so the servants, transported

from South Lambeth, determined to accompany him. The party, which included Mary, Elizabeth, Ann, Thomas and the coachman, were guided by George Hardy, the Grasmere grocer, who was so impressed by Cockney jollity that two years later, on his first visit to London, he called at Caron Place. While the laughing party scrambled, slipped and refreshed themselves with champagne[1] Aunt George was left a victim to all the alarms of the unprotected. She 'had an awful fright as she thought she heard someone getting into the house. She called us and then Mr Gooch. He went down but it was all quiet; so we all settled down again, when at about three o'clock Aunt George came into our room again; she felt so ill. Louey went and lay down on Aunt George's bed; she was very bad for some time. We felt as tired this morning as if we had been up Helvellyn with Mark.'

The Beaufoys and Minnie were omnivorous sightseers, but unfortunately the run of warm, dry summers began to break in 1872. 'Wet, wet, wet' frequently set the holiday note in Minnie's diary, and the party were reduced to reading, playing battledore and shuttlecock and brooding over their ailments.

To penetrate the wildness of Wales was adventurous, to visit Rydal Mount and the Lodore Falls was to establish claims to sensibility, and to take a holiday in Scotland was fashionable. Queen Victoria's marked predilection for the country set the pace. On leaving Balmoral in October 1858 she wrote, 'altogether I feel so sad, as you know and feel for me, at the bitter thought at going from this blessed place – leaving these hills – this enchanting life of liberty – and returning to tame, dull, formal England and the prison life of Windsor!'[2]

The English went to Scotland to enjoy a life of liberty for a few months; but, to live at all, thousands of Scots were forced to emigrate every year. Once they settled, and quickly prospered, in India, Australia and New Zealand, the English did not find them nearly so attractive as when they roamed their

[1] After climbing Scaw Fell on 2 August 1872 'Mark was quite knocked up after his long walk (champagne, etc)', so it is unlikely that the ascent of Helvellyn was made without similar sustenance.

[2] R. Fulford, *Dearest Child: Letters between Queen Victoria and the Princess Royal*, 1964, p. 139.

native glens. Ellen felt obliged to apologise for marrying a Scot in India; while the Thornhills mixed as little as possible with their Scottish fellow settlers in Otago.

Aunt George was not one to lag behind the fashion and on 2 August 1869 she set off with her entourage for Scotland. Her spirit did not fail her even on the tedious night journey to Glasgow: 'Aunt George sported a very swell night-cap, Louey came out in a little shawl, Rita had her red hood, Mark his cap and Mr Gooch tied a handkerchief over his head . . . Nothing disturbed Mr Gooch, he slept soundly through it all, breakfast and sunrise too.'

But Gooch knew that having escorted the party to Glasgow he would be returning almost immediately to the comforts of London. The lochs and mountains of the west coast along which the Beaufoy party toured were not unobserved, but it was the poverty of the inhabitants that most struck them. Greenock appeared 'the dirtiest and most beastly place' Minnie was ever in, and swarmed 'with filthy children and awful old women'. Greenock, like other towns along the west coast had received early in the nineteenth century an influx of Irish labourers. They undertook the lowest paid and hardest work in towns and farms while the Highlanders, also dispossessed of their land, made every endeavour to emigrate. That their efforts were so often successful was largely due to the establishment at the end of the seventeenth century of village schools. Education enabled many to rise but not necessarily to succeed. On the banks of Loch Esk the party passed a mansion 'in a lovely position just in the valley with such a beautiful hill at the back. It is a very large house, the stables are a little way off. Our driver told us Mr Patrick was once a porter about here. He went to America, made a large fortune, and came back and built this splendid mansion. It is let now as he joined some company that failed, and he is now in prison for debt.'

The tour of the western coast was not altogether pleasurable to Aunt George who, bereft of her satellites, was out of sympathy with the austerity which distinguished the scenery, the religious outlook and often the accommodation in the Highlands. To sustain their spirits the party felt obliged to 'have always a portion of whisky toddy before going to bed.' On 23 August Aunt George turned thankfully southwards;

and Minnie joined her cousins, the Grants of Rothiemurchus, whom she again visited in 1871.

The Grants were Minnie's cousins on the Siddons side of the family. Sarah Siddons' eldest son, Henry, married the charming and gifted Harriott Murray of Covent Garden. It is never easy to follow in the footsteps of an illustrious parent and Henry, weighted by his studious and diffident disposition, was not financially successful as an actor or as manager of the Theatre Royal, Edinburgh. When he died in 1815 little provision had been made for his wife and three children. One of Henry's daughters, Sarah, married William Grant, Laird of Rothiemurchus, an alliance which would have satisfied her Grandmother Siddons. The lively and talented Elizabeth married John Mair of the Army Medical Service who was retired on half-pay in 1850. The Mairs had one son, four daughters (Sarah, Ellen, Harriet and Elizabeth), and a small income.

Despite the large gatherings in the summer of the Siddons, Mair and Murray families the shadows, like the rain, never quite lifted from the mansion amidst the hills and pine forests of Rothiemurchus for the Grants were childless. The 'plain modern building situated on the bank of the Spey, in the most beautifully laid out grounds and thriving plantations',[1] the church and the school house all proclaimed that the legal career of the founder, Sir J. P. Grant, and his connection with the East India Company had not been without profit; but he had built in vain as an heir was lacking.

The magnificence of the Strathspey scenery only appeared fitfully through the mists. The description of one scrambling walk to Loch Morlich could have been applied to most of the expeditions Minnie made: 'The rain tried to come down all the time. We had to put our umbrellas up, but it was very jolly.' Nearer home conditions were no better: 'We played croquet this morning in spite of the rain. I went out, but soon came in again as I did not see the fun of getting wet through.' Minnie was equally unable to appreciate the service at the kirk at Rothiemurchus: 'It is a Presbyterian Church, of course. I did not like the service at all; but the singing and the church altogether were far better than at Alvie.' Except for the rains which blotted out the countryside so quickly, for the kirk

[1] S. Lewis, *A Topographical Dictionary of Scotland*, 1846, Vol. II, p. 436.

services and for the flocks of white birds that settled at dusk on the lawn 'like a tremendous snowstorm', there was little in the daily life at Rothiemurchus that was unfamiliar to Minnie. The house party organised the annual treat of the Rothiemurchus school children and were delighted, but not altogether surprised, when a baby cousin, catching the topic of conversation, lisped through the afternoon 'ou [rheu] matic gout'. They tried to play croquet and succeeded in playing chess and paper games in the evening. The most popular was 'Words and Questions'. There were many variations of this game; at Rothiemurchus a question was put to all the players who had to answer in rhyme bringing in a given noun. Family jokes and topics of the day were aired during the game. Harriet Mair voiced a generally-felt grievance when she answered: 'Are you in favour of woman's rights?', bringing in the noun 'dumps':

'If women are frights
Let them look to their rights
For this I am sure is quite true
Men are such sad dumps
They won't stir their stumps
Unless for the beautiful few.'

Elizabeth Mair, who had been forced to part with her grandmother's portrait by Gainsborough to purchase her son's commission, might have been expected to feel strongly about the Army Bill of 1871 to abolish the purchase of commissions. She had to answer the question, 'Do you like gas light?' and bring in 'Army Bill' about which she was surprisingly half-hearted:

'I like light of every kind
Wax light, gas light, sunlight.
So I cannot bring my mind
Now to fix on one light.
But the Army Bill I fear
(And I greatly rue it)
Is so very far from clear
No light I can see through it.'

Scotland had many attractions for the sportsman, the romantic and the antiquarian, but few for the invalid for whose patronage resorts in the 1860s were competing. But hope was in sight. Priessnitz's water cures at Gräfenberg in Bohemia were attracting an assemblage of *kurgäste* who included many Almanach-de-Gotha families. As his patients went through a course of bathing and wet bandaging, slept in straw-filled cribs, took regular walks and fed mainly on milk and sour bread, Priessnitz achieved many cures of the malaises of those leading indoor lives. Doctors in other countries were not slow to adopt this treatment for patients who needed to be entertained as well as re-animated. Highland hydropathic establishments which could offer plentiful water, bracing air, and splendid walks came into their own. As most of the hydros had over twenty-five patients they could offer indoor entertainment during bad weather. The standards of Gräfenberg, where interesting invalids appeared in 'grand toilette gossamer dresses with short sleeves and waists a *little lower* than I thought waists were ever worn',[1] were not quite achieved. Visitors to hydros in more northern climes were advised: 'Your dresses may be neat and fashionable, but they need not be gay . . . but good warm, all wool underwear, and plenty of that is essential.'

It is not surprising that Aunt George who, as Ellen wrote, 'never seems to be very well long together', should spend one summer at a health resort. By taking a summer holiday in 1870 at Buxton, she hoped to enjoy the rugged beauties of Derbyshire from a base which also offered mineral waters and social diversions. Had Aunt George read Granville she might have been less optimistic as regards entertainment. The doctor found Buxton gloomy, but attributed this to the character of the English visitors: 'It is either dull gaiety or gay dulness with them all'.

When Granville arrived at the Grand Hotel, Buxton, 'the very first *coup-d'oeil*' showed him the necessity of taking some pains with his toilet. Aunt George's party felt a similar anxiety before dining at the table d'hôte of the Palace Hotel: 'It was rather formidable going down to dinner . . . I sat next to such an amusing little Frenchman; he was very much amused at the waiters. First of all they shot all the jelly off the dish on to the table; then an old gentleman just opposite us had a butter

---

[1] Elizabeth Blackwell, *Pioneer Work . . . Autobiographical Sketches*, 1st ed., 1895, Everyman ed., p. 130.

knife dropped on his shoulder.'

The news of the relentless Prussian advance in north-east France had not yet reached this lively Frenchman. But even when he learnt of Napoleon III's surrender, his sociability was undiminished, and he insisted on escorting the Beaufoy party round Manchester where he had business connections. On the 'wet, wet, wet' Monday, 12 September:

> 'We went to Manchester today . . . We had breakfast at Green's Hotel, Manchester and we went over Watts' Bazaar, it is one of the largest warehouses in England. The Assize Courts are well worth seeing; we were nearly turned over going to them, though. The horses got frightened going up to the doors, and the coachman tried to force them against their will. Thomas came to our rescue just in time, he and coachman and Elizabeth were following in a cab. After that we had an omnibus (a small one to carry eight). We drove a little about the town and . . . then we all went together to Mr Belhouse's cotton mill [a Mr Belhouse was staying at Buxton] . . . It was very interesting seeing all the different stages of the cotton; first there was the dirty cotton-wool, and lastly it came out so clean, and in such fine thread. They send most of it to Nottingham for lace-making. Some of the rooms were so hot! Seeing over the mill took some time; we then went to the Hotel, had some claret and then, after having a little turn, walked to the station and . . . got back in time to dress for dinner.'

No Colonial viewing for the first time the architectural splendours of the Old World could have maintained a more determined *nil admirari* attitude than that displayed by most Britons when faced with their industrial achievements.

The mid-Victorians envisaged themselves as a race of country gentlemen. When the Scottish porter, Patrick, made his fortune he established himself like a laird beside Loch Esk. Retired Anglo-Indians, according to Thomas Pearce, the sporting vicar of Morden in Dorset (1853–1882), were often to be found shivering in shooting lodges with their paraquets and 'bilious-eyed' children; and retired manufacturers took to beagling in frock coats.[1] The ordeal by country life to prove the

---

[1] *Idstone Papers,* 2nd ed., 1874, pp. 207–11, chapter on 'Varied Shooting'.

attainment of gentility was only possible because hard times were forcing old-established landowners from their estates; and the popular play, 'New Men and Old Acres', was being enacted almost daily throughout the countryside. The letting of country mansions was a desperate, and often ineffective, attempt to avert selling up. For three summers Anne Beaufoy rented such houses: New Canonteign House in Devon, Iwerne House in Dorset and Donhead Hall on the borders of Dorset and Wiltshire.

When New Canonteign House was built in the early nineteenth century there seemed little likelihood of lean years. Both the mansion and its builder, Edward Pellew, first Viscount Exmouth, expressed the most pleasing and lively characteristics of their age. A feeling for the countryside and good taste guided Pellew to build a mansion which, though of noble proportions, in no way marred the magnificent landscape of the Teign valley. There was no attempt at the ostentation to which Lord Wolverton aspired when he rebuilt Iwerne House in Dorset. But Pellew's renown did not depend on his wealth but on the furious courage with which he rushed to the help of the unfortunate, whether those in danger of drowning or 'in helpless captivity in a heathen land.' In 1816 he freed 31,000 Christian slaves held in Algiers. With the down-to-earth piety of the age, Pellew's exploits are commemorated on his memorial in Christow church which concludes:

> 'So, when the mighty orb in dread alarm,
> Shall crash in ruins, at its God's decree;
> May thy Redeemer, with triumphant arm,
> From the vast wreck of all things – rescue thee.'

The Beaufoys were able to rent this mansion as Lord Exmouth was on visiting terms with the family at South Lambeth; but the reasons why an increasing number of landowners were letting their country seats for the summer months were manifold. The most cogent was the realisation in the early 1870s that the profits of high farming depended on an increasing expenditure on large-scale improvements, such as drainage, and on retrenchment in domestic management. When later in the decade rents stopped rising the summer flitting was often the sad prelude to selling-up. The propensity to roam, always strong in the Pellews, and the desire to join the fashionable summer activities of deer stalking in Scotland and fishing in Norway also accounted for the search for summer tenants.

The September rains of 1871 were a prelude to the wet seasons which were to wash the profits out of high farming later in the decade. As Christow was primarily a grassland district the dairy farmers could view with equanimity the September rains; but the tenants of Canonteign found it hard to resign themselves to indoor activities. Furthermore the varying tastes of the five adults and the three young people in the Beaufoy party and of their visitors were bound to clash. Aunt George was in the country for her health and insisted on her daily constitutional walk. Only Minnie would accompany her in the pouring rain on the prescribed route march, three times to the Lodge and back; the others demanded either more restful or more lively entertainment: 'wet – wet – wet. We . . . did our best to amuse the children. We pretended to mesmerise Lewis and Rita with a black saucer, and took them in most beautifully. Lewis was perfectly taken in; we made him sit behind the curtain while Rita was being done.'

While the rains lasted the boys would put up with being mesmerised and with being dressed up as 'a lady and gentleman . . . from Exeter', but as soon as the clouds lifted they escaped. One day the young rector of Christow, George Bird, took them shooting. Mark returned to tell his relations that 'he had shot three brace of birds which turned out to be three tomtits, a chaffinch and two yellow hammers.' Hedgerow birds were victims not only of amateur sportsmen but also of birdcatchers who could not keep pace with the demands of taxidermists, town dwellers and milliners. In the early issues of the *Boy's Own Paper* the editor gave almost weekly information on how to make bird-lime, to build and maintain an aviary and to stuff birds. Encouragement was not lacking: 'We are glad indeed to know you are assisting your sons in the beautiful art of taxidermy. There is nothing like a hobby for passing away the time pleasantly and profitably. 1. Let the bird cool; there will then be less chance of an accidental bleeding and soiling cut. 2. 26 wire you are not likely to want unless for the humming bird or golden headed wren. Finches 20 or

21, blackbirds 19, jays 17, magpies, partridges and grouse, 16.'

But even before W. H. Hudson revealed the excitement of adventures among free-flying birds, some naturalists felt doubts about 'the beautiful art of taxidermy.' The Reverend John Woods, the popular naturalist who stole Alfred Wallace's thunder while both were lecturing in the United States, wanted 'equal protection for *all* British Birds during their close season, without reference to their supposed beneficial, harmless, or noxious qualities.'

Mark's onslaughts on the hedges were cut short by his return to Eton. Just before he left the party enjoyed 'one of *the* most beautiful drives since we have been here; through Ashton and Belvidere (the tower on the hill). The ground is very high and the view is splendid, too grand to attempt to describe.'

In September the exuberant vegetation of banks and tree-studded hedgerows still concealed the greatest charms of the lanes around Canonteign; the views of late Gothic church towers and the countless falls of water. These ranged from the majestic waterfall in the Canonteign grounds to the ubiquitous trickles splashing over grey stones and under ferns. In this smiling and well-watered countryside memorials recording more stirring scenes were not lacking. With a fortune made in India the Palk family erected the eye-catching Belvidere in memory of the military exploits of Stringer Lawrence (1697–1775) in India. A memorial in Canonteign church shows how in his short life Barrington Reynolds Pellew (1833–1858) took part in the chief forward thrusts of British expansion overseas,

> 'he had served with distinction in the Cafir War, South Africa, at the siege of Sebastopol, the storming of Canton, in China, and at the final assault and capture of Lucknow, at which place he died of dysentery, in the 26th year of his age, beloved and deeply lamented.'

Hardly had Aunt George recovered from the setbacks of rain, difficult guests and badly-kept croquet lawns incidental to summer holidays spent in country houses when she was ready for the winter excursion to Torquay. By the 1870s other resorts besides Brighton were establishing claims to winter honours. Foremost among these was Torquay, which had tra-

velled a long way since the sociable Dr Granville dismissed
Torbay society as consisting of 'eighty-two spinsters, nineteen
medicals, twelve divines and only two attorneys'. The credit
for the changed image of Torquay must be shared by Philip
Gosse, whose descriptions of the rock pools he loved signed
their death warrant, and by visiting royalty either functioning
or exiled.

The drawback to the winter season at Torquay was the
weather. Everything possible was done to give an impression
of gaiety and warmth. Bands played on the Strand in the evening 'to enliven the inhabitants and cheer the invalid to his
early couch'; and in the 1840s the Royal Hotel had the public
rooms lighted by gas. But the ex-Emperor Napoleon III and
Mark Thornhill were not deceived by this adventitious
warmth. In March 1877 Thornhill wrote dismally from Torquay: 'Our hopes of fine weather appear again disappointed. I
do not mind fog and gloom when at home but these are not
pleasant when one is travelling.' Aunt George endorsed this
opinion. Having made the round of tea parties, or kettle-
drums, and of local beauty spots, the party in shivering des-
peration 'drove all over Torquay . . . in and out of almost
every street, constantly coming to the end of the road and
having to turn'. Soon these culs-de-sac were to stretch into the
surrounding countryside where Beatrix Potter found: 'The
suburbs of villas and gardens are pretty, but not so much as
Roehampton, and very steep walking.'[1]

When the Italianate towers of Osborne triumphantly arose
they marked the capitulation of the Isle of Wight to the
tourists. The fishermen retreated from the shore and those
working on the small farms, finding that the royal visitors provided pageantry rather than work, withdrew to the mainland.
A native of Binstead remembers watching the slow progress of
Queen Victoria in her open carriage, preceded by outriders in
scarlet; but he had to travel as far afield as South Lambeth to
find work.

Until the last decades of the eighteenth century the Island
had only provided fishermen and small farmers with a livelihood and a few large landowners, like the Worsleys, with
rents. The exuberant landscape of the Undercliff, the coastline

[1] Beatrix Potter, op. cit., p. 308.

between Luccombe and Blackgang Chines, could not fail to
attract those with a taste for romantic seclusion. 'Sea Cottages' appeared particularly in the vicinity of the 'rude and
frightful' rock formations between St Lawrence and Ventnor.
The luxuriant vegetation that invaded the fissures of the rocks
proclaimed 'an Italianate atmosphere'; and the evidence of
long-flowering myrtle, verbena and rose convinced many doctors, particularly Sir James Clark, that the climate was ideal
for consumptives. But memorials in the Undercliff churches
suggest how hopeless was this last search for health. In the
pleasing and unpretentious church of St Catherine, Ventnor, a
Nottingham man recorded his grief at the loss of his two sons,
both aged twenty-seven, in the 1840s. The 'genial warmth' of
the Undercliff did not save the poet, John Sterling, who was
buried at Bonchurch.

If the climate could not stay consumption, it was certainly
beneficial to the delicate and the aged. The flourishing flora
attracted many sun-starved Anglo-Indians to the Island. Mr
Lock, the friend of Henry Thornhill who was killed at Sitapur,
settled in Ventnor; and Mark Thornhill, with whom Lock had
a prolonged dispute over Henry's estate, died at Bembridge.
Those seeking only a comfortable retirement, like the widow
of the wealthy Charles Francis of South Lambeth, were not
disappointed. The de Cerjats, also London friends of the
Thornhills, settled at Ryde in 'the sweetest little house possible' called, almost inevitably, Rose Bank. The sea cottages
which had once provided couples with a hide-out where they
could assure each other that the world was well lost for love
had become respectable. Though deploring the origins of
these rustic retreats, the new residents were anxious to maintain their seclusion. Their aims were not shared by lodging-
house and hotel keepers who by the 1870s were concerned to
meet the needs of visitors for man-made attractions, and for
'celebrated things that ought to be seen'. High on the list of
notable places was Carisbrooke Castle. Despite the inclement
season Frances Lock and Minnie travelled to Newport in the
approved style on top of a coach. They drove through a 'bitter-
ly cold fog and . . . were nearly frozen.' With the help of
refreshment in Self's well-warmed rooms they were able to
stay the course of a visit to Princess Elizabeth's monument in

St Thomas' church and the castle. The ivy leaves which Minnie brought away to remind her of 'a very jolly day in spite of the weather' are still unfaded. That Charles I and King Arthur were the idols of the age was due to the abhorrence of many mid-Victorians of their industrial heritage and to the genius of Tennyson and Henry Irving. Minnie wrote after seeing *Charles I* at the Lyceum: 'Irving's rendering of that beautiful character was most touching and affected almost everyone in the theatre to tears'; while King Arthur's last journey seemed pleasingly remote from the practical funeral arrangements of the time: artisan's funeral with patent carriage at £2 15s 0d, tradesman's with hearse and coach £6 and removals from public institutions at 5s.[1]

When Thomas Pennant referred to the 'rude and frightful' scenery of the Undercliff he had in mind the deep ravines cut in the dark clay by water falling to the sea. The ferns and mosses growing in these ravines were eagerly sought in the 1850s and 1860s by enthusiastic collectors; later holiday makers demanded something more than mud and ferns as Minnie and Ada Francis found when they visited Blackgang Chine: 'Ada and I drove to Blackgang this morning. We had our luncheon in the Bazaar in the Whale's Room. Ada sat on his tail . . . it cleared in time for us to go part of the way down the Chine. It is very wild and grand, but so dirty and slippery.'

When she had collected ferns at St Lawrence and ivy at Carisbrooke, had descended Blackgang and Luccombe Chines and had braved the grazing cows, amongst which a bull was always suspected, on cliff-top walks, Minnie had achieved the chief goals of the holiday-maker on the Island. An entry in her diary shows that she had learned not to put too much trust in the 'Italianate atmosphere':

> 'Very, very wet day
> Sorry to say
> Nothing particular
> Happened today'

The summer peregrinations of the Caron Place household suggest that the wet summers which recurred so persistently in the 1870s did little to check the growth of the holiday-

[1] *South London News*, 18 August 1855, advertisement for Field's General Economic Funerals.

makers' empire in Britain. Outpost resorts, such as Buxton, Torquay and Grasmere, initially settled by invalids, naturalists and admirers of natural beauty, were being clamourously occupied by regular tourists. Sir John Kaye and other men of good will were rightly concerned that during at least one month there should be 'a lull in the mighty clatter of the machinery of life'. But the reformers could not foresee the magnitude of the task of ensuring that every man had a chance of recreation and also that the quiet, space and solitude necessary to rebuild spirit and body were preserved. Some, notably John Ruskin and Hardwick Rawnsley, were conscious of the difficulties and were feeling their way towards a solution; but the majority were unwilling to envisage that Kaye's happy groups, 'radiant with the expectation of a day's pleasure', would become a mighty army whose insistence on the provision of urban amenities would preclude the enjoyment by future generations of the peace and beauties of the countryside and seashore.

CHAPTER SEVEN

Travel on the Continent:
Prejudices and Tea-Kettles

Notwithstanding Kotzebue's affirmation, that the English carry their prejudices and tea-kettles everywhere, the
traveller may dispossess himself so far as he can of the
former, but he is strongly advised not to forget the latter.

R. T. Claridge, *A Guide Along the Danube*, 1837

English travellers in the mid-nineteenth century still clung to
the prejudices which Kotzebue had observed and Byron had
ridiculed fifty years earlier. Never lenient towards his
countrymen's idiosyncrasies at home, the poet had little
patience with their mannerisms abroad. These he particula-
rized when he complained of his manservant's 'perpetual
lamentations after beef and beer, the stupid bigoted contempt
for everything foreign, and insurmountable incapacity of
acquiring even a few words of any language', and his 'long list
of calamities, such as stumbling horses, want of tea!!! and
etc.'[1] Though these aversions did not diminish with time, the
numbers of travellers increased to the extent that in 1866
Thomas Cook was directing their comings and goings in the
New as well as the Old World.

Foreigners did not fail to detect this paradox and wondered
why the Englishman set forth at all since he spent 'most of his
pleasure trip (cursing to himself, for neither the Bible nor his
respectability allows him to curse aloud)... he does not
understand foreign languages; he finds the food strange;
everything which is foreign – customs, clothes, ways of thinking – shock him'.[2] By following in the footsteps of these uneasy
travellers an attempt will be made to discover why they over-

[1] T. Moore, *Letters and Journals of Lord Byron*, 1830, Vol. I, p. 245.

[2] Eça de Queiroz, *Letters from England*, trans. 1970, see pp. 14–16 on the travelling season.

ran the continent to the extent that Cannes was 'regarded completely as an English Colony' and Norway 'as a playground for the peoples of other countries, but especially for Englishmen'.[1]

The most cogent reasons accounting for the mass exoduses of mid-Victorian tourists stemmed from the Industrial Revolution. Industrialism produced the smoke and fog which drove many sufferers from pulmonary complaints to seek relief in less polluted climes; and also the faster pace of living which allegedly gave rise to nervous disorders and to the desire for solitude which was to become the hallmark of the English eccentric abroad. Above all, wealth from mines, foundries and factories made possible these wanderings in search of fugitive health and peace of mind, and also of pleasure. Concerning this last pursuit those who crossed the Channel, as did Trollope's Samuel Rubb, to escape from 'decorum' at home were not so outspoken as the invalids and eccentrics concerning their objectives. Like tourists of every age the mid-Victorians were seekers after a state of well-being that seemed unobtainable at home; but their numbers also included those who, often disregarding their own comfort, sought for information so as to increase the well-being of others. The activities of these fact-finders reached a zenith in the mid-nineteenth century when controversies at home, particularly those concerning religious practices and the Eastern Question, depended on facts collected abroad by eager, if not always objective, tourists. The English traveller with his ever-open notebook was a source of amusement in most European countries, including his own, and of dread in a few. His activities are worth considering not only because they were typical of the age, but also because their effects on Government policy were not negligible.

As medical practitioners from Sir James Clark to Morell Mackenzie had nailed their colours to the mast of climate, the health seekers moved southwards in steadily widening circles. Lord Brougham discovered in 1831 the village of Cannes which he afterwards visited regularly as he enjoyed warmth

[1] W. Miller, *Wintering in the Riviera*, with Notes on Travel in Italy and France and Practical Hints to Travellers, 1879, p. 148 and J. C. Pythian, *Scenes of Travel in Norway*, 1877, p. 113.

and quiet. The more earnest mid-Victorians followed in his footsteps as a duty imposed by their doctors. As will be seen from Minnie Thornhill's journal the sun shone, but the train-loads of visitors created their own furore and many, like Bishop Morrell and his wife with whom Minnie travelled, were 'quite knocked up' by their cures. The congestion on the Riviera caused well-to-do invalids to move further afield. By 1868 there was a sanatorium at Thebes, where half a century earlier a French traveller, stepping boldly into the unknown, had recoiled in disgust from the sight of an English lady's maid in a pink spencer among the tombs.[1] Where the masters and mistresses went the servants necessarily followed to be squeezed into boxrooms and to drag around museums and galleries with the young ladies. Noble, the maid who accom-panied the Morrells to the Riviera and Italy, only came up for air at the Bon Marché emporium in Paris where she 'was delighted with the fine show of dresses etc.'

While pulmonary complaints accounted for many of these southward flittings, some were due to nervous disorders. These particularly afflicted overwrought clergy like Charles Kingsley, Frederick Maurice and even Anthony Huxtable from deepest Dorset. Other sufferers were misunderstood younger sons of wealthy parents and women exhausted by tasks manufactured to fill long and empty days. One patient worn out by idleness was told by her doctor: 'I must send you to the glaciers'.[2] Earlier these icy stretches had attracted only those with a superabundance of energy like Mark Beaufoy (1764–1827), Sarah Siddons and Byron. Half a century later climbing in Switzerland was being cut down to a scale suited to invalids and to those climbers who believed 'every fellah does Mont Blanc now, and what every fellah does, of course another fellah is obliged to do.'[3]

Whether seeking to recuperate in the shadow of the Alps or on the shores of the Mediterranean, invalids often underwent considerable hardships in reaching their destinations. The

[1] *Blackwood's Magazine*, March 1845, Vol. LVII, pp. 286–287, Review of Mrs Poole's 'Englishwoman in Egypt'.

[2] *Girl's Own Paper*, 9 July 1898.

[3] H. and A. Mayhew, *Mont Blanc*, first performed at the Theatre Royal, Haymarket, on 25 May 1874.

most bracing of all family doctors, William Gordon Stables (1840–1910), might declare, 'the journey itself has sometimes a good effect on important internal organs, besides exciting for good the whole vascular system';[1] but the experiences of a lady travelling to Bordighera in 1873 suggest that the excitement was too much for some vascular systems. A heavy snow-fall and a 'furious mistral' brought the train to a standstill at a small station near Orange. Here there was a 'filthy little caba-ret' where the *patron* was understandably overjoyed by the influx of clients. 'He cocked his hat on one side and winked one eye till it was more convenient to keep it shut, and could hardly keep from dancing for joy'. Three nights were spent in an icy waiting room among 'Piedmontese of the very roughest, commonest sort'. The narrator described her experiences on the third night. 'I was very sleepy but dared not go to sleep, lest the hands which were within three inches of me should steal up and catch my throat, and get my little money-bag or pick my pocket . . . at 2 am down came the inspector in a rage, and then it seemed we might have got off the previous night; but they wanted to compliment the inspector by making it appear he had sent us off!' When the train at last reached Orange the writer concluded: 'A poor gentleman who had been in our train died there suddenly; the cold and fatigue killed him. A lady was also struck by the cold and was not expected to live over the day when we left.'[2]

As the Channel had to be crossed few journeys southwards had a propitious start. This Minnie discovered when, on 22 October 1873, she set off with Bishop Morrell and his wife, Francina, on their journey to the Riviera and Italy:

> 'I never saw anything so awful as the sea looked. When we were about halfway across the waves were like huge mountains and seemed as if they must have swallowed up the little steamer . . . Nearly everyone was ill on board (all the basins were employed); so a French sailor kindly brought me a pail. I could not help (in spite of my misery) having a good laugh. Everyone did look so utter-ly helpless. The greatest fun was Franzy and the bishop

[1] *Girl's Own Paper*, 20 October 1894.

[2] Cutting from an unnamed and undated newspaper in H.S.T's diary, October 1873.

were both shot off their seat on to the floor. The bishop
sat there sometime; the boat rocked so fearfully it was
quite impossible for him to get up.'

The party had hardly recovered from the effects of the crossing when they received another shock in Paris. Tourists who
crossed the Channel before the smoke of invasion and civil war
had drifted away were dismayed to find that such activities
leave a mark on humans as well as buildings:

'We looked into lots of shops and longed to have our
pockets full of money. It is most sad to see the destruction
caused by the war, all the beautiful places pulled down
and windows broken and the monuments in
ruins . . . Paris is Radical to a degree just now . . . and
Republicanism is written on every face; the people are
barely civil and treat you with a contempt not to be
tolerated . . . With a very few exceptions, every person
among the under classes expressed as plainly as they
dared: I am as good as you and I would not put a little
finger out to do anything for you. Though not in so many
words, they made you feel it; and it was quite a relief to
get into the train and leave it all behind.'

The atmosphere in the train to Cannes was certainly more
homelike, but hardly cheerful. The sad search by consumptives was filling the hotels of the Riviera as it had done those of
Ventnor and Bournemouth; and among the many English
passengers was 'one poor young man we particularly noticed.
He looked so fearfully ill; his sister and a gentleman were with
him. They were taking him to Cannes.' On 11 December 1873
Minnie recorded: 'Poor Mr Cave died this morning at 1
o'clock, so peacefully; he must have been a very good man. It
is very sad for his poor brother and sisters. They have nursed
him so tenderly all through his illness. It has cast a sad gloom
all over the hotel . . . They say he has been ill for years, last
winter was the first time he missed coming to Cannes for the
cold weather for six years.'

As might be expected in a 'British Colony' the home routine
was followed at Cannes with only a few variations. Croquet
was played on 'hard mud', English visitors brought their dogs
which fluttered the French barn-door fowls and a better

dinner than usual appeared on Sundays. British tastes were also catered for on that day with a choice of one Presbyterian and three Anglican churches. Minnie sang in the choir at St Paul's as no 'English boys were handy at Cannes.' This shortage was particularly noticeable at the Hotel Beau Séjour where the Morrells stayed: 'We had a little tea party in our salon; there are no nice gentlemen to be had. This is quite a ladies' and old gentlemen's hotel. However, we had a nice quiet little party and lots of tea and talking – talking'... 'I feel so like one of the old ladies in Cranford! This hotel with all its old maids is just like Cranford!'

The Cranford atmosphere explains why more adventurous invalids were attracted by the 'health stations' of Norway; and why Bishop Morrell frequently disappeared with a 'bun and bottle luncheon' for a day's solitary walking.

The journey to Italy and the first impressions of Genoa were more exhilarating, even though the party divided their time between visits to the Campo Santo and to the Mercier family, associated with Lyston days. Old Mrs Mercier constantly relived 'the happy days she spent with Dearest which are still fresh in her mind'. The bishop was also reminded of home by having his pockets picked so losing £10 and all his papers which 'he most imprudently put ... into his coat pockets behind'. He was in no mood to appreciate the scenery around Sestri, the next stopping place, or the clean but 'rough and ready' hotel where the party stayed. Here straw was piled under the few carpets that were laid: 'No carpet in the *salle à manger* except under the table where there is quite a bed of straw with a carpet over it forming a huge stool.' Matters were little better on the table:

> 'The dinner was a dreadful production, sour bread, water soup, beef with all the goodness boiled out of it, very funny stringy chicken, cutlets of garlic etc. The only passable dish was stewed apples. The wine was very bad though the waiter told us it was 'très bon, très bon'. Certainly he did try to make the best of everything, even of having a most frightfully ugly old woman, the *femme de chambre*, for his only companion. He told Franzy with a wink, 'that it was a little hard for him, he would like something younger.'

Franzy was unaccustomed to such confidences and to garlic cutlets; so when the party ventured on an excursion, 'she was sick nearly all the way with a dreadful headache.' Minnie forgot her malaise in admiring the skill of the coachman, 'a first-rate whip . . . dashing along and passing everything on the road . . . he turned the corners so beautifully which was by no means easy with such a heavy carriage and five horses to guide.'

At Florence, despite the roar of the Arno and sick head-aches keeping the visitors awake, the party was able to enjoy the gala procession of carriages on 11 February 1874. This sight cheered even Francina who had been in 'such low spirits . . . and so homesick': 'We had lots of sweets (not good for much) and a bunch of violets thrown into the carriage . . . I saw one gentleman make a splendid shot, he aimed a bouquet past the head of a young lady who was standing on the balcony. It struck the walls and exploded and a little book (it seemed to me) fell at her feet. She looked so delighted, and laughed and nodded to him as she picked it up. The carriage was full of bouquets so I am afraid this was not the only one he intended to throw that day.'

In Rome Minnie was alone in her longing to see the sights. The Bishop and his wife feared the unwholesome air by night and cold winds by day. Francina, however, ventured to take Minnie to an audience at the Vatican. The benign old Pius IX well knew how to make himself affable to English ladies by asking if they 'would like a blessing from the old Pope etc', and assuring them that, 'he always prayed for the Protestants that they might be turned to the right faith'. Franzy, who had pronounced Tractarian views, did not consider herself a Pro-testant and took a ring she was going to give her husband and a locket with her brother's hair to be blessed.

At Milan the party, joined by Rose and Henry Eland from Bedminster and escorted by a canon of the cathedral, picked up amazingly: 'The bishop is much better so is Franzy. It is all dear Milan'. The charms of Milan included the staggering structural beauty of the cathedral, the shops in the Galleria, the homelike atmosphere of the Hotel Cavour, 'clean and so comfortable', and the dignity of the cathedral services: 'The religion in Milan is quite different from the rest of Italy. They will not here acknowledge the Pope in the same way as they do in Rome. They look up to him merely as we do the Archbishop of Canterbury' . . . 'They are so much more reverent here, and look like gentlemen. You do not see them taking snuff and spitting during Divine Service as they used to do so dreadfully at St Peter's in Rome.'

The party were escorted by Canon Bignani, whom the bishop found 'a most charming man', and whose polite attentions made Minnie decide: 'I am not at all disappointed in the Italians; they are so polite and attentive . . . to *all* women. The Canon is a perfect pattern of Italian gallantry. He takes the greatest interest in the most trivial wish you express. He took Rose to a shop to buy a dress and if it had been for himself I am sure he could not have taken more trouble'.

Everyone regretted leaving 'dear Milan . . . such a cheerful, clean, beautiful city with every living thing so happy and basking in the warm sunshine . . . not the fierce heat and cold wind of France or the sultry closeness of Rome, but its own sweet cheerful softness' for Pallanza. Here, despite the spring sunshine, the spell of Milan was broken. Soon after the party's arrival there was 'a great fuss last evening at dinner about windows. The Germans would have them all shut and the Bishop wanted them open.' Although English tourists made no secret of their penchant for draughts, effective drainage systems and decorum, it was some time before Continental hoteliers were able to meet their needs.

After their arrival at Dover the party went to Ascension Day service at St Mary's: 'We were very pleased and thankful to be able to go to such a beautiful service, and the first thing when we returned home after seven months' absence. It was the very thing I had so longed for.' Minnie could have whole-heartedly given thanks for months of great interest and pleasure, Franzy that she was once more in 'dear old England' and the bishop may have included in his thanksgivings the thought that next time he would go abroad alone.

When the Morrells were seeking fugitive health and happiness in the South of France and Italy, many Britons were beginning to think that the cure for their malaises lay in Norway where they could enjoy 'the recreation of travelling far from everyday surroundings, everyday customs, everyday snobbery'.[1] Wearied by industrial civilisation, some holiday makers longed for the solitude of the mountains and 'the simplicity of the patriarchal order of society' in the villages. To find these primitive blessings, tourists followed the trail which had been blazed by the British traders, miners and industrialists who had made their way up the west coast of Norway. As the pattern of the tourist following the trader was not uncommon, its development in Norway is worth some consideration. Trading relations between Dundee and Trondheim were well established by the mid-eighteenth century so that the Norwegian port was not altogether unprepared for the influx of British tourists a century later. An English iron-master gave Narvik a welcoming appearance by planting a public garden, and James Small supplied Bergen with gas. As these pioneer industrialists took with them their foremen and skilled workers the humble were able to observe simple and self-supporting societies before the well-to-do. The verdict of the artisan was not altogether favourable to those dwelling under 'the patriarchal order': 'They don't know much, the poor creatures, and as to work, Lord bless you, they have no notion of it; but they are a good set of fellows, and we hit it off very well together.'[2]

When Thomas Robert Malthus (1766–1834), a pioneer in search of facts to benefit his fellows, visited Trondheim at the end of the eighteenth century, he had been preceded by a manufacturer's agent. This factor had been 'collecting moss for an English Company: it is . . . used for a scarlet dye. When it was first discovered the price was only £3 the tun, and now is 28'.[3] As was the case in south-east Europe, Norway was opened to the tourist by industrialists and by thoughtful men in search of information. Malthus travelled to northern Norway not to escape industrial society but to discover how to dispel the cloud of overpopulation which he considered overshadowed its prospects. In every respect Malthus was the

[1] Beyer's *Guide to Western Norway*, 1887, p. 9.

[2] C. Boner, *Transylvania, its Products and Peoples*, 1865, p. 270. This was an Englishman's opinion of Wallachian bricklayers working on the erection of a gasometer at Kronstadt (Braşov).

[3] *The Travel Diaries of Thomas Robert Malthus*, ed. Patricia James, 1966, p. 73.

ideal tourist in search of facts. He worked systematically, taking thermometer readings and filling notebooks, he never complained of hardships and communicated readily and pleasantly with all whom he met. Knowing something of the rapid growth of manufacturing towns like Cromford in Derbyshire, Malthus particularly admired the wide and well-planned streets of Trondheim. He was also pleased to find that the lavish board spread by his hosts in this city appeared also in peasant homes. In one of these the sight of 'seven men eating a most comfortable breakfast, of fried bacon and veal, some fried fish, large bowls of milk, and oat cake and butter' gave the economist food for thought.[1] In fertile England only bread remained on the agricultural labourer's table.

The questing spirit which sent reflective men like Malthus into the little visited parts of Europe also accounted for the wanderings of British naturalists and botanists in the first half of the nineteenth century. Their accounts of bears and reindeer in Norway, of the splendour of alpine pastures in spring and of the abounding waterfowl at the mouth of the Danube did not a little to encourage tourists many of whom were also amateur naturalists and sportsmen. That the two interests often merged is illustrated by the short life of William Dawson Hooker (1816–1840), the eldest son of the great botanist, Sir Joseph Hooker. William, who was an enthusiastic ornithologist, albeit much attached to his gun, visited northern Norway in 1836. Most of his time was spent at Hammerfest where an English acquaintance was manager of the nearby copper mines at Kaafjord (plate 27). The short journal of William Hooker glows with the sunset radiance which is often apparent in accounts written by consumptives overseas. Hooker was intoxicated by the fragrance of the *Linnaea borealis* in the woodland, and by the midsummer gaiety of a people who spent the winter in total darkness. At Hammerfest 'the fun was . . . kept up for a whole dozen hours. . . . I soon hardly knew whether it was upon my head or heels that I stood, or rather staggered'.[2] This summer abandon was an even more

[1] Ibid., pp. 147–8 for description of Trondheim and p. 142 for the labourer's breakfast.

[2] W. D. Hooker. *Notes on Norway*, or a brief Journal of a Tour made in the Northern Part of Norway, 2nd ed., 1839, 123 pp.

powerful attraction to many British tourists than the carnivals in the South of France and in Italy.

By the 1850s steamboats were sailing regularly up the west coast of Norway carrying climbers, sportsmen, artists and those whose strange impulses could not fail to escape notice:

> 'Englishmen are objects of great wonderment to the Norwegians. The steward told me of an English lady who has a farm hereabouts [near Lillehammer], who rides bare-backed horses, and cuts her own timber in a silk gown; and of Sir Something Somebody, who hired a special steam packet in order to avoid meeting five people he had travelled with; also of another Englishman who for some years past has lived in a lonely hut with no other associate than an old woman, his housekeeper; and who spends all his time in hunting wolves and bears, and does not catch any.'[1]

Tales are current of an English recluse of more recent date whose obsession with the Nordic ethos was such that he had his own excellent teeth replaced by those of an elk. The hopes of shooting an elk, or a bear kept many an Englishman in the Norwegian wilderness until he was loath to part with the habits bred in solitude.

These solitary habits explain why many mid-Victorian travellers were considered eccentric on the Continent. In over-crowded England where neighbour jostled neighbour individual taste did not have the same scope as it did on the large and isolated estates of central and eastern Europe. Many well-to-do individuals, therefore, sought to follow their own life styles in the less congested areas of the Continent. But the possession of wealth, which made this course possible, was in itself an abnormality in poor countries like Norway. A Norwegian historian recalls 'the first great days of tourism, when English travellers of the upper classes, with their precious sovereigns and eccentric habits were one of the sights of the town.'[2]

The town in question was Trondheim which by the 1880s

---

[1] W. M. Williams, *Through Norway with a Knapsack*, 1859, pp. 40–41.

[2] *Trondheim Bys Historie*, Vol. IV, 1958, R. Danielsen, The New Society, 1880–1914, pp. 114–15.

had acquired aspects not altogether pleasing to the eccentrics. The three leading hotels, Britannia, Angleterre and Victoria, attested to the growing popularity of northern Norway with English tourists. Though yearning for solitude the eccentrics did not shun the solid, and comfortable, respectability of the Britannia which still stands as a monument to the strange marriage of the Knightsbridge Dutch and Classical styles of architecture. In seeking to break the exigent bonds of industrial society by visiting northern Norway, mid-Victorian tourists, like the silent and chained convicts whom Mark Thornhill saw escaping during the Mutiny, dragged their shackles with them. Though many enjoyed watching, and even entering into, 'the simplicity of the patriarchal order of society . . . for a time', tourists took with them the standards and needs engendered by an urban civilisation. These tastes changed the favoured ports of call along the west coast of Norway, as surely as they had done the Riviera resorts.

The travellers who declared in 1857 that 'the English are lords and masters in Bergen, all they do is imitated'[1] were exaggerating but by the 1890s Bergen was ceasing to be a typical Norwegian town (plates 28 and 29). Impressive stone built houses, such as those in Parkvei, might have been transplanted from the more prosperous areas of Kensington; but the 'prettily draped lace curtains at the windows, looking neat and fresh, as though Spring cleaning had just finished' could be seen in few coal-burning English towns. These 'tastefully draped' curtains also appeared at Trondheim,[2] where shopkeepers were quick to take the measure of British tastes. Skins were displayed in polar settings to tempt unsuccessful sportsmen longing to take some trophy home; and silversmiths learned the value of 'national style' tableware and trinkets.[3] The services in Trondheim cathedral, as in other Lutheran churches, also had something to offer British tourists of both High and Low Church parties, though neither approved of the notices: 'Worshippers are requested to spit in the platters'. At Hammerfest William Hooker was struck by the carved Crucifixion and by the 'huge

[1] Anon, *Unprotected Females in Norway*, 1857, p. 154.

[2] Lizzie Vickers, *Old Norway and its Fjords*, or a Holiday in Norseland, 1893, p. 24 for description of Bergen and pp. 53–61 for that of Trondheim.

[3] R. Danielsen, op. cit., p. 115.

gilded wax tapers' on the altar, and by the orderly deportment of the congregation which resembled that 'of a Scottish Country Kirk'. Another observer ecstatically described the celebration of Holy Communion at Trondheim with altar lights, the eastward position, vestments, hymn singing and the sign of the Cross at Benediction.[1]

With so many Anglican parsons scaling the heights, or plumbing the depths, of Lutheran practices in Scandinavia and Roman Catholic ones in France and Italy, the Orthodox Church was inevitably drawn into the orbit of English theological polemics. Eagerness to obtain ammunition for this warfare partly accounts for the prominence of clergy among Galton's 'vacation tourists': they rode in Palestine, climbed Mount Sinai, visited Moscow and penetrated into Serbia. So enthusiastic was the geographer and eugenist, Francis Galton (1822–1911), about information collected on holidays that he edited between 1861–3 a series of reports entitled *Vacation Tourists*. In his *Hints to Travellers* (1878), Galton showed how high were his expectations from well-spent holidays. The tourist was assured that sextant, compass, thermometer, aneroid and other instruments would 'travel excellently when packed in *loose, tumbled* clothes' and that the notebook was best carried in a 'leather pouch secured to the waist-belt'. The attitude of Continental officials to these heavily-laden travellers ranged between bewilderment and suspicion. It is impossible not to feel some sympathy with the Serb confronted by the indomitable Mary Durham who was ready to shoulder the whole burden of the Balkans: ' "I have come to see Serbia" said I, in return to the enquiry of a police officer. "But what do you see?" he asked, gazing wildly round. "I see nothing!" '[2]

The infant principality of Serbia offered a good starting point for investigating the complexities of Orthodox practices and of the Eastern Question. The area was small compared with the daunting vastness of Russia; and by the 1860s, many of the Serb people were freed from Turkish suzerainty so travellers were not subjected to the delays and confusions of Ottoman administration. Furthermore, thanks to the

---

[1] *The Guardian*, 2 July 1890, letter from R. Strutt.

[2] M. E. Durham, *Twenty Years of Balkan Tangle*, 1920, p. 47: Mary Durham's *Burden of the Balkans* was published in 1905.

Romantic enthusiasm for hajduk chiefs, giaours and pashas and to Sir John Bowring's translation in 1827 of Serb popular songs, the reading public knew something of 'the popular and passionate spirit' of the South Slavs.[1]

Something of this spirit appears in the accounts of two English clergymen, William Denton and Walter Greive, who visited Serbia in the early 1860s. Having first-hand knowledge of industrial society, both men felt that in Serbia they were living in a golden age, long lost in England, when all who toiled shared the rude plenty of the countryside and those who worshipped did so from happiness rather than from guilt. Since the clerical visitors held this view their sympathies lay with the 'long-trampled' peoples still struggling to free themselves from the Turkish yoke. That an influential section of the British public sympathised with this aim was due to the voices of English travellers crying after a sojourn in the South-Slav wilderness.

Among the most objective of these travellers were, as Gladstone acknowledged, Georgina Mackenzie (later Lady G. M. Sebright) and Adeline Irby. On their way to Greece in search of 'a warm yet bracing climate for the winter', the two friends heard tales of Slav misfortunes which induced them to start in 1860 a series of investigations into the state of the Slavs under Turkish suzerainty. Though Miss Mackenzie was delicate and died soon after her marriage, the two jolted in wagons from the Aegean to the Adriatic. They learned Serb and travelled from village to village making careful notes and sleeping in Turkish *khans*, or inns, or in the equally primitive houses of small officials. The first of their publications, 'Christmas in Montenegro', appeared in 1861 among the accounts of Galton's vacation tourists. As well as collecting information, the travellers endeavoured to encourage female education. Here they met much opposition from local dignitaries one of whom declared, 'that if women could write they would be forever inditing love letters'.[2]

---

[1] *The Westminster Review*, July–October 1826, Vol VI, pp. 23–35, review of 'Popular Serbian Songs' collected and published by V. S. Karadžić 1823–4, and translated by J. Bowring, 1827.

[2] G. M. Mackenzie and I. P. Irby, *Travels in the Slavonic Provinces of Turkey-in-Europe*, 1877, Vol. I, p. 207. This view might be expected in the town in question, Pristina, which remained under Turkish control until 1912.

Even before Miss MacKenzie and Miss Irby started distributing reading primers changes were beginning to threaten the lives of peoples seemingly forgotten by Time. The inception of steam navigation on the Danube in the 1830s caused optimists like John Murray, with the sale of his guide books in mind, to forecast a glorious future for riparian peoples who would be reached at last by civilisation in the shape of trade and tourists. Hopeful as he was concerning future improvements in the steamboat services, Murray felt constrained to mention certain disadvantages such as delays, dirt, insects, 'the filthy habit of spitting' among Hungarian passengers and the lack of accommodation at the riverside clusters of huts which had been elevated to the status of ports.[1]

The regulation of the Danube and the introduction of steam navigation was due to the forceful energy of the Hungarian Count István Széchenyi (1791–1860) and to the skill and initiative of two Englishmen who operated the first steamship company running boats from Pressburg to Galatz at the mouth of the river. Britons were as at home on the Danube as on the Ganges or the Rangitata in New Zealand. They commanded and manned the steamships and they were to be found at the keypoints along the river. In the desolate village of Svinjište a British traveller found a fellow countryman, 'a very intelligent though humble adventurer in the engineering line' who operated the diving-bell used to clear obstacles impeding navigation.[2] Despite the many evidences of British skill which accompanied a voyage down the Danube from Pressburg, aspects of the journey were not calculated to attract the mid-Victorian paterfamilias. Some of these may be seen through the eyes of ubiquitous Charles Elliott who, having retired from the Bengal Civil Service, entered the church. His pastorates, however, were frequently interrupted by prolonged searches for health which took him from the Baltic to the Bosphorus. In Autumn 1835 the vicar of Godalming embarked at Pressburg for a voyage down the Danube 'in the hopes of curing' a 'complaint of the throat which inhibited him from fulfilling the

---

[1] Murray's *Handbook for Travellers in Southern Germany*, 1838; for descriptions of the Danube between Vienna and the Black Sea see pp. 353–387.

[2] M. J. Quin, *A Steam Voyage down the Danube*, 1836, pp. 83–84.

duties of his profession.'[1] Elliott must have begun to wonder if he had chosen the right cure for parson's throat as soon as he entered the men's cuddy 'fraught with unsavoury odours, almost suffocating'. The floor was strewn with mattresses 'alive and almost moving', and several passengers as well as the steward were suffering from tertian fever. Matters did not improve in the dining saloon where passengers, mostly Germans and Hungarians with a few English and Italians, were obliged to remain all day as carriages crowded the decks. A frugal breakfast was followed by 'a little pelting of orange-peel and all the concomitants of the most essentially vulgar mirth' which filled the time until, in response to 'a Bacchanalian yell' from the Germans, midday dinner appeared. After the meal 'cards and tumultuous mirth' filled the time until the appearance of candles heralded the scramble for sleeping places. These amenities (not including food) could be enjoyed at the cost, according to Murray, of £11 18s for the voyage from Vienna to Galatz, which lasted approximately fourteen days.

Improvements were effected, but perhaps not to the extent that the long-suffering Elliott anticipated: 'When the Danube becomes a fashionable resort, a better arrangement will, doubtless, be effected.' Even in the 1860s steamboat services had a long way to go before they could compete with those offered by tourist boats on the Rhine or sailing up the west coast of Norway. Nevertheless more than one visitor to Serbia wondered why British tourists remained faithful to the Rhine, where the scenery seemed 'made by contract for the express purpose of attracting tourists', when 'grander scenery and equal historic character' awaited them beside the Danube.[2] Few could resist the fascination of the river's green waters whether they flowed gently between osiers and islands covered with sweetly scented shrubs or raced down from Orsova, a village where an inn offered a bed for 10d, breakfast 6d, dinner 1s and supper 9d.[3] Despite these inducements, most tourists who

[1] C. B. Elliott, *Travels in the Three Great Empires of Austria, Russia and Turkey*, 1838, Vol. I, p. 9. For descriptions of conditions on the steamboat see pp. 71–9.

[2] *The Field*, 12 February 1870, Templar 'A Ramble in Serbia'; see also W. Denton, *Serbia and the Serbians*, 1862, pp. 103–4. The old spelling, Servia, has been changed in these titles and in quotations.

[3] R. T. Claridge, *A Guide along the Danube*, 1837, p. 56.

ventured to Belgrade travelled overland by rail, a journey which took in the 1860s just over four days of continuous travelling. So long and tiring a prelude to a holiday was more than the average tourist cared to face; and, furthermore, few of his tastes were catered for in Serbia. The ancient monasteries and Roman remains were too little known to attract sightseers; and the country's many spas could not tempt invalids from the more fashionable springs in Germany and Austria. The reluctance of sportsmen to visit the country is hard to understand since bears, the most sought-after prizes of Britons on the Continent, were more plentiful than in Norway. In the autumn, according to William Denton, a bear could be 'occasionally seen shaking the wild-plum tree for his favourite food'; while ortolan, quail and snipe abounded beside the Danube. The journey, however, was too expensive for would-be sportsmen, and the terrain too alien for those accustomed to hunt in the shires, shoot over the Scottish moors and fish in Norway. The forests of Serbia were often impenetrable, and the riverside haunts of wildfowl infested by insects. Well-trained sporting dogs were at a disadvantage for the density of the undergrowth prevented the use of a pointer, and the other dogs were corrupted by the 'yelping curs' used by Serb hunters.[1] In the 1860s most travellers left Britain for Serbia to search for new sources of minerals and coal, or for information generally touching some aspect of the Eastern Question. The quests of these searchers were facilitated by the regulation and navigation of the Danube which opened up Serbia to enterprising industrialists and to the fact collectors.

Although claiming that he visited Serbia in April 1861 'partly in search of health', William Denton, the vicar of St. Bartholomew's, Cripplegate, was impelled by the desire to help the Christians under Ottoman rule, and to enlist British interest in the Eastern Church. He wisely prefaced his appeals for the sympathy of his countrymen by stressing the many resemblances between England and Serbia. He assured his readers that: 'Those who endure, as part of the necessary evils of travel, the dirt of Germany, and the petty and vexatious inconveniences with which some continental Governments

---

[1] *The Field*, 19 February 1870, Templar, 'A Ramble in Serbia'.

annoy the traveller, will be charmed with the cleanliness of the
Serbian people, and the perfect freedom which is enjoyed in a
country where the constitution is as free and the franchise
more extended than in England.'[1] Furthermore, the natural
vegetation was 'almost entirely English'; but Denton's compa-
rison of the weighted bushes dragged as harrows by Serb peasants with 'our common bush harrow' cannot have been
acceptable to English cultivators who followed high-farming
practices and prided themselves on their array of metal
machinery. Even the fort-like Romanesque churches were
drawn within the home orbit, for Denton observed that the
monastic church at Manasija had pillars which were 'Early
English in character like those at Islip.'

A year or so later Walter Greive, chaplain of the House of
Mercy at Clewer, with three companions followed in Denton's
footsteps. As befitted Galton's 'vacation tourists' the party
were prepared for every hazard. In Serbia they travelled in
'white linen coats', and with white cotton 'arranged in flowing
folds around their wide-a-wake hats so as to convert them into
something like turbans.'[2] So garbed, Greive and his companions were disconcerted to find the main roads 'macada-
mised' and 'generally bounded by admirable fences'. They
only began to feel themselves pioneers when their light and
springless wagons took to tracks winding through forests
where great herds of swine were grubbing beneath the trees;
and when they found caviare and lemon 'no bad relish for
brown bread or white at a roadside breakfast.'

To Greive it seemed the vast forests dominated both life and
death in Serbia. Concerning the small graveyards in their
shadow he wrote: 'There is something very impressive and
affecting in the loneliness of these quiet resting places . . . One
loved to linger in quiet amid those who seemed so peacefully
waiting for the Lord of the Forest to appear, as if even now
they were engaged in silent communication with Him, and,
beneath the dancing sunlight, were exulting in their beds.'
The Serb graves, often overrun with 'large green lizards,
besides troops of small brown ones' also fascinated Denton as

[1] W. Denton, op. cit., p. 104.

[2] *Vacation Tourists* 1862–3, ed. F. Galton, pp. 417–456, W. T. Greive, 'The
Church and People of Serbia'.

a folklore enthusiast, since they provided an explanation for the Eastern belief that lizards symbolised the spirit of man.

Not only did the clerical visitors feel conscious of the spirit

A scene in a Serb forest.

of the forest, but when they stopped in isolated and log-built villages they recaptured their own past. It seemed natural to Greive that the priest should be 'scantily educated', and that: 'His face, weather-beaten and tanned, his hands hard with manual labour, all witnessed to the soil wherewith he earned his bread and eked out a scanty subsistence'. So had the priest appeared in English medieval villages, and Greive forgot the quite different standards by which his fellow clergy at Clewer were judged. He also forgot the repressive Sundays at home when he watched the sports, singing and dancing that took place outside the church after the Sunday service.

Although by the 1870s British tourists were bringing no mean profit to France and Italy, they remained fringe groups of interest only to hoteliers, shopkeepers and guides. The few who moved into south-east Europe were more closely observed; and even the least assuming were believed to have important political contacts in England. In Hungary an indefatigable fact-finding tourist, Julia Pardoe (1806–1862), secured an interview with the Anglophil Count Széchenyi, and also with the Prince Palatinate. The Prince, smarting under adverse criticism from foreign visitors, besought her not to heed ' "travellers' tales" disseminated by hurried and prejudiced tourists'.[1] Among developing nations 'the chield . . . taking notes' was both feared and courted.

The clerical visitors to Serbia, therefore, had no difficulty in visiting the ruling prince, Michael Obrenović (1839–42 and 1860–8), and the Metropolitan in Belgrade. The politically-minded prelate took care to entertain Greive and his party in a style that 'befitted the establishment of a great ecclesiastic' and to send cordial messages 'to the Lord Bishop of London, the Lord Bishop of Oxford, and the Reverend William Denton.' Prince Michael, an outstandingly able ruler with an attractive personality, was equally pleased to receive British travellers whose presence in Serbia indicated their pro-Slav sympathies. Though preparing for defensive action against the Turks, the prince wisely confined his conversations with Denton and Greive to 'social, commercial, and agricultural topics'. To impress visitors from a country renowned for its advanced farming practices, Obrenović produced in April a full ear of barley grown on his own farm.

The glowing accounts given by Denton and Greive of the Prince's moderation and benevolence helped to foster in England an awareness of the Slav claims even if they carried little weight with the Government, still intent on bolstering up the

---

[1] Julia Pardoe, *The City of the Magyar*, or Hungary and her Institutions in 1839–1840, 1840, Vol. I, p. 263 for description of Count Széchenyi, and p. 315 for that of Archduke Joseph, the Prince Palatinate.

Sick Man of Europe. Kotzebue's description of English tourists was accurate as regards those travelling in south-east Europe. They took with them their tea kettles and, as a rule, their prejudices against Ottoman rule. They also took their notebooks which they filled to good, if not immediate, effect.

A Scottish observer in the mid-nineteenth century rightly regarded the mass tourist exoduses as one of the phenomena of the age. Among these he placed 'the contest of labour with capital', the growth of ritualism and the 'penchant' of the Government for 'conquering remote provinces stern and wild or insalubrious'.[1] These disquieting forces were all derived from the Industrial Revolution which, by expelling many from their ecological niches, created the 'footloose and expansionist race' whose activities as tourists and colonists amazed the Portuguese consul at Newcastle and many other foreigners.

British travellers remained enigmas on the Continent until the First World War. After 1918 their presence ceased to attract attention among the moving peoples of Europe. Only some of the imposing hotels, Angleterre, Britannique and Victoria, and the Anglican churches, trying to look both English and Gothic among the palms and eucalyptus trees, remained as monuments to the golden days of British tourism.

[1] W. Miller, op. cit., p. 1.

CHAPTER EIGHT

India: 'The Glorious Glowing Land'

India, the glorious glowing land, the gorgeous and the beautiful; India, the golden prize contended for by Alexander of old, and acknowledged in our day as the brightest jewel in Victoria's crown; India the romantic, the fervid, the dreamy country of the rising sun; India the far-off, the strange, the wonderful, the original, the true, the brave, the conquered; India, how nobly does she show in the Palace devoted to the industrial products of the world!

The Illustrated Exhibitor, 4 October, 1851.

This ecstasy was not simulated to puff the Great Exhibition of 1851. The press of visitors in the 'gorgeous tent' of the East India Company indicated a general longing to forget the workaday world in 'a bit out of the Arabian Nights'. No praise was too high for the Illustrious Company which had succeeded in securing 'the golden prize'; and in bringing not only wealth to the homeland but also a reflection of the heart-warming splendour of the Orient. Yet within six years the East India Company had become: 'The Great Indian Pickle Warehouse' in which were to be found 'various green things, such as incompetent judges, cruel tax-gatherers, and over-bearing military officers.'[1]

This *volte-face* was due primarily to the Indian Mutiny for which the suspected incompetence of the Company was blamed and also the angry bewilderment over the shattered image of 'India the romantic'. In the harrowing 1840s and 1850s this land of promise was the only glimmer on the horizon of many machine-bound Britons.

The Indian legend had been built up during the century

[1] *Punch*, 15 August 1857.

177

preceding the Mutiny. Those who had served in India did not hide their lights under bushels when they came home. The architectural displays of nabobs, such as Robert Palk's Belvidere overlooking the Teign valley, blazoned the news that fortunes had been made. Even the old British soldiers and servants who often returned from India destitute could not forbear to vaunt the glories they had known. As many of these took to the roads as beggars, like the couple who called at Lyston Hall and refused to leave unless they were given more than is, or strolling players, their yarns were heard in servants' halls, cottages and taverns throughout the country. Some substance was given to these travellers' tales by the number of Indians who amazed street-corner audiences by their conjuring tricks or frightened housewives with their dark looks and mysterious words into buying trash. Cold and cowed though their appearance often was they expressed, even when selling tracts, something of the magic of distant lands (plate 30). When they attempted to earn a livelihood as 'musicianers', however, these aliens failed to charm. George Augustus Sala voiced a general opinion when he described, 'a shivering Hindoo, his skin apparently just washed in walnut juice, with a voluminous turban, dirty white muslin caftan, worsted stockings and hob-nailed shoes, who, followed by two diminutive imps in similar costume, sings a dismal ditty in the Hindostanee language, and beats the tom-tom with fiendish monotony.'[1]

But royal patronage could almost make the Ethiopian change his skin: in a high place among the entertainers offered by the Army and Navy Stores in 1907 were Wallah and Jarhoo the Royal Durbar Entertainers. Most of the Indians in Britain were servants who had been jettisoned in the first half of the nineteenth century. The feelings of pity and alarm with which many, like Mrs Siddons, regarded 'these poor Orientals'[2] hardened as the century progressed. On 6 March 1869 *Punch* referred to the 'Oriental vagabonds who scowl about our streets' and approvingly noted that Captain Stacpole had demanded in the Commons 'why the wholesome Indian rule

[1] G. A. Sala, *Twice Around the Clock*, 1859, p. 105.

[2] Gwendoline Beaufoy, *Leaves from a Beech Tree*, 1930, p. 265 quoting from letter dated 10 May 1814.

that provided for the return of exported servants were [sic] broken.'

Even the woebegone aspect of scowling Orientals did not dispel the popular image of India as a golden treasure chest of which the East India Company held the key. For in the service of the Illustrious Company even needy boys, if they were able and adventurous, had a chance to rise to positions of authority and affluence. After the Mutiny this great escape route for poor but ambitious boys was closed. With the Company disappeared the dreams of those who hoped to rise from humble homes, since imperial service was restricted to the well-educated, and also the seemingly do-nothing yet profitable days of Britons serving in India. Despite Lord Mayo's criticism of lax district officers, who were not achieving 'constant association with the people, perfect accessibility and a thorough knowledge of the language',[1] the official pace of imperial servants quickened after the Mutiny. This point was clearly made by a young engineer starting his career in the Punjab in 1872: 'We work like horses, and a good deal harder, none of your old *Company* days for us – all play and no work. One has to *work* now.'[2] The languid ways of many retired Company servants were largely responsible for giving this impression of idleness which was not necessarily universal. Old Cudbert Thornhill could have told a different tale when he recalled his struggles with white ant in the timber of Company vessels, with runaway seamen and with drunken pilots. He worked quite as hard as his great-grandson, Henry Beaufoy Thornhill, who was Sanitary Officer for Lord Curzon's Durbar at the turn of the twentieth century and also at the great Coronation Durbar of 1911. He had been responsible for the erection of 'many square miles of tents and gardens – a hundred miles of main roads – all this in a jungle place where partridges, hyaenas and jackals normally dwell. Pipewater is arranged for 500,000 people.'

From a study of the Thornhills in India something may be learned about the relations of Company and of imperial ser-

[1] Cited by W. W. Hunter, *Life of the Earl of Mayo*, 1875, Vol. II, p. 249.

[2] From a letter dated 17 March 1872 written by Edward Lang (1849–1880) to his father, Arthur Lang, who had been a judge in the East India Company.

vants with the Indians; and of the continuation of the old system of government by empirical manoeuvring. This alone made British rule possible, but after 1858 with an aspect of greater efficiency and uniformity. These two qualities produced tangible benefits for India but made any rapprochement between the two races impossible. A brief survey of British rule in India must be made before the careers of the six generations of Thornhills who served in the subcontinent can be seen in perspective.

In the seventeenth century the servants of the East India Company merely strove to hold their own as traders; but the need to protect their interests against the French forced them to extend their influence by becoming tax collectors and administrators in the following century. Finally, under governors like Bentinck and Dalhousie, officials found themselves having to act as torch-bearers of western civilization. Though service in the Company was often a valuable legacy from father to son, there was little uniformity in the private or official conduct of its servants. They ranged from the ministerial nominees, one of whom Clive allegedly greeted with the question, 'Well, chap, how much do you want?' and paid him £10,000 to leave the country, to men of outstanding ability and integrity, many of whom were also ministerial protégés. Even the scrupulous Cornwallis was glad to oblige his friend, the Marquis of Lansdowne, by employing the able and hardworking John Fombelle. The prolix and frequent instructions of the Company's Court of Directors in London bewildered, amused or angered officials in India but seldom directed them. Despite the ineffectiveness of their control the directors resented the authority often exerted by the men on the spot, the governers. The interests of the two authorities often only coincided when their powers were threatened by the government intervention made possible by the India Acts.

The efforts of the Company to achieve some settlement with dependent rulers may be likened to the struggles of an European trying to shrug himself into an *achkan*. The submission of a ruler often necessitated the Company collecting his taxes and this, in its turn, entailed the administration of justice. So the anomaly of the Company's collector and magistrate appeared. With the forces at their disposal the Company had not the means, even if they had the wish, to alter the laws or the financial structure of the dependent states. Throughout India revenue was derived mainly from the land, so that collectors were necessarily concerned with questions of land tenure. Unfortunately, as Mark Thornhill (1822–1900) pointed out, Company officials had little understanding of the Indian belief that, 'rights in land were invested with a degree of sanctity.'[1] The English had developed, under the wayward tutelage of the Plantagenets, a remarkably sure instinct for flexible and efficient administration. But, as they lived in the most feudal of West European countries, their understanding of the rights of land tenure was moulded by autocratic rulers determined to maintain a hold on the lands of their own vassals. In their turn these tenants-in-chief tightened their grip on their land-holding dependents. So Englishmen early learned to stand up for their rights as taxpayers but not as landowners. The inability to comprehend the sanctity of land ownership overshadowed all England's dealings with Ireland, and, to a lesser extent, with India. Under the guidance of Lord Cornwallis (Governor-General of Bengal 1786–1793 and 1805) an honest effort was made to fit the English official into the jacket of Bengali laws of land tenure. That such an effort could be made was due to the greater control secured over the Company's activities by the India Act of 1784, and to the character of Cornwallis. Energy and disinterestedness have been common characteristics of English rulers in India, but the commonsense and compassion of Cornwallis were never rivalled.

As a great landowner himself, Cornwallis has been blamed for achieving a settlement based on an European and aristocratic model. But if the Governor erred, it was in making a permanent settlement in which an over-scrupulous consideration was given to the laws and customs of Bengal. The

[1] Unless otherwise stated, all Mark Thornhill's quotations have been taken from his two accounts of India: *The Personal Adventures and Experiences of a Magistrate during the Rise Progress and Suppression of the Indian Mutiny*, 1884, and *Haunts and Hobbies of an Indian Official*, 1899. According to Henry Beaufoy Thornhill, Lord Roberts considered the account of the Mutiny to be 'the best book he ever read of its kind'; while the *Athenaeum*, 31 January 1885, praised its 'spirit of fairness, not too common in writings upon the Mutiny by men who took part in it'.

revenue from the land in Bengal was collected by hereditary agents, the *zamindars*, who were often, but not necessarily, landowners on a large scale. As he was struggling to get into another man's coat, it is understandable that Cornwallis retained the *zamindari* system; and that he endeavoured to achieve a measure of financial stability by making his settlement of tax liability permanent. The fixed levy on the *zamindars* was not great as Cornwallis over-optimistically hoped, 'that they would be induced to devote their energies, and some of their means, to the improvement of the condition of the peasantry.'[1] Overburdened as the peasants were their land, at least, was protected by Indian law from seizure against their debts. This alien conception was not readily grasped by Company officials so that, according to Mark Thornhill, 'Under our rule this was changed; land was made liable to sale in the same manner as other property'. This liability gave the *bunnisah*, or money lender, a hold over both the burdened peasant and the spendthrift *zamindar*. Where *zamindari* had not been established, as in Madras, revenue was collected by the Company direct from the *ryot*, or cultivator. Only in Oudh, annexed in 1856, were all attempts to get into the *achkan* abandoned. The disorder in this state that had been a stumbling block to Warren Hastings and a grief to Cornwallis was a challenge to the brisk and doctrinaire officials of the mid-nineteenth century. To them the landlord, whether great or small, was the demon to be exorcised; so the annexation of Oudh was followed by a policy based on the determination 'to root out the *talukdars*' or landlords. It was easy to achieve a province-wide dispossession by regarding *talukdar* rights as office not property, and to make a thirty-year settlement with the cultivators. Throughout Oudh was enacted a scene, not unknown in England during the enclosures, where documentary evidences of possession were demanded from landholders whose family acres had been so long occupied that the need for papers was forgotten.

From the banks of the Jumna to the foothills of the Himalayas dispossessed *talukdars*, with whom the perverse peasantry often sided, promotion-hungry sepoys, debt-ridden *zamindars* and devout Hindus and Muslims, who feared Chris-

[1] J. D. Hooker, *Himalayan Journals*, 1848–1851, 1891 ed. p. 273.

tian proselytism, all nursed their grievances. Moving from district to district in the discontented provinces the four sons of John and Henriette Philippine Thornhill, Robert, Cudbert, Mark and Henry, ascended the Company's ladder of promotion from writers to magistrates and inspectors. It seemed as if their uneventful lives, disturbed only by leisurely journeys through their districts would end, as their father's and grandfather's had done, with a comfortable and well-respected retirement.

Encounter in an Indian jungle.

On the eve of the Mutiny Europeans and Indians were closer than at any other time during their long association. Many of the Company's servants belonged to families who had been long established in India, and who had absorbed something of the fatalistic attitude of those among whom they lived. Also, the oriental taste for display appeared as a characteristic Anglo-Indian attribute. Soon after his first marriage in 1852 Mark was promoted to the position of magistrate at Muttra, an ancient Hindu stronghold. Here Mark, who readily conversed with those he met in the city, on journeys and round camp fires, developed a sympathetic understanding of the Indian temperament with which his own had many affinities. He willingly sank into the 'calm tranquillity' of oriental life, and lived in a style befitting a minor potentate: 'Our house was large and handsomely furnished, we had many horses and a great retinue of servants, besides a guard of soldiers and numerous attendants on horse and foot, who were provided for me at the expense of the Government. I had a chest full of silver plate, which stood in the hall, and . . . a great store of Cashmere shawls, pearls, and diamonds.'

In May 1857 rumours of the restoration of the Mogul dynasty at Delhi reached the fairy-tale city of Muttra. Living in a dream world, Europeans gathered to discuss the developments with pleasurable excitement. 'Their talk was all about the ceremonial of the palace, and how it would be revived. They speculated as to who would be the Grand Chamberlain, which of the chiefs of Rajputana would guard the different gates, and who were the fifty-two Rajahs who would assemble to place the Emperor on the throne.'

Even when the mutiny of the Ulwar cavalry was a threat to Muttra, Mark riding to Agra for assistance felt 'something rather exhilarating in our position. It was such a pleasant change from our usual confinement indoors to be in the open air, and riding over the country at the head of a band of horsemen seemed like acting a part in a fairy tale. All possible adventures might be before us'.

If, as Thornhill believed, the Indians mutinied to escape from 'the disciplined order of English rule' to the pre-Company days which they imagined to have been 'full of poetry, full of romance – wondrous rumours, vague anticipations', the Anglo-Indians had also sought to escape into a 'glowing land' of adventures, ceremonies and intrigues.

Another dream world awaited Mark Thornhill when he followed his family to the fortified city of Agra held by John Colvin who was Lieutenant Governor of the North-West Provinces. Colvin's appointment in 1853 as head of the Agra government marked his emergence from the shadows into which he had been thrown as a result of his fervent support for the ill-fated Afghanistan expedition. Under this unhappy man who suffered all the anguish, which eventually killed him, of being unable to rise to the occasion, Mark and Cudbert Thornhill served throughout the Mutiny. Cudbert, who acted as secretary to the governor's council, was by nature and principle reticent; while Mark being communicative and untrammelled by office in high places, was not inhibited from reporting what he saw rather than what should have been seen. Even at this early stage Mark wondered at Colvin's 'sad, wearied expression', and at the determination of Agra officials to treat the district reports as unduly alarmist. Despite official complacency, refugees steamed into the city which soon assumed the 'stuffy, stewy, and vermin-infested aspect' and atmosphere of unreality associated with ship-board life. Agra was a city cut off from reality where English soldiers used their leisure and much-needed ammunition to fire at vultures, where every military officer knew how the revolt could be suppressed, and where civilians gossiped endlessly while uncollected filth and rubbish around the well seeped into the water.

English writers on Indian history liked to dwell on the confusion and mismanagement in high places. Had the spirit of Akbar returned to his fort, as an old attendant of Mark's alleged it regularly did, the great emperor would have smiled at the Agra scene during the rains of 1857. Mark noted that:

> 'There were disputes about the militia, disputes about the rifle corps, disputes about the Moti Masjid, disputes about the marble hall, disputes about the Sunday service held within it – disputes, in short, about every conceivable subject. The civil authorities disputed with the military, the militia with the regulars, and all among themselves; and, as if this were not enough, some of the civil officials made a very unprovoked attack on the Roman Catholic bishop and clergy. As Christians of all denominations were then in danger of common destruction from the Mohammedans, the time selected for this was generally regarded as inopportune.'

On one point only was there unity: Colvin was blamed for everything. Calcutta was bombarded with complaints of his inefficiency which the Governor-General, Lord Canning, contemptuously described as 'screeches from Agra'. The Government, however, paid some attention to Agra. Colvin was sent a reprimand for delays in returning the last year's administration report and for not answering correspondence. Even gentle, reserved Cudbert was moved to exclaim, 'what manner of men must they be in Calcutta, who, at a time like this, when they ought to be straining every nerve to save the Empire, are thinking only of unanswered letters?' (Plate 33.)

With some reason Colvin could not always agree with his magistrate, Robert Drummond, who, like many of his colleagues, was 'partial to Mohammedans' for their manliness and independence, qualities greatly admired by the mid-Victorians. Drummond's partiality induced him to countermand the Governor's order to stock the fort for a six-months siege by forbidding the sale of grain to the commissariat contractor. The well-trusted Muslims of Agra eventually showed their virility by murdering the Indian Christians in the city, and their independence by joining the mutineers in plundering the treasure chest.

Looting throughout the Mutiny was widespread on both sides. In 1860 an officer at Gosport observed the return of the troops from India: 'And every man-jack of them was possessed of valuable jewels. Where the worthy rogues had captured the loot needs not to enquire, suffice to say that oriental stones worth hundreds were retailed for a few shillings'.[1]

Not only was the unfortunate Cudbert an intermediary between the Governor and his staff, but on the morning of the battle of Shahgunj he had to inform Major Weller of the Engineers that Brigadier Polwhele, after refusing to make a sortie, had decided to assemble the troops for an attack on the mutineers.[2] Polwhele got his men into the field but their advance was hampered by lack of effective artillery or cavalry support.

[1] One of the Old Brigade, *London in the Sixties*, 1st ed., 1908, 1914, p. 3.

[2] The account of the battle of Shahgunj is based on J. W. Kaye, op. cit., III, pp. 384–394. Kaye's description is more detailed than the account in *The Indian Mutiny*, pp. 177–202, since Mark Thornhill was mainly concerned with the repercussions of the battle on the civilians in Agra.

The British could only put into the field 'some sixty mounted militiamen', among whom were 'horse-riders of a wandering circus from France', whose leader fought '*pour l'honneur d'alliance*'. Even this manifestation of the Entente Cordiale could not see the old Brigadier through; he ordered a retreat which was hampered by his omission to arrange for bearers for the wounded or water carriers. The thirst-maddened men stampeded into the canteen at the fort, uncaring that the city police had mutinied, the jails been thrown open and the cantonment set on fire. The women 'with the skirts of their gowns stuffed through their petticoats' did what they could to relieve the wounded and thirsty. Ellen, Cudbert's wife, was one of those who endeavoured to make life more bearable in the fort. Wearied by the exigences of Anglo-Indian life, Ellen later became an over-anxious and not always amiable member of the family. Her children could not know and her contemporaries forgot how cheerfully and readily she had worked during the dark days at Agra.

After the rioting in the city almost six thousand men, women and children were packed into the fort. Anglo-Indian officials and their families were crowded with French nuns, Italian priests, missionaries, rope-dancers from Paris and pedlars from America into the galleries of Jehangire's old palace, where once the ladies of the zenana had played hide-and-seek. This atmosphere was recaptured when Company servants foregathered at dusk:

> 'Chairs were placed on the terraces and tables arranged, charcoal fires began to glimmer, kettles to boil, and soon the square presented the appearance of a great tea garden. This was our time for social intercourse and enjoyment. The fare was as simple as the invitations and each guest brought his own contribution, very often also his chair. Very charming were those evening gatherings, very pleasant they arise to memory. We talked, we chatted, often we sat silent, enjoying the slight coolness that the night had brought, gazing on the delicious moonlight ... When there was no moon our tables were lighted by little coloured lamps, and the square glistened with all the rich tints of a cathedral window.'

Even the most hard-headed were affected by the moonlight

on the ancient fort which 'had once contained half the wealth of India'. Though food supplies were running short excavations for hidden treasure were officially sanctioned. Expectations of treasure or of disaster no longer concerned Colvin whose health, since the battle of Shahgunj, rapidly declined. On the afternoon of 8 September 1857 Mark was struck by 'the immense number of birds that were hovering over the fort – thousands of crows, and whole flights of kites and vultures.' That evening he directed his servant to make enquiries concerning Colvin. 'The man dropped his eyes, and replied quietly that it was unnecessary, he had just heard . . . that his spirit had commenced its march from this transitory world'. Never had a spirit started more willingly on this journey.

As no reliable news reached those incarcerated in the fort Mark and Cudbert did not know how their brothers at stations to the east of Agra were faring.

Robert, the eldest son of the Old Director's second family, was in 1857 completing his service in India as civil and sessions judge at Banda (plate 32). The 'tall, thin, fair youth' had grown into a portly man, but in disposition remained 'still like a boy, so full of fun and games!' The cheerfulness of his wife, Mary, whom her grandmother Siddons had found 'a clever and sociable and fascinating creature' as a child, was somewhat dimmed. She had known all the upheavals of an Anglo-Indian childhood; and, she was racked by the anxieties of Anglo-Indian mothers. She feared that the children sent home might suffer as she had done; and she had some reason to dread the effects of climate and diet on those in India. The Thornhills lost five babies, whose death Robert commemorated in verses which he wrote for his wife on their wedding anniversary:

> 'My love your health – another year's flown by
> Again, when looking o'er the date, my eye
> Sees that the day our marriage knot was tied
> Your public assent to my vows was sighed.
> Little Georgie now, our only pride,
> Talking so sweetly by his mother's side
> Alas! our others died – so willed by Heaven.

*   *   *

> Our Babes, now Angel spirits in the sky
> For them, let not escape a single sigh,

Thrice happy they, who never sorrow knew
Such lot is given but to few.

*   *   *

We who topped the many years of grief
Would give a world for such blest relief.
I know for certain that when called by death,
And feel we soon must draw our latest breath,
That we shall straightway go to Realms of joys
And meet in Heaven our dear infant boys.'[1]

Three children, George, Minnie and Edward, survived their infancy in India and also the passage home to their Grandmother Thornhill; and two were with their parents at Banda when the Mutiny broke out. On 22 May 1857 Mary wrote: 'What a fearful butchery has taken place; it quite makes one's heart bleed for the poor victims and the sufferers from this bloody transaction. But God grant that in a couple of days we may hear of the massacre of the mutineers at Delhi . . . we have been in terror here, as reports were abroad that we were to be attacked; and I shall never forget the agony of mind I endured for two nights dreading to hear the signal guns which were to warn us to fly to the fort.'

On 3 June the signal guns were fired and boats carried civilians, women and children from the Farrukhabad area to the fort of Futegur. Long abandoned as a place of defence the fort was vulnerable at all points to the thousand or so sepoy besiegers. Desperate and unavailing appeals were sent for help. One, on a slip of paper thin enough to be rolled inside a quill, was signed by the commanding officer and Robert Thornhill. As no response came from the paralysed headquarters at Agra, the boats were lowered to take about a hundred Europeans to the safety of the great cantonment at Cawnpore. Loyal Indians fully realised the dangers of trusting to boats. When Mark Thornhill was escaping from Muttra an aged follower, clasped his knees and implored him 'not to set foot in the boat.' Had the old man's advice been followed in other districts many deaths might have been avoided on nightmare river journeys, when boats ran aground or were raked by fire

[1] These verses were found in the recaptured Futegur fort in December 1857.

from hostile villagers on the banks. Of the three boats that left Futegur only one, in which were Mary, Robert, their two children and Mary Long, their 'very good, cheerful young European nurse', reached Cawnpore. The garrison had been occupied by the rebel leader, Nana Sahib. After days of waiting in unbelievable squalor and in alternating fears and hopes of a safe conduct the whole garrison and the men, women and children who had taken refuge in Cawnpore were massacred.[1]

When the Nawab of Farrukhabad's palace was fired on 7 January 1858 a book belonging to Mary Thornhill was salvaged. It was called *The Afflicted's Refuge*, or Prayers Adopted to Various Circumstances of Distress. Whether in Oudh, the North-West Provinces or Lower Bengal, risings which Mark Thornhill considered to have been popular rather than military in origin, followed the same pattern. Successful attacks on the treasuries and record offices were succeeded by the release of prisoners, whose silent flitting Mark Thornhill described:

> 'I looked and saw a line of figures coming one by one out of the darkness, and passing close by me, so close that I could have touched them. I held my pistol ready to fire should they attack us. They seemed to have no such intention. They neither turned their heads, nor quickened their pace, nor indicated by any sign that they were aware of our presence. They moved on like the others, with the same slow, silent, shuffling steps, and like them vanished in the darkness; at each step their chains rattled. They passed on as might phantoms from another world – dimly seen, silent, regardless – issuing from the darkness, gliding by, and re-entering it.'

After securing the treasure and releasing the prisoners insurgents attacked the defended posts where 'ladies, women and children' were so mistakenly herded together. Had they been left in their own homes their chances of survival by the help of friendly sepoys or servants would have been greater. Unfortunately the house in which the women and children of Sitapur were made 'all secure' lay in the bend of a *nullah* or

---

[1] A family tradition has it that Robert Bensley Thornhill 'was shot in the boats because he would not betray his countrymen'; but according to J. W. Kaye, *History of the Sepoy War*, 1876, III, fn. p. 303, W. H. Fitchett, *The Tale of The Great Mutiny*, 1915, pp. 130–140 and the family memorial in Lyston Church it seems he was killed with his family at Cawnpore on 15 July.

dried water course. When defence was no longer possible the refugees had only one route for escape so the families who accompanied the officials, the chief targets of the insurgents, were mown down. Among those slain at Sitapur were Henry Bensley Thornhill, deputy commissioner, his wife, Emily, their infant child and 'their faithful nurse', Eliza Jennings.

Lucknow was not only a stronghold for the protection of those Europeans who could reach the city, but it had also been the capital of the dispossessed rulers of Oudh. Fighting around the city, part of which the British managed to hold throughout the Mutiny, was, therefore, fierce and prolonged. Among the besieged was John Bensley Thornhill, eldest grandson of John Thornhill by his first wife. The year 1856 had been an auspicious one for him; he had been promoted to an assistant commissioner in Oudh, and in December married Mary Havelock, a connection of Henry Havelock who effected the first relief of Lucknow. She had hardly doffed her bridal finery which, according to Mary Thornhill had cost over 1000 rupees, before the siege started. On 27 August her prematurely born baby died, and on 12 October her husband succumbed to wounds received on 26 September. 'A splendid fellow', John Thornhill volunteered to lead a party to bring in the wounded left by Havelock's relieving force. The wounded, among whom was Havelock's son, were picked up; but, bewildered by the mass of murderous lanes, the party attempted to return by a passage way loopholed by sepoys, who immediately opened fire. Severely wounded, John managed to crawl back and lingered on for over two weeks in the defences where 'there was no spot . . . where a dying soldier or an ailing woman or child could feel an instant's security.'[1] John Thornhill's widow with other survivors from Lucknow set sail from Madras on 10 February 1858. In the evening the vessel struck a rock. Stunned by this culminating misfortune, the passengers, nearly all women and children, took to the boats in silence; 'not even a child cried'.[2] Mary lived to see happier days and married again.

[1] J. W. Kaye, op. cit., III, fn. p. 537, quoting from notes of George Couper whose wife, Emily, was a close friend of Mary Thornhill. Two of the three existing letters written by Mary were addressed to Emily Couper.

[2] Lady Inglis, *The Siege of Lucknow*. A Diary, 1893, pp. 215–216.

John Thornhill's younger brother, Edmund, only arrived in India in 1854 and at the time of the outbreak was assistant magistrate at Moradabad under James Cracroft Wilson whose daughter he married. Wilson was respected and loved by Europeans and Indians alike. When uneasiness was apparent in the lines he rode, waving his hat, up to the guns manned by hostile sepoys who from astonishment forbore to fire. Time was gained and by his energy and decisiveness Wilson enabled military officers and covenanted civilians to reach in safety the hill station of Naini Tal.

By the end of September 1857 Delhi was captured, and the Mutiny was virtually over. When early in 1858 Mark Thornhill was posted to Dehra Dun, in the foothills of the Himalayas 'the clouds cleared and displayed the vast peaks of the snowy range . . . looking down, as it seemed to me, on the war and turmoil below calm and indifferent, as they had centuries ago on the hordes of Timor, or, long ages before, on the armies of Alexander.'

In their triumph the British people forgot General Medows' noble words: 'An enemy defeated is an enemy no longer.' The passive suffered with the active. Peasants who took advantage of the disappearance of the records and *bunniahs* were, Mark Thornhill considered, 'punished in accordance with the laws which, at the time when the disturbances occurred, had ceased to exist.' Ancient buildings suffered with the 'rural disturbers'. The palaces at Delhi and Lucknow were pulled down; even 'the majestic ruins of the fort of Juanpore were blown to pieces to satisfy the idle crochet of an engineer.'

This was the beginning of the onslaught on the Indian countryside made in the interests of agricultural and industrial development and of sport. During his service in India Mark Thornhill observed how some animals, like the rhinoceroses which had roamed around Peshawar, had disappeared and others, like tigers, were decreasing (plate 35). Though in Thornhill's time the 'barbarous destruction of the elephant' was apparently 'unknown', contemporary drawings suggest it had started in the 1870s.

The savagery of the British suppression of the rising was partly caused by the clamour at home. If the hysterical cruelty of the sepoy was due to an inner conflict between loyalty to his

Indian past and to his British officers[1] the English demand for reprisals owed something to anger over the loss of an image as well as over the ill-treatment of women and children. India no longer appeared as a glorious and glowing land full of promise; and the noble Indian had become a treacherous native. In the crucial 1850s both Britain and India reached a crisis in their civilisations; and, as often happens, those in the same boat turned and rended each other.

In their horror-struck consternation over sepoy excesses at Delhi and Cawnpore, Englishmen forgot that they themselves had decided, some fifty years earlier, to throw women and children into the front line of the battle for industrial supremacy where their sufferings had been prolonged and great. The bewilderment of the nation passing through the darkness of early industrialisation found some outlet in the demand that

'. . . terrified India shall tell to all time
How Englishmen paid her for murder and loot'.

No words were too hard for those who tried, as did 'Sepoy D'Israeli' and 'Clemency Canning', to slake the popular thirst for vengeance. This frenzy owed not a little to popular literature and sensational spectacles. The performance of 'The Taking of Delhi' at Astley's in December 1857 sent away 'the audience most confirmed anti-sentimentalists'.[2]

In their demands for retribution these 'anti-sentimentalists' overlooked the number of European victims claimed by India in times of peace. During the Mutiny eight Thornhills, including three infants, were killed by violence; Mary Thornhill lost a prematurely born baby at Lucknow and one of Mark's children died at Agra. Before 1857 five babies of Robert's and two of Cudbert's had succumbed to the hazards of Indian life. These were later to carry off Cudbert Thornhill, one of his sons-in-law, his daugher, Ellen, and her cousin, Thornhill Lane. Truly Ellen wrote, 'it is quite wonderful how soon people get knocked down with illness out here, and how long it takes them to pick up again'.

[1] *The Manchester Guardian*, 10 May 1957, P. Spear 'The Indian Mutiny: A Creative Explosion.'

[2] *Punch* 26 December 1857. The demand for a 'terrified India' appeared in the issue of 12 September 1857.

The likelihood of not picking up again partly accounts for the langour that inhibited the many portents of unrest before 1857 being taken seriously. At the beginning of the century George John Siddons had no official support in quelling the frequent disturbances which broke out among the sepoys in the dilapidated cantonment at Fort Marlborough. The hazards of living in India and the climate militated against sustained endeavour. Few lived, or stayed in India, long enough to see their undertakings completed. Cudbert Thornhill was lucky in this respect. His dream of seeing 'the trains skimming through the air supported upon what looks no stronger than a thread' was fulfilled; before Thornhill left India to die on the voyage home his 2,988-foot railway bridge at Allahabad was completed. Bringing himself at last to visit a province that had caused him much trouble, Lord Canning congratulated in person the bright-faced Cudbert.[1]

The sudden, and often terrible, deaths of so many Europeans long haunted their relatives and, in many cases, they provided a rich quarry for lawyers. Wills of the Mutiny victims could not always be found and, if discovered, it was difficult to establish whether the husband or the wife died first. Some wills were brought to light by lawyers who specialised in this grave-digging work and caused disputes which did little honour to the dead. After the murder of Henry Thornhill at Sitapur his estate, including his share of the Old Director's legacy, passed to his mother, Henriette Philippine. As Cudbert, the father of six children, had undertaken the care of Robert's orphans Henriette assigned Henry's money to him. But Cudbert only took a portion for himself, and, after his death, claims to the unappropriated balance were put forward with equal vivacity by Mark on behalf of his own and Robert's children and Ellen Thornhill. Her claim to the whole sum had not been established by 1880 so that the estate was probably eaten up by the costs. This was the case with Robert's estate which was settled in 1910 with the three legatees receiving £17 18s 11d each. Great but unfulfilled hopes had been raised in 1903 by a Calcutta solicitor who claimed to have discovered a sum owing the Thornhills 'after it had been practic-

---

[1] J. W. Sherer, *Havelock's March on Cawnpore 1857*, 1898, p. 324.

ally buried for half a century'. He modestly claimed one third of the sum the amount of which was not specified.

That much of Captain Cudbert Thornhill's fortune should have melted away in the country of its origin is but one instance of India's way with invaders. She submitted and left time to take the sting out of conquest. When the Old Director's legacy, made up of his father's money and that of the Bensleys, seeped away as a result of the Mutiny the widowed Ellen Thornhill was hard pressed to provide for her two younger sons, Henry Beaufoy and John. That she got Henry into Eton and both into the Indian army shows she had not lost the resolution that kept her active during the siege of Agra. Inheriting his mother's determination Henry also possessed a buoyancy of spirit which enabled him to overcome the constant ill-health of his youth. He suffered from all the symptoms of an over-highly strung constitution: nervous exhaustion, stammering, backaches and insomnia. No ill-health, however, could check the exuberance of the boy who wrote: 'How are you? How am I? Grand!!! Eton is the jolliest place I ever was at . . . but I had no one to tell me what I ought to do . . . I flatter myself a good deal on my tea making and ham etc. cutting'. John lacked his brother's high spirits and soon drifted from India to try his luck in South Africa. But it was lack of will power rather than a sphere for his activities that inhibited John from succeeding.

When in September 1873 Henry Beaufoy Thornhill was ordered to India with the 5th Foot a brisker pace was being enforced on military men and civilians at home and in India. The purchase of army commissions had been ended, and examinations were the carrots dangled before ambitious youth, whether in the army, in Board Schools or in the Indian Civil Service. By the 1870s the military engineers in the Public Works Department in India were having to make way for men who had been trained at Coopers Hill, King's College, London and the Scottish universities: seats of learning which army men considered to subsist in the marchlands of civilisation. Nine of the twelve candidates who qualified in 1870 with Edward Lang came from King's College, London, from Trinity College, Dublin and from Scottish universities. Without any specialised training Henry Beaufoy Thornhill applied himself to the problems of sanitation with such good effect that he was Executive Sanitary Officer at the Durbars of 1902 and 1911. For this work he received a knighthood. Despite his application to sanitary problems, Henry retained something of the waywardness that had characterised his Uncle Mark, whom he considered 'a clever man but what an eccentric!' At the end of his career in India Sir Henry confessed: 'I am mad on trees; they appeal to me. I have collected every sort of seed I came across for years.'

In one respect Company and imperial officials were alike. Most of them spent one third of their lives dreaming of the moist English countryside and another third in shivering idleness. Even buoyant Henry Thornhill sensed this chill before his retirement in 1913: 'Everyone writes to me to say what with Lloyd George and servants, England is no place for a white man now-a-days. Unless the nation wakes up and borrows £100,000,000 for its Navy, Germany will go on competing with us and eventually . . . "go" for us. Serve us right, too, just as it will to lose India as we assuredly shall if Morley-Crewe and Co go on playing the fool and giving into the seditious and disloyal native.'

The spectre of the 'seditious and disloyal native' was the legacy of the Mutiny. Half a century of imperial rule had not restored the confidence of Company days when India was 'the wonderful, the original, the true, the brave'. The golden opportunities offered by life in India, however, were not seized by all Company officials; many, like Thackeray's Joseph Sedley, were bondsmen to their lonely, swamp-surrounded stations. Nevertheless it is not unfair to suggest that the lives in India of the many Company servants who were prepared to learn were more rewarding than those of their successors who were chiefly concerned to teach. Those who were ready to develop the gift, which Mark Thornhill described as essentially Indian, of enjoying 'the minor beauties of nature' took pleasant memories home. Mark's retirement started stormily with an unsuccessful second marriage and the attempted management of five headstrong daughters and one difficult son. Henry Mark eventually sailed to America where, according to family tradition, he landed in a beer barrel.

Mark Thornhill finally settled happily with a home-keeping

daughter and his memories of India which for him was always 'the strange, the wonderful'. This was not the impression of a tourist struck by temples and a rioting vegetation, but of a man who had soaked himself in the Indian countryside. Thornhill recognised its underlying melancholy when he described a riverside wader, which was not unlike a Bengali peasant: 'it has an odd attractiveness. With its dingy plumage and melancholy aspect, it seems the embodiment of the dreariness of the great, sandy waste. Its quietude, its utter inoffensiveness, excite, too, for it a sort of sympathy. One can almost fancy it oppressed by some great sorrow.' He also rejoiced in the gaiety of the Company's early tea plantations in the valley of Dehra Dunn: 'There were fruit trees of all kinds, green lawns, hedges of aloes and hedges covered with roses, beds full of gayest flowers, long, low white buildings that glistened in the sunshine and everywhere small canals and watercourses, through which flowed the clear, sparkling water of some mountain torrent not far away . . . the climate was so delicious, the scenery so charming, no wind, no dust, no unpleasant heat or glare, always bright sunshine and a clear blue sky.'

This was the countryside about which Britons were beginning to dream in the 1850s whether they gazed at grey skies from the windows of offices, tenements or hovels in villages. The longing, often only expressed by an escape into garishly lit gin palaces, for an environment in which man's soul could expand was the leaven causing society to rise and overspill into foreign parts.

If tourists escaping from industrialism left their imprint on favoured resorts how much more did the British alter the face of the countryside where they settled or made long sojourns. Railways, roads, telegraph poles and canals showed British zeal to add lustre to 'the brightest jewel in Victoria's crown'; they also put an end to any thoughts which imperial servants may have had of sinking into 'oriental calm' and made it harder for Indians to maintain their quiescence. Steam may have been, as Emerson asserted, almost an Englishman but it certainly was not an Indian. Steam power enabled the British to embark on undertakings which seemed to many Indians to be directed at the very heart of their civilisation. The widening rift between the two races was caused not so much by the resentment of the ruled towards the rulers as by a seemingly impassable gulf between two philosophies of life. The catch-phrases which severed the sub-continent were Western material progress and Eastern mysticism. Neither side would concede that something might be learnt from the other.

The give-and-take of Company days and the sudden out-bursts of reciprocal ferocity between the two races found little place in the imperial framework. The magnificent establish-ment and the all-embracing benevolence of Captain Cudbert Thornhill could be easily understood by the Indians, so could the vagaries of Mark Thornhill as from under a padded umbrella he studied the comings and goings of ants on the banks of the Ganges; but not the drive of imperial servants to compass engineering *tours de force*. Another factor which im-peded the rapprochement between the two races was the increasing numbers of wives and daughters who joined hus-bands and fathers serving in India. At a time when women's rights were considered to be at their nadir, these newcomers had the opportunity to fashion a new society. Their efforts in this direction will be considered in the next chapter.

If unable to agree on questions of hygiene or material pro-gress, many Indians made efforts, which were reciprocated, of understanding an alien civilisation. Even these men of goodwill found themselves giving a new twist to old themes. Increasing numbers of higher Indian students passed through the hoops of English Literature; but a performance of *The Merchant of Venice* given by the students of St Columba's College, Hazaribagh, suggests that a new pudding was being served on a familiar dish:

> 'The first night we were treated to a very spirited version in Urdu of The Merchant of Venice . . . Robbers, con-stables, dancing girls and servants, Khalasis and messen-gers followed each other's heels in almost bewildering confusion. Hardly had we ceased shuddering at the grue-some aspect of ferocious bandits waylaying their victims in a lonely part of a dense jungle than our susceptibilities were put on the rack by the horrors of a house on fire.'[1]

[1] *St. Columba's College Magazine*, December 1911, Vol. III, No. 3. St. Columba's was a college associated with the Dublin University Mission at Hazaribagh in the province of Bihar and Orissa.

Britons were not more successful in their endeavours to catch the lyricism of Indian poetry which, like the call of the night hawk described by Mark Thornhill, sounded like 'musical glass or the softest of bells'. Still the attempt at rapprochement was made, however haltingly:

'Upon the City Ramparts, lit by sunset gleam,
The Blue eyes that conquer, meet the Darker eyes that dream.
The Dark eyes, so Eastern, and the Blue eyes from the West,
The last alight with action, the first so full of rest.

Brown, that seem to hold the Past; its magic mystery,
Blue, that catch the early light, of ages yet to be.
Meet and fall and meet again, then linger, look, and smile,
Time and distance all forgotten, for a little while.'[1]

Attempts to forget time and distance seldom succeed; only the acceptance of differences makes good understanding possible.

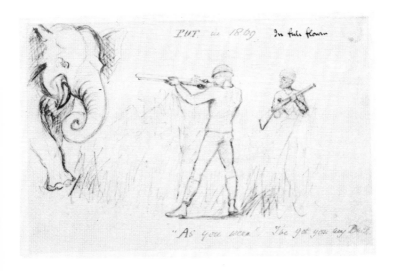

---

[1] *The Garden of Kama* and other Love Lyrics from India, arranged in verse by Lawrence Hope, 1902, p. 144.

CHAPTER NINE

'An Avatar of Fair Young English Maidens'

English news, English books, above all, English gentle-
women made their way freely and rapidly to
India . . . and an avatar of fair young English maidens,
with the bloom of the Western summer on their cheeks,
yielded attractions beside which the gossip of the lines
and the feeble garrulity of the old Soubahdar [Indian
officer in the British army in India] were very dreary and
fatiguing. . . . With the appearance of the English gentlewoman in the cantonments there grew up a host of new
interests and new excitements, and the regiment became
a bore.

Sir John Kaye, *A History of the Sepoy War 1857–1858*

Kaye was not too dazzled by his vision of English maidens to
realise that the presence of large numbers of English women
would lead to the isolation of the British in India. But the optimism of the nineteenth-century historian outweighed the commonsense of the man when Kaye forecast that this withdrawal
would be offset by the wives of imperial servants diffusing an
enlightenment which would re-animate Indian society. He saw
the leaven already at work in the 1850s when, inspired by the
'enlightened female companionship' in Anglo-Indian society,
'the courtesans of the Calcutta Bazaars taught themselves to
play on instruments, to sing songs, and to read poetry, that
thereby they might lure from the dreary environments of their
vapid homes the very flower of Young Bengal.'[1]

Had he lived long enough Kaye would have seen that the
influence of the petticoat invasion left the Bengali homes

[1] J. W. Kaye, *A History of the Sepoy War 1857–1858*, Vol. I, pp. 187–8. Kaye
was an unblushing optimist who held that: 'One of the lessons which we
learn by growing old is that all things work together, not for evil, but for
good.' *Essays of an Optimist*, 1870, p. 183.

untouched but created a new social force; the self-contained Anglo-Indian community. Living under the shadow of the Mutiny British wives were unwavering in their resolve to maintain a society isolated from a people whose disregard for human life sprang not so much from savagery as from an acceptance of values completely alien to Western conceptions. To step out of the compound was to be confronted with a disturbing insouciance concerning life and death. A pleasure excursion was spoiled for Ellen Thornhill when 'a whole lot of natives brought out a dead man on a charpoy [a light bed] to bury him, and they set it down about 20 yards from our tent. So we sent out (thinking it was a Hindoo being carried to the river to be burned) to tell them to take it further; but they only took it a little further and after a long time buried it. It was disagree-able finding ourselves unawares in a burying ground, and while it was going on a grand procession passed with three ponies, one after another, and a fly in front and a lot more natives, and this turned out to be a wedding.'

Before this confounding of the quick and the dead, Anglo-Indian women recoiled and endeavoured by an over-insistence on order and regularity within the British communities to forget the confusion without. Order within Anglo-Indian societies largely depended on the punctilious regulation of the social position and daily activities of every member of the community. Many might feel, as did Ellen Thornhill, that they were 'shut up in a box'; but imprisonment at least implies security. Like the ever-busy ants watched so intently by Mark Thornhill Anglo-Indian women assembled, scrap by scrap, the ordinances which regulated precedence, hours of visiting and entertaining in general. The fact that these social prescriptions often entailed some hardship gave members of the community the comforting sense that they were doing their duty rather than pleasure seeking. Writing from Simla (plate 31), after her marriage to Huntly Garden, Tal, Ellen's sister, announced with some pride that 'both visits and visitors are innumerable . . . we have used up the 200 cards each that we brought out.' This social marathon started at noon when, as Ellen observed, 'it is really quite boiling out of doors at that time . . . I find it awfully hard to cook up small talk and shall be tremendously glad when it is all over.' Winston Churchill was determined never to start it and wrote at the end of the century: 'The vulgar Anglo-Indians have commented on my not "calling" as is the absurd custom of the country'.[1] Rigid adherence to prescribed orders of precedence was another custom of the country. This concern with social rank provided the one common interest of East and West since, as Cobden pointed out, 'the insatiable love of caste . . . in England as in Hindostan, devours all hearts'.[2]

After 1858 men went to India to rule not to create a new way of life. Knowing that their sojourn in the sub-continent would last, at most, four decades they were content to leave the moulding of Anglo-Indian society to their wives. When men emigrated to Australia, New Zealand and Canada they were determined to build a new society for themselves and their children as well as earn a living. Women were necessary in these new societies as home keepers not as participants in any wider sphere. In India, where servants abounded, women were freed from household tasks to direct the daily life of the Anglo-Indian community. Even the elaborate social practices which they evolved allowed the memsahibs long hours of leisure many of which were spent in writing home. Despite the daunting postal rates to England in the 1860s – 8 annas (approximately 1s) for every ½ oz. – relatives were teased by receiving long and crossed communications on thin paper every word of which had to be painfully deciphered. These communications give the best insight into the everyday life of Anglo-Indian communities; and this short study has been based on letters from three girls, Ellen and Tal Thornhill and Hebe Prior, all of whom married in India. As Tal and Ellen belonged to the fourth generation of Thornhills to pass through India and as both married officers in the Indian army, they were, like Mrs. Merdle in *Little Dorrit*, entitled to speak for Society. Hebe Prior also had family connections with India, and she married Edward Lang, one of the go-ahead imperial servants in the new Public Works Department. Though the women set the tone of Anglo-Indian society, the

[1] Quoted in J. Morris, *Pax Britannica*, 1968, p. 222.

[2] R. Cobden, *Collected Works*, 4th ed., 1903, Vol. I, p. 102. The passage quoted appears in an essay on England, Ireland and America published 1835.

male voice was not unheard, so extracts of letters from Edward Lang have been used to amplify the account of the formative years of British hegemony in India.

The backgrounds of the three girls were similar, but their tastes and temperaments differed widely. Thoughtful, well-informed Hebe had a marked talent for painting flowers, Ellen was gay and musical, while Tal's dogmatism was in no way checked by the fact that before her marriage nothing more had depended on her than 'occasionally making a few dusters for Mama'.

That the activities of so many girls had been as restricted as Tal's explains some of the langours of Anglo-Indian life. The education of many of the girls who sailed eastward hardly differed from that received by the Indian wives who presided over the 'vapid homes' of the 'very flower of Young Bengal.' Those educated in India fared little better. A glance at the girls' schools of Calcutta in 1857 will indicate the educational trend that persisted through the century, and moulded the outlook of many pupils who were to set the tone of Anglo-Indian society. First in the field was the institute which provided 'female orphans chiefly of H.M. Regiments' with 'a plain and useful Christian Education . . . as Nursery Governessess, or Upper Domestic Servants.' That as early as 1815 such an orphanage should have been established is a reminder of the numbers of soldiers' wives who made their way to India. Though seldom mentioned by contemporaries their influence in the cantonments cannot have been negligible. There was no doubt about the spheres which the 'female orphans' were to fill. Even the hard-pressed governessess and maidservants of Britain were unwilling to travel to India, so the orphans were sure of situations. Numbers were killed in the Mutiny; the 'young and cheerful' Mary Long and the 'faithful' Eliza Jennings who were murdered with the Thornhills at Cawnpore and Sitapur probably came from this orphanage. The future of the daughters of Indian Christians receiving 'a good Christian education in Bengali' at the Native Female Institute (1833) was not so clear cut. These girls were isolated from the Hindu community by their faith, and from the European by their race and by the general disinclination to employ Christian servants. Problems were posed rather than solved by the secular education offered at the Bethune Institute for 'the daughters of Brahmins of the Higher Class'. Fearing western liberalism and Christian proselytism, the Brahmins looked askance at the Institute and at Lady Canning's carriage which was often seen standing at its entrance.

As the lives of so many Indian girls were hidden from sight,the most earnest efforts towards their education could make little progress. To the memsahibs Indian women were ayahs and to the missionaries 'sisters'; they seldom appeared as individuals. That the light had dawned on enclosed lives is suggested by a poem, allegedly written by a woman who was a follower and contemporary of Buddha:

> O woman well set free! How free am I,
> How thoroughly free from kitchen drudgery!
> Me stained and squalid 'mong my cooking-pots
> My brutal husband ranked as even less
> Than the sunshades he sits and weaves alway.
>
> Purged now of all my former lust and hate,
> I dwell, musing at ease, beneath the shade
> Of spreading bough – O, but 'tis well with me!
>
> Tr. Mrs C. Rhys Davids[1]

That all was not so well with Anglo-Indian girls in the mid-nineteenth century is suggested by the curriculum of the Young Ladies Institute at Calcutta. This seminary established in 1855 as a rival to the Roman-Catholic Loretto House, tried to meet all shades of conviction by assuring parents that governesses had been selected by an interdenominational committee in Edinburgh – a venue with a direful sound to Anglicans. An unspecified 'general education' was offered at the two leading Calcutta girls' schools, Loretto House and the Young Ladies Institute; but the emphasis was on the extras: dancing, singing, painting, piano and guitar playing, French and Italian. Only Miss Young, who ran a smaller seminary, realised her young ladies might have to talk as well as play; and she stressed the inclusion of British and Indian history in her curriculum. A product of an Anglo-Indian education was described in 1874 by Hebe Lang as

> 'childish in character and manner . . . she is pleasant
> and friendly enough and nice in many ways but only

[1] *Poems by Indian Women*, ed. Margaret Macnicol, 1923, p. 44.

cares for the most trivial topics of conservation . . . When we were staying with them, I used to wonder what she did all day for she never reads, not even a novel, hardly does any work, never practised, never seemed to sit down to any occupation whatever. She never seems to know or care about anything that goes on in the world, did not even know the name of the Ashanti War, when it was beginning and the papers were full of it, but then she says she never looks at anything but the Births etc in the paper'.

Many Anglo-Indian women recognised and deplored their lack of solid education. Unable to alter her husband's ill-fitting shirt collars, Mary Thornhill wrote in 1854: 'I wish my daughter [Minnie] to be better educated than her mother in this and every other respect.'

By the 1870s some eddies from the whirlwind at home concerning women's rights and missions were reaching India. Neither the new ideas nor their exponents were welcomed in the Anglo-Indian communities. Charlotte Tucker's missionary activities were accepted because she made a name for herself by her writings as A.L.O.E. (A Lady of England), and because she belonged to a family long and honourably connected with India. The zealous endeavours of the wife of Charles Powlett Lane, an officer in the Indian army and a grandson of the Old Director by his first marriage, did not arouse much enthusiasm, at least among her relatives. Ellen wrote, 'up at Simla we heard that she is going in for having soldiers to a sort of tea meeting and reading the Bible to them first and afterwards regaling them with tea and cake. I believe she is liked, but I did not hear that she is at all pretty.'

Certainly neither Simla nor Calcutta had much sympathy with Mary Carpenter (1807–1877) who travelled in the subcontinent in the interests of education for Indian women. Her schemes were supported by the viceroy, Lord Lawrence, but not by the Anglo-Indian wives. In December 1866 Mary Carpenter wrote from Calcutta: 'Scarcely any ladies have come near me, partly perhaps from fearing that I should meddle with their plans, chiefly probably because they were afraid of my heterodoxy.'[1] Even to be enthusiastic was suspect or, perhaps even worse, slightly ridiculous. Feeling all the fear and

[1] J. E. Carpenter, *The Life and work of Mary Carpenter*, 1879, p. 342.

little of the excitement of the unknown, the interests of the memsahib contracted to 'the personal world of Anglo-India'.[1] Few shared the zest of the governor's wife whose arrival at Rupar Hebe Lang described: 'Mrs Davies is a lively sprightly lady apparently desirous to go everywhere and see everything . . . Eddy declares she nearly knocked him down on the platform when they arrived, jumping out of the carriage and clearing it in two bounds. The next day she . . . joined in a boating excursion up the river to see some mahseer fishing. She was very eager after this, springing off the boat quite by herself on to the river bank regardless of the soft mud into which she sank over her boots directly.'

The obsessive fears of the unknown and the heterodox started, not altogether without reason, on the outward voyage. All may have been shipshape on board but the dangers were never distant. When she sailed in the *Columbian* Tal wrote from her heart, 'have the hymn "For Those at Sea" sometimes for us.' In the mid-nineteenth century the passage of the Red Sea was still as dangerous as it had been in Captain Cudbert Thornhill's time. In 1859 the Peninsular and Oriental Steam Navigation Company lost the screw-steamer *Alma* and the *Northam* in this sea; while a few years later the *Carnatic* ran upon a reef near the entrance to the Gulf of Suez. All the adventure-tale misfortunes of shipwreck were experienced by the passengers of the *Alma* in June 1859. As the water poured into the ship 'the women and children were dragged from their berths and from the cabins now filling with water, and hoisted upon the decks; but very few of them had on more than their night-clothes, and none saved any of their apparel.' Among the women, who first shivered in their sodden night wear and were then scorched 'by the terrible power of the Red Sea sun' beating on a waterless coral island, were Mrs Ferguson and Mrs Anne Mackey. Neither women recovered from the shock. On her journey to India Ellen Thornhill was irked almost past bearing by the anxieties of her chaperon, Mrs Ferguson; while Mrs Mackey suffered during a long life, not only from the shock but also from the grievance that her presentiment that the *Alma* would sink was unheeded by her husband. Mabel

[1] Sara Duncan, *The Simple Adventures of a Memsahib*, 1893, Nelson ed., 1908, p. 379.

Siddons-Downe remembers how her youthful complaints about this exacting old lady were stilled by the injunction: 'Remember she was shipwrecked!' Having survived revolutions in Europe and poisoning in Hong Kong the philologist and radical, Sir John Bowring, was able to take the wreck in his stride. On the island he observed the Spanish idioms used by some Philippine passengers and the admirable resourcefulness of the Indian army officers. The crew and passengers were rescued after four days on the island and their tales were dramatised in *The Overland Route*.[1]

On long voyages in the mid-nineteenth century those who escaped shipwreck were faced with monotony and all the discomforts of overcrowding. Despite their many disadvantages, sea voyages were becoming fashionable as cures. George Henry Kingsley was a determined advocate of voyages for health; his account of such a journey had the unintentionally apt title of *South Sea Bubbles*. Patients suffering from some nervous complaints and tubercular infections may have been jolted out of their ailments; but such bracing methods only hastened the deaths of those who, like Cudbert Bensley Thornhill, were seriously ill.[2]

The monotony and discomforts of sea voyages filled the letters of Ellen Thornhill, who sailed in the paddle steamer *Syria* in 1866, of Edward Lang who left in 1870 in the *Massilia* and of his betrothed, Hebe Prior, who followed him a year later in the *Candia*. Ellen, with all the happy bustle of Lyston and the gaiety of Caron Place fresh in her mind, was most conscious of the vexations of shipboard life: 'I'm so awfully tired of board-ship, we sit in a row all day long and work or read. In the evening we take a little walk up and down the deck and watch the moon and the dancing, and that's all from day to day.'

Meals often provided employment rather than pleasure. On the *Simla* which she boarded at Suez Ellen found that: 'The

[1] Accounts of the wreck of the Alma have been obtained from the *Annual Register*, 12 June 1859, Sir John Bowring, *Autobiographical Recollections*, 1877, pp. 95–96, and Bowring's account, signed J. B. in *Once a Week*, 3 September 1859. For information concerning the *Alma* and other P and O steamers I am grateful to the Peninsular and Oriental Steam Navigation Company.

[2] As late as the turn of this century the writer's father was sent to Australia in a sailing ship to cure a tubercular complaint. In this case the cure was efficacious.

food here is beastly, you can scarcely get enough to eat. The curry is made up of all the bones and the fowls are like brick bats. Fortunately the claret is pretty good, for the tea is undrinkable and they put no milk in the coffee; however there is some jam and I generally "go in" for that. I am afraid I am getting thinner and then all my swell dresses will be too big, but I shall stuff as much as I can and I will tell you the result . . . I shall be very thankful to get on land again, I hate this sort of life, it's so unsettled.'

Some ships, like the *Atrato* in which Edward Thornhill sailed to New Zealand in 1866, carried a cow. The milk was kept for the children; but on long voyages nothing short of laudanum quietened the babies whose screaming was 'something frightful from morning to night, if one begins they all join the chorus.'

As well as the poor food Ellen had another grievance on board the *Simla*. The captain, John Squire Castle, refused to allow dancing 'unless they sing as well'. The reason for this regulation was that among the passengers in the *Massilia*, whom Ellen met at Cairo, three engagements were contracted in ten days. Captains were blamed for imprudent shipboard matches so Castle tried to keep his young passengers occupied between dances. As he had saved the burning *Sarah Sands* in 1857, Castle was a brave man but, like Lord Ullin's daughter, he could face the raging skies 'But not an angry father.' The captain's safeguards were considered inadequate by Mrs Ferguson who only reluctantly allowed Ellen to join the square, but never the round, dances towards the end of the voyage.

The danger of shipwreck, the certainty of seasickness, the heat, the bad food, the lack of laundries, which necessitated wearing paper collars that 'came to pieces in $\frac{1}{2}$ hour' and overcrowding all explain Edward's heartfelt comment on a sea voyage: 'Never undertake it unless you can help it.'

At the ports of call on the journey to India many passengers had their first contacts with those strange and importunate beings, the natives. This encounter was not unprofitable to those who sold their fruit, lace, Turkish delight, ostrich feathers and tortoise shells or put to good account their skills in bargaining, diving, conjuring, and acting as guides. Their first reaction of distaste towards the dark, shouting and gesticulating crowds on the quayside was often retained by travellers during their whole life abroad. At Calcutta Edward Lang, who liked to get things done quietly and quickly, found: 'These natives here are the most extraordinary people I've ever seen, perfectly exasperating with all the fuss they make.' On the voyage out Ellen, who was later to share this irritation, found some points in favour of alien peoples. In Egypt 'a good many of the men had really handsome features', while she had a fellow feeling with the Singhalese men 'standing at the doors doing up their back hair'.

A feeling of isolation was common to most young arrivals in India. Even Tal and Ellen, who had grown up in the Anglo-Indian orbit felt that life was '*so different*' from what they had imagined at home. The absence of Valentines on 14 February made Ellen, at eighteen, feel her age, 'people don't keep it up out here they are all too old . . . you can't imagine how horribly old and stupid I feel, everybody is so fearfully serious'.

Tal and Ellen were lucky in that they joined their parents at Allahabad where, despite Ellen's complaints of the dancing men being 'all fat boys . . . and one or two very old duffers', social life was not lacking. Hebe Lang's destiny took her to isolated stations on the Sirhind canal in the Punjab where her husband was working. The solitude did not worry Hebe who, when the time came to leave for a larger station, observed that, 'we shall miss a little the perfect freedom and independence which we have enjoyed up here. Society has its restraints as well as its pleasures.'

The Thornhill sisters would not have agreed with Hebe's aphorism. They only came alive when released from the boredom of Allahabad to the freedom and fun of the hill station at Naini Tal.

Going up to the hills was one of the 'new excitements' which owed its popularity, if not its origin, to the 'English gentlewoman'. Heavy losses from sickness among unseasoned troops were among the reasons that induced the Court of Directors to sanction the purchase of land in Sikkim to build Darjeeling. The renown of Dr Campbell's health resort was such that the needs of European families soon took precedence over those of the army. The necessity for Europeans to recruit their health accounted for the establishment of the other stations in the

Himalaya foot hills at Naini Tal, Mussoorie, Simla, Dehra Dun and Murree; the pursuit of pleasure was responsible for their rapid development (plate 34). Seasoned seekers after health and pleasure could compare the advantages of the different resorts. For Ellen the gaiety of Simla was offset by the obligation to endure 'long joggling about in a jampan [a sedan with two poles]' to pay calls; and the beauty of Murree by the visitors being 'such utter snobs'. Naini Tal, the only hill station where she had felt really well, had first place in her affections.

In June 1867 the Thornhill family set out from Allahabad on the four-day journey to Naini Tal. They were conveyed by rail, by horse-drawn carriages and by porters. Ellen described how the ladies sought a little ease in the long, narrow gharry, or carriage: 'We all took off our crinolines and Tal and I put on our white dressing gowns with an out-of-door jacket over; so we had nothing on but chemise, drawers, and little and big petticoats beside the dressing-gown skirt and jacket. We looked such rag bags. The heat was something awful. We had tatties at the two doors but they got dry directly from the hot wind. A tattie is a grass screen that is wetted to make the wind cool that comes through it.' To stretch out in the dhoolie, or litter, gave Ellen no relief for she was 'bitten to death by bugs; . . . and pussy miaowed a good deal and would not be comforted.'

In the train this unfortunate cat had tried to jump out of the window, so that Ellen and Tal 'were obliged to take it in turns to hold her tail while she stood on her legs and looked out of the window like any Christian'. If Ellen's concern for her cat is considered excessive, it should be remembered that Lady Macnaghten had dragged her two Persian cats with her on the nightmare retreat from Kabul;[1] while Samuel Butler had carried his cat in a bag while travelling on horseback in New Zealand.

Anglo-Indians who reached Naini Tal had every reason to amuse themselves with the frenzy of the reprieved. The young danced, played croquet and rode while their elders, according to Ellen, started to 'invent a frightful quantity of scandal'. Invention was hardly necessary in the 1867 season. The rivalries between the ladies' rowing crews provided enough ill feeling, as

[1] P. Macrory, *Signal Catastrophie*, 1966, p. 245 and p. 248.

Tal explained, to start 'quite a battle raging between the 2 Mrs Drummonds; and Mama, of course, had to help . . . I'm afraid as there seems to be a sort of squabbling begun that it will last out all the season, and that's rather a pity for it will make it uncommonly disagreeable.' Exactly ten years ago Mama had learned in Agra the tactics of the 'sort of squabbling' that was endemic in Anglo-Indian communities.

Conscious of their fetching clothes, the crews of the *Undine*, the *Effie* and the *Hilda* were not averse to being the centre of attention. Ellen and Tal rowed in the *Undine* the most select of the boats captained by the Lieutenant-Governor's daughter, Marianne Drummond. Though their mothers might be at loggerheads the daughters of a prominent official like Cudbert Bensley Thornhill could not be overlooked. The Drummonds created a little world of their own in Anglo-Indian society; the eleven members of the family who held prominent civil and military positions in 1873 well illustrated, after the passage of nearly a century, how effectively Lord Dundas had secured votes for Pitt the Younger and Scottish officials for the East India Company. Not only was an invitation to row in Miss Drummond's boat a social triumph, but the boating dress was the most becoming,

> 'they have a very swell costume of dark blue stuff trimmed with scarlet braid and looped up with 15 scarlet anchors. The jacket is . . . blue serge . . . trimmed with red braid. The shirt is striped red and white with studs of anchors down the front, and an anchor for a buckle. The jacket is trimmed also with sailors' gilt buttons with an anchor and crown on them. The hats are white straw with blue ribbon round them and *Undine* worked in scarlet in front. We all wear sailors' knots of blue ribbon. I think on the whole it is a very pretty dress.'

The parents' refusal to provide such an expensive outfit would have marred their daughters' chances; but Ellen Thornhill, thinking of the younger children to be educated at home, could not view the outlay with equanimity or wholeheartedly rejoice when the *Undine* defeated the *Effie* in 'the first ladies' race that was ever rowed'.

The sparkling air of the hill station brought little refreshment to Mrs Cudbert Thornhill who, night after night, tried to keep awake in ballrooms from which one of her daughters was inclined to disappear. Ellen resented, and often evaded, her mother's surveillance. She was constantly pressed for dances by Captain James Drummond, the eldest son of Lord Strathallan and nephew of Robert Drummond, whose intransigence had so harassed officials at Agra during the Mutiny. Family disapproval only encouraged Ellen who found 'Captain Drummond was very amusing but a little too cheeky. He craned his neck more than usual, it's wonderful that it doesn't crack as it is continually being bent nearly double. He took me into supper . . . luckily Mama did not look at my card or she could have been horrified to see that I had 4 dances with Captain Drummond and 5 with Mr Kay, but one of these was a square. She thinks three times too much which I consider very hard lines. You can scarcely get into anyone's step in only twice. How many do you allow yourself?'

Captain Drummond's cheek carried the day and a week later Tal wrote: 'Ellen is over head and toes in love with a Broken Neck, and is so foolish there is no doing anything with her.' It was almost impossible not to get engaged at Naini Tal where the stage was elaborately set to give every chance to Kaye's 'fair young English maidens'. For once Ellen approved of an 'old duffer' when General Storey gave a ball at his establishment where 'they had the gardens lighted up and they looked awfully pretty. I went out several times for a turn; once with Mr Kay, Frank Drummond and Captain Drummond though I caught it when I got home for going out at all. I thought it by far the nicest part of the whole affair'.

For a girl 'over head and toes' in love, Ellen announced the Broken Neck's proposal remarkably coolly at the end of a long letter to Minnie: 'Tal has I think told you all about Captain Drummond. Papa will not give his sanction to an engagement until Captain Drummond hears from his father which he expects to do about December, so then I will tell you all about it and send you his picture. I warn you beforehand not to expect a handsome man for I don't think him at all so, nor does anyone else I think; but he is very nice which of course makes up for all that.'

Cudbert Thornhill was not enthusiastic about an alliance with the Drummonds which might give his daughter social prestige but not financial security. Worn out by the painstaking fulfilment of his duties in a climate which had never suited him, Thornhill had all the forebodings of a sick man about the future of his own six children and of the three orphans, Minnie, George and Edward, for whom he was responsible. But, as Tal pointed out, Lord Strathallan was unlikely to withold his consent except 'on the score of tin, for the Drummonds hoped, it seems, that he would marry some heiress as their place is in debt and all that.' When the consent came Ellen reported 'that his relations out here . . . are awfully sold he has fixed on me'; and on her own side she had some regrets: 'I am sorry to say he is Scotch but doesn't talk a bit differently to us fortunately'. Neither the unflattering suggestion that he spoke English as well as his fiancée wrote it nor the chilliness of both families daunted James Drummond; so the wedding took place at Allahabad on 11 February 1868. Ellen would have given a great deal to have been married in England as she agreed with Tal that 'Indian marriages are melancholy scuffles.'

In her last letter before the wedding Ellen wrote, 'make haste dear and tell me what you think about my future husband. We are going off by the 12 o'clock train on Tuesday morning, after the most approved fashion, to spend our honeymoon at a place belonging to the Rajah of Benares. I will write you a long letter by the next mail from there. The pony has gone down and Jim's horse so we shall get lots of riding; and we are taking down my beloved cat and lots of books and Jim's two dogs, as we are going to amuse ourselves by making a happy family.'

High-caste Indian women may have marvelled at the freedom and variety in the lives of European girls on the voyage to India and at hill stations, and of married women who were at liberty in large towns to spend the hottest part of the day paying calls; but had they entered any small-station residence the scene would have been familiar to them. The greatest advantage that English brides had over Indian was freedom from the supervision of their elders. They were, as Ellen put it, 'off on their own hook'. This emancipation seldom went to their heads, as the first concern of young married couples was to reproduce their English homes in India. Splendidly regardless of the climate, they crammed their bungalows with furniture,

ornaments and pictures. At Rupar the walls of the Langs'
drawing room were hung with twenty-two big pictures and
thirteen small ones, and Edward Lang would have liked 'any
amount more'.

The Drummonds were equally determined to anglicize their

An Anglo-Indian home in the 1860s.

'very ugly' bungalow at Sialkot in north-east Punjab. But even
the most approved home trappings sent from Howell and
James could not shut out the desolation of the surrounding
plains which seemed to seep into the bungalow so that familiar
objects and meals assumed a sinister aspect. When the pressed
beef ordered by Ellen appeared on the table she had never seen
'anything more beastly looking, just like 4 or 5 lbs of worms all
jammed together.' The three tables covered with books and
wedding presents brought little comfort to the bride as the long
slow-moving day seemed to allow little time for the drawing-room pleasures and ploys which she had enjoyed at Lyston.
Writing home, Ellen tried to express the weariness of these
days:

> 'I do not think you would like the monotony of the life
> out here, at all events not at this station, Sialkot. It is the

same thing from day to day. I make the ayah call me and bring my tea before 6 and sometimes I turn out directly but not when I have had a bad night, as the heat keeps one awake. Then I have my bath and the ayah does my hair, that is combs and brushes it for more than an hour and I read some stale book while she is about it. When I am dressed I go to the store room and order breakfast and dinner; then I have my *chota nagree*, a cup of tea or cocoa and bread and butter and boiled egg or something of that sort. Jim is all this while at work, he comes in and has his *chota nagree* separately. Then I work till breakfast at 1 o'clock in the drawing room, and Jim reads or writes or sometimes takes a nap when he has been up early. After breakfast I feed the cats and then work and play the piano till past 4 when I go and take off my clothes and lie down and read; sometimes I go to sleep then for an hour but not often. Then at 6 o'clock I dress, bathe and have my hair done, and generally Jim takes me for a drive after racquets, that is 7.30 o'clock. Jim generally works from 3 to 5 when he goes to racquets. When I go to croquet I start at 6.30 and don't get back till past 8. We have our dinner at 8.30 generally, and afterwards I read some story book, and so does Jim when he is at home, till bedtime about 10 o'clock. And this is what I do every day and I hope you are not as sick of it as I am.'

Poor postal services contributed to the sense of isolation in small stations. Charges were high, deliveries uncertain and losses frequent. Parcels from home, which later cheered so many exiles, could not be posted until in 1865 the cheaper rates allowed for sending trade patterns were extended to 'articles of intrinsic value'. This was virtually the establishment between Great Britain and India of parcel post which the Director General of the Indian Post Office complacently pointed out 'has in India been for many years a recognised part of the mail services'.[1] At home Britons had to wait until 1883 for a parcel post. Though pattern post eased the transit of goods, Anglo-Indian shoppers still felt they were being cheated; as indeed they often were. When the Drummonds ordered

[1] Communication No. 2309 of 11 November 1865 from H. B. Riddell, Director General of the Post Office in India, Home Department, a copy of which was kindly supplied by the Departmental Record Officer, Post Office Records.

a gold locket costing £5 they were sent one priced £12; a considerable setback to an impecunious couple. Matters were no better in India where Edward Lang complained: 'Those Calcutta people are such ruffians, they get one's money and then jeer at you.' Relief came when the doctrines of self-help made an unexpected impact on some serving officers who were goaded by delays, over-pricing and neglect into acting without reference to the regulations. In 1871 'a plodding captain of the foot', F. B. McCrea, undertook to establish a co-operative enterprise, the Army and Navy Supply Depot in Victoria Street, to provide military and naval members serving overseas with provisions and wines of good quality at reasonable prices. Further services were soon supplied and McCrea was rumoured to have enlisted his father as a laundry man. These activities found little favour with the Old Brigade who considered them and also the 'bonnet shops and costumiers springing up in every fashionable street' under military direction as manifestations of the huckstering spirit let loose in the army with the abolition of the purchase of commissions.[1] These critics overlooked the brisk buying and selling of commissions a century earlier when the notorious John Calcraft as well as dealing in commissions privately advanced money to officers who were thus doubly in his power.

A service so widely needed as the Army and Navy Stores could not long be confined to the forces or to liquor and comestibles. Within a decade civilians could obtain tickets, and amidst mosquito nets, hurricane spirit stoves and tropical medical kits, the most home-keeping Briton could feel himself an imperial auxiliary.

The paraphernalia of the Empire had no charms for Ellen Drummond whose spirits were further depressed at Sialkot by a series of deaths. In 1871 she complained, 'it really seems as if I were never to be out of mourning again. I have only been in colours 6 months since poor Papa died [11 July 1868]'. The burden of mourning fell on the women who did double duty for their own and their husband's relatives; in 1871 Ellen was in black for Jim's aunt. To wear mourning clothes may have been a genuine expression of grief; it was certainly a social

[1] One of the Old Brigade, *London in the Sixties*, 1st ed. 1908, 14th ed., 1914, see pp. 144–5 for the activities of McCrea and of the 'military Mantalinis'.

obligation. The intensity of grief was exactly measured: two years for a husband or parent, six to nine months for a brother or sister, three for an uncle or aunt and six weeks for an uncle or aunt by marriage. In India not only was mourning garb exceptionally oppressive, but it had to be repeatedly donned. The frequency of deaths and of ill health impeded any continuity in Anglo-Indian life so that it seemed impossible to establish a way of living between the frantic gaiety of the stations in the hills and the do-nothing monotony of those in the plains.

With little to do in the house but hand out the stores and with few interests to take them beyond the compound many Anglo-Indian wives indulged in the corrosive gossip of the under-occupied. Even Ellen, a warm-hearted girl, could write that one of the Sialkot balls 'was given by a very dark couple; the Colonel (and his wife) of a native regiment here. She is an awful creature, quite coffee coloured, and powders and paints herself but still it shows . . . it was a capital party and some of the dresses were very pretty. 2 or 3 ladies here wear their hair in *enormous* chignons, quite ridiculous as it makes their heads miles too big for their bodies. The supper wasn't very tempting and I came home quite famished at about 3 o'clock'. Half a century earlier Ellen's grandmother, Mary Fombelle, had been proud to make it known that 'she had in her veins the blood of the Mogul Emperors.'[1]

It was not only the wives who found the slow-moving life of small stations wearisome. Husbands also grew restless; even steady, hard-working Edward Lang felt 'one has a vague longing to have some rushing about and get kicked, in fact anything wild.' He could hardly express his contempt for a colleague who felt skittles would meet the need: 'He is a German – and wants to make a skittles alley – and us to subscribe to it, catch me!! It's all skittles, he can't play English games, he is a great big fair man . . . and throws and hits like a girl – and skittles!!! oh my!!! actually making a skittle alley!!!'

The games barrier obviated the necessity for any restrictions on the employment of Continental Europeans in

[1] *Maga*, Blackwood's Magazine, April 1968, pp. 363–5, D. Shaw, 'My Indian Hunt for Mrs Siddons'.

British service in India.

The longing for an interest and employment in many Anglo-Indian establishments meant that children came into their own. Relegated at home to nurseries, they held the centre of the stage in India and tyrannised over indulgent ayahs and admiring parents. As Ellen explained, 'in India one doesn't leave them with servants as you do at home, and I wash and dress mine every day and put him to bed myself, and he is in the drawing room with us all day long.' Ellen at last had found employment for a room which had previously been given over to cats and bric-à-brac. When the children reached a companionable age they were sent home to be easily recognisable by their yellow faces and peevish, imperious ways. The little Anglo-Indian was immortalised in *The Secret Garden* where the sickly Mary Lennox learned to enjoy fresh air and to show consideration to those around her. Many Anglo-Indian children were not able to re-establish themselves so successfully. Dispossessed of a home, many grew up ill at ease with themselves and their surroundings and lacking in confidence.

Ellen lost her first baby, Henrietta Alice (1869–1870). There was not an Anglo-Indian home where the voice of Rachel was not heard weeping for her children:

> 'It began quite suddenly. She was not quite well on Sunday morning and the doctor ordered her some powders but told me there was nothing much amiss with her . . . All Monday Baby was in bed moaning with pain and nothing seemed to do her any good. In the evening Dr Harrison called another doctor who lanced her gums and ordered her to take some ether in milk which we gave her 3 times but she was sick directly every time till 2 o'clock at night and then she kept it down; and Jim and I, thinking she had turned the corner and was better, both of us lay down to get a little rest; the doctor was in the house. I hadn't been asleep a quarter of an hour when the ayah called me and I found my poor little darling just dying. I called Jim who fetched the doctor but it was too late. Her hands were quite cold but when I took her hand she squeezed my finger as she used always to do, my dear, dear little girl . . . She was buried on the Tuesday afternoon . . . in a quiet corner of the cemetery under a lilac tree.'

The Drummonds' second child, William Huntly, survived to come home, to serve in the Black Watch, to grow 'a big flame-coloured beard' and to become the fifteenth Earl of Perth.

Soon after William's birth Ellen started the 'nasty cough' she was never to throw off. After the birth of little Ellen in 1872 she grew steadily weaker. In February 1873 she wrote a note in pencil to assure Minnie that she had 'taken a decided turn for the better . . . I shall be thankful to get well . . . it is dull work being so seedy'; but it was now clear Ellen was in the advanced stages of consumption, and a passage home for the whole family was booked in the *Khedive*. On the journey home James Drummond tended his dying wife and the two children, both of whom were ailing.

The family reached London, and on 19 May 1873 Minnie was allowed to visit her cousin and dearest friend: 'She is fearfully altered, I only stayed in the room a few minutes and she said very little to me, she is in bed and looks so thin and her face is quite changed, her eyes brightened when I first went in, and then she had such a fit of coughing'.

Never forgetting Lyston, Ellen begged that her old nurse, Martha Snazzle, should look after her children who were taken to South Lambeth. Here the two miserable and sickly infants 'screamed like anything' until young Henry Beaufoy Thornhill, ever kind-hearted, 'pretended to talk Hindustani' and quietened Willy. May 28 was Derby Day and, as usual, the Caron Place household stood at the gates, one pillar of which still remains embedded in the front wall of the Vinegar Factory, to watch the passers-by. On Derby Day seven years earlier Minnie wrote in her diary: 'Ellen and I were together . . . and we had a little pincushion thrown to us from a gentleman on the top of a four-in-hand, another took off his hat'. Watching racegoers returning from the Oaks a few days later 'Ellen and Miss Mercier had a bow from the Prince of Wales. They stood at the gates, they had a doll thrown to them, and roses etc from some fast young men'.

During her first year at Sialkot Ellen had written to Minnie: 'I so often wish for you out here; it would be so nice being together again and what lots we should have to talk about. Almost every other night I dream that I am at home again, fighting with you like cat and dog, it is a most absurd thing.' But when Minnie visited Ellen on 31 May four years later,

'Dear Ellen hardly spoke today. She only said that we had not had one talk together, she stroked my cheek'. On 5 June, the day after Ellen's twenty-fourth birthday, Minnie wrote:

> 'Our dearest Ellen died this afternoon at about five o'clock. Jim, Aunt Ellen, Tal and I were with her to the last, she knew us all quite well, poor darling and seemed to like to have us with her . . . she seemed so ready to die there was no fear of death. Poor darling she kept saying "Father take me" and "When will it come". She suffered very much, was in great pain all night, poor darling, her gasping for breath was most distressing. Jim read the 23rd Psalm and Tal afterwards read the 332nd hymn "A few more years shall roll". Her cough was very bad at this time and at last she did not seem to have strength to cough.'

The next day the weather 'turned so cold'. Alone, except for the servants, at Caron Place Minnie tried to dispel the feeling of being in a 'dreadful dream' by taking out her old diaries and reading about 'dear Lyston'. But comfort only came next day when 'Tal took me in to see Dearest Ellen and she looked so beautiful . . . Tal had a cross of all white flowers and put it on her breast and lovely roses. She looked so sweet and the upper part of her face is quite like her old self, there is no expression of pain now. It seems to take away so much of the dread and awfulness of death to see her lying there so lovely. It quite realises those beautiful words "They also which are *fallen asleep in Christ*". She only looks as if she was asleep, a pure and Heavenly sleep'.

After the calm of Ellen's room, the desolation of Caron Place seemed greater. Little Ellen, who was soon to join her mother, 'screamed all night'. When at last Minnie stumbled up to her room 'a horrid rat came into her bed'. So the short June night passed and Ellen was buried at Woking Cemetery on 9 June. Life only became normal when Aunt George and the housekeeper returned and 'were at it all day' setting Caron Place in order.

The remembrance of the thousands of girls who endured all the sorrows of Ellen's short life makes it hard to pass judgment on the activities of European women in India. Most of them entered the arena armed with accomplishments but without the awakened understanding which might have secured victory over monotony. The vital energies of many began to ebb after a few years in India; and all lived under the shadow of sudden death. In a few hours the fingers of Ellen's baby were cold; and falling beneath the assassin's knife Lord Mayo, whom no exertion could tire, brushed his hair from his eyes and died. This shadow was most menacing in the years after the Mutiny when increasing numbers of European women began to arrive. To preserve life and sanity they felt compelled to build a fort rather than a dwelling place. But they were the first victims of the restricting punctilio and social ritual which they themselves had established. It was the great misfortune of Anglo-Indian women that their opportunity to create an out-ward-looking society in India came in the fear-dominated decades after the Mutiny. In these years any deviation from the accepted pattern seemed a step towards social disintegra-tion. Their education had not prepared young wives to think independently; and, after a few years residence in India, their energies were often sapped by ill-health. It was inevitable, therefore, that they should be more concerned with the appearances than the foundations of Anglo-Indian society. It could be said of their activities, as it was of a type of embroi-dery popular at the time: 'One of the advantages of the Anglo-Indian, or Brocade, embroidery is that it is easily done, and is more effective than almost any other kind of work on which so little labour is lavished'.

CHAPTER TEN

New Zealand:
The Unhappy Shepherds

> I am very sick of New Zealand and would give no small
> sum to get away, but I am afraid it is fated that I shall
> waste the best part of my existence in this uncivilised
> place.
>
> W. R. Thornhill
Centre Hill, 10 October 1869

> Unless we can transplant into our Colonies, as happily
> we have translated into New Zealand (where men are
> found reading Dante while they are shepherding their
> flocks), not merely the young noblemen, but the noble
> young men of England . . . what is to become of them?
>
> William Sewell, speaking at the annual
dinner of Old Radleians, 22 June 1872

New Zealand was the ultimate refuge of those unable to survive at home. If emigrants failed to secure a foothold in this
antipodean outpost, their case was hard indeed. To move on
either to the west or to the east only brought them back to
their starting point where no second spring of hope awaited
them. Although forced abroad by the conditions in a country
which could only offer stones to many of her children, colonial
settlers were anxious to recreate the setting they had left. As
emigrants ranged from boys from the city streets shipped off
with a suit of clothes, the Bible and good advice: 'Remember
time is short – eternity long'[1] to Sewell's 'noble young men of
England' there was little identity of background. Nevertheless,
some familiar aspects of the homeland were introduced: English weeds, rodents, white clover, sectarian wranglings and
land speculations. Before considering how the New Zealand
nation was created from these diverse elements something

[1] *Ragged School Union Magazine*, April 1851, Vol. III.

must be said about the land from which the immigrants, and particularly the four young Thornhills, hoped so much.

The silence, the sombre green shade beneath the great ferns and the ferocious mien of the Maoris did not endear New Zealand to early travellers, most of whom had still in mind the gaiety and abundance of Tahiti. That the islands were annexed by Great Britain in 1840 was due to the needs of the Australian colonists for flax and timber, of the whalers for bases and of the British Government for an outlet for those, like the agricultural rioters in the 1830s, whom poverty was driving into crime.

Faced with the menacing problem of pauperism at a time when industrial expansion was steadily increasing the nat-- ional wealth, the Whig governments could only pass Bills and hope that God would send administrators. Their optimism was not ill-founded: Edwin Chadwick oiled the grinding machinery of the Poor Law Amendment Act at home; and the erratic fervour of Edward Gibbon Wakefield inspired the New Zealand Association of 1837 which founded the first British settlements in that country. The early settlers arrived in a foreign land amidst a suspicious, and often hostile, population. The acceptance by the Maori chiefs at Waitangi of the sovereignty of Queen Victoria and of her right to purchase their lands only postponed the conflict that was inevitable between two races whose single common aim was to hold land. But the singleness of their purpose was the only effective weapon with which the Maoris could combat the Europeans.

On their arrival many settlers felt that they had returned to the morning of time; but sectarian wranglings continued as briskly in the solemn and passionless landscape of New Zealand as they had done in the crowded villages and streets of the homeland. As the contestants strove to increase their influence overseas, one colony after another provided a new battleground. New Zealand, where neither climate nor terrain overpowered the settlers, offered all the possibilities of a promised land to the militants of the churches in England and Scotland. The Free Church of Scotland was first off the mark with settlements in Otago; while two years later, in 1850, Canterbury was founded to revive the zeal, purity and architectural nobility which High Churchmen believed had characterised the fourteenth-century church in England. Cudbert Thornhill may not have known much about medieval ecclesiastical history, but his Radley training enabled him to take a clear cut view of church affairs in New Zealand during the 1860s: 'Canterbury is by far the best settlement of the lot. The people are better educated and there are more gentlemen; it is High Church, too. Otago is principally Scotch and very Low Church, no Church at all, in fact; and most of the swells there are roaring cads.'

Radley men could hardly view dispassionately the Otago scene where cattle drovers from the Highlands made fortunes, and where church services and ways of living were unadorned and down to earth. Cudbert confessed that: 'Everyone knows I was not fond of work at Radley', but he had thoroughly absorbed the ethos of this school established in 1847 by William Sewell (1804–1874). The strange and fitful abilities of Sewell would have found a scope in any age, but they were particularly suited to directing a school for boys who were to fill the colonies and mould the destinies of India. Brains were not overtaxed as Sewell despised 'narrow-minded, parrot-like book-worms from the treadmill cram of competitive examination'; but perhaps the pupils' health was. Sewell got his boys up at 5.45 a.m. and gave them bread and butter for breakfast, after one and a half hour's work, and also for tea at 6. p.m. to fortify them for the evening's study. Meat appeared with the bread at midday dinner and, on three days a week, pudding.[1] Sewell was determined that his pupils should be well able to face the rigours of colonial life especially in New Zealand where the diet often consisted of 'damper [unleavened bread], tea and mutton – mutton, damper, tea.' Even more important than hardiness to a settler's success was self-reliance which Sewell did not encourage. Indeed, he overstressed the need of boys to cultivate *verecundia* or 'an instinctive feeling of inferiority in themselves', forgetting that true modesty can only stem from self-confidence. Haunted by the uprisings of youthful revolutionaries in 1848, headmasters of the mid-nineteenth century were determined to keep boys in their places. To Thomas Arnold all the turmoil and disorder of the student riots on the Continent were due to 'that proud notion of per-

[1] A. K. Boyd, *A History of Radley College*, 1847–1947, 1948, see pp. 86–7 for description of Sewell's regime at Radley.

sonal independence which is neither reasonable nor Christian – but essentially barbarian. It visited Europe with all the curses of the age of chivalry, and is threatening us now with those of Jacobinism'.[1]

Mild and persistent encouragement would have helped the Thornhills better than the vehement exhortations of Sewell who brought everything to the sweating point. Because they were physically active few realised that the Thornhills were incapable of sustained effort. Possibly this failing was due to lack of parental support. The parents of George and Edward were killed during the Mutiny, and those of Cudbert and William only saw their sons during home leaves which were chiefly devoted to family business and visits to medical practitioners.

Sewell's methods may be criticised but the school registers show a remarkably high record of achievement overseas, particularly in India and New Zealand. The careers of the crew which almost defeated Eton at Henley in 1858 indicate how effectively his pupils were fulfilling the Founder's ambitions. This Radley crew provided South Africa with a prime minister, British Guiana with a receiver-general and Madras with a judge; two of the crew left written records indicating their careers: a treatise on the manufacture of guns and the *Reminiscences of an Old Sportsman*; one took Holy Orders, and advantageous marriages enabled three to settle as country gentlemen; only George Thornhill failed to establish himself satisfactorily. His cousin, Henry George Fombelle Siddons, who was also at Radley, served with distinction in the Burmese War of 1885–9, so that the inertia of the Thornhills in New Zealand cannot be altogether attributed to their inheriting the langour characteristic of long-established Anglo-Indian families.

When George left Radley in 1860 and Cudbert a year later, the responsibility of settling their futures fell on Cudbert's father. Oppressed by family sorrows and ill health, he was at a loss as how best to provide for young men with no outstanding preferences or talents. For parents and guardians, particularly of Radley boys, in such a quandary New Zealand was a

[1] A. P. Stanley, *The Life and Correspondence of Thomas Arnold*, 1890, 3rd ed., p. 67.

Heaven-sent solution. The way of living in the thriving Anglican province of Canterbury seemed but an extension, and a
profitable one, of life at Radley. Not quite sharing their elders
optimism, George and Cudbert sailed for New Zealand in
October 1861, at the ages of nineteen and eighteen. Exactly
five years later but with much less flourish, since he had failed
to get into Oxford and the Lyston home was broken up,
Edward followed his cousin and brother (plate 38). Finally with
no ceremony at all William, who had been sent down from
Oxford and had contracted a hasty and imprudent engagement
with Marion Russell of South Lambeth, was bundled off early
in December 1867.

Though Cudbert Bensley Thornhill bore the brunt of
making all financial arrangements. Aunt George Beaufoy also
assisted in speeding her nephews to New Zealand. But it was a
long time before her man of business, J. R. Turner, cleared
himself from all the entanglements which this assistance
involved. Turner escorted to Southampton William who,
having spent all his journey money on an engagement ring for
his 'little darling', found himself 'in a peculiar maze' and at
the last moment had to be reimbursed. Later dunning letters
arrived for Edward who, shamed by his sister's offer to pay his
debts, eventually sent a draft of £14, and urged Minnie to 'try
and get Mr Turner to knock off the interest, as I think it is
bosh; the man ought to think himself lucky in getting it at all,
as he hasn't the shadow of a hold on me, as I was under age at
the time.' William continued his new life in the 'peculiar
maze' in which he had started it since he felt sure that Aunt
George, who refused to correspond with him, would eventually
come down handsomely. He ran through all the usual blan-
dishments of a necessitous nephew to a wealthy aunt. He
besought her 'not to run on too fast . . . she had no nephew now
to look after her interests with a careful eye.' He begged her 'to
write directly, at once, if not sooner' and, in a final effort, sent
his 'love and a kiss – a good smacker.' But Aunt George's
response was a donation to a missionary society which Edward
dutifully acknowledged: 'It is most awfully kind of Aunt George
to assist in the good work of propagating Christian literature in
these heathen countries, and I hope you will thank her very
much.'

The propagation of Christianity in New Zealand, according to George Henry Kingsley 'met with that hopeless death-blow, the contact of different sects of missionaries, which invariably inspires the sharp Maori with a distrust of them all.'[1] Sometimes, as in the case of George Augustus Selwyn, Bishop of New Zealand, the Maoris felt they could trust the man if not the missionary. The last words of Selwyn and of Sir George Grey were spoken in Maori; on their deathbeds the thoughts of both men were with a people they admired and a country which had drawn out the best from both the bishop and the governor.

An observant passenger on an emigrant ship could have easily picked out the winners in the colonial stakes. Success in the new settlements largely depended on being a good neighbour. It was not so much the self-reliant man who was likely to prosper as the man who was willing not only to help his neighbours but also to keep up their spirits. Mark Tapleys were the founding fathers of every thriving settlement. In this rôle unexpected figures came to the fore. One was Samuel Butler (1835–1902) who, although seldom regarded as a philanthropist, came out as strongly as Tapley had done as a model emigrant. He organised and conducted a shipboard choir so that for some hours every week emigrants could forget their discomforts and apprehensions for the future. On arriving at Christchurch he helped some of the passengers to settle in their new home where he 'scrubbed the floors of the two rooms with soap, scrubbing brushes, flannel and water, made them respectably clean, and removed . . . boxes into their proper places.'[2] Inclination not lack of success caused Butler to abandon sheep farming in 1864.

With no lack of good heart, the Thornhills never achieved a happy relationship with their fellow voyagers or settlers. The chief reason was their great expectations. Always hoping that the Old Director's estate would be finally settled in their favour or that Aunt George would relent, they made but little effort to master sheep farming or to accept their neighbours. Their natural diffidence also prevented them from making friends easily. The barriers might have been overcome as the Thorn-

[1] G. H. Kingsley, *South Sea Bubbles*, 1872, p. 304.

[2] S. Butler, *A First Year in Canterbury Settlement*, 1863, p. 33.

hills were, from inclination and Radley training, musical; and in all settlements musicians were particularly in demand. But, as Cudbert pointed out, 'most of the music one hears out here is such beastly Scotch stuff that one can hardly appreciate it.' So when their 'jolly' songs arrived from home, such as 'Weeping Sad and Lonely', 'Hark 'tis the Vesper Bell' and 'Orpheus and his Lute', the Thornhills kept their fun to themselves: 'Cud, I [William] and Eddy have regular concerts . . . as we are the musical ones we keep it up here. We have some awful fine songs and choruses.' Even in the most riotous music halls of the 1860s mournful songs pleased and held audiences. Young men of 1860s had, according to *Punch*, 'a faculty of depreciation quite unparalleled in history'; but juniors seldom please their elders. Looking back over a century, these 'cool young satirists' appear to us as being highly inflammable and earnest. This point is well made by a writer who had a long acquaintance with schoolboys: 'There was in the early-Victorian public schoolboy none of the studied concealment of emotion, the phlegmatic reserve, or the stoicism which marks his modern counterpart. Affection, too, lay nearer the surface, and not in the deeps where it now lurks'.[1]

In 1862 George and Cudbert started their shepherding career in the Rangitata valley, where Butler had taken up a run almost two years earlier. The treeless, terraced landscape around the Rangitata river, described by Butler as 'that torrent pathway of destruction' and by Cudbert as 'a most loathsome affair' was not welcoming. No settlers in New Zealand could remain indifferent to the rivers or the winds which, it often seemed, dominated their lives with an active and persistent malevolence. There was little to choose between the 'howling nor'wester' and the 'southerly buster'. The first harassed the humans by shaking the houses and raising the sand from-river beds, the second scattered the sheep. Nor'-westers were often followed by heavy rains which, though they brought on the grass, caused freshes that turned rivers into impassable torrents. The elements not only harried the sheep and bullocks struggling to drag loads across swollen rivers, but took their toll of human lives. The youngest son of Cracroft Wilson, the Thornhills' agent and connection by marriage, was drowned

[1] A.K. Boyd, *op. cit.*, p. 193.

in the Rakaia which, in flood, was a seething mass of cloudy yellow water. The frequency of such tragedies gave rise to a saying that in New Zealand people only died from drink or drowning. As menacing a hazard as the rivers was the bush. Even in sunshine the silence of these forests and the twisted, creeper-hung trees appeared alien and unfriendly to settlers, but when swept by gales the bush had the fearful quality of a nightmare. The bush stretched into the Centre Hill run which the Thornhills eventually bought. Their shepherd's boys, aged seven and eight, wandered into the forest where Edward happened to be carting timber. He described the developments:

'I had heard the father of the children calling after them for some bit, but didn't think anything of it for some time, as they often stop out late; but he went on calling for so long that at last I remarked to Cud that I thought they must be lost. So we went out; it was quite dark then, and blowing very hard, and we hunted about until about four o'clock in the morning, when it began to get a little light. I then walked down to the house where George and I live, about four miles, to get more men to search. George and I then came back having got our horses; and we met Cud, who had been looking about all the time. This was about half past five. Then George went over to a neighbouring run and got a lot more men; and we scoured the country high and low for miles, and the Bush as well. There were between seventy and eighty men out searching, and we didn't find either of them for two days. Then we only found one; he had been out two nights and nearly two days, when we found him; but he didn't seem any the worse for it. We kept up the search for the other one for a week or ten days, but we didn't succeed in finding him. His body, or the remains of it, were found the other day by a shepherd, about ten miles from his home.'

The golden air of New Zealand gave many settlers 'the sort of joyous light-heartedness which only young children have'; but in this colony, as throughout the Empire, the greatest sufferings of the pioneering days were borne by the children.

George and Cudbert were probably employed on the Rangitata run as cadets, working for their keep to learn the business of sheep farming. On the whole, this system was unsatisfactory since it often resulted in the 'half-and-half work' of an unpaid amateur.

Rightly or wrongly, the Thornhills felt by 1864 that they

Lost in the New Zealand bush.

had learnt enough about sheep farming to start their own run. The immediate problem was to find land; this difficulty would have been unthinkable thirty years earlier. The land problems of all colonial settlements were similar. The first settlers felt that centuries would pass before an impression was made on the seemingly limitless lands before them; yet after a few decades immigrants were jostling each other in their race for holdings. In New Zealand settlers were not only competing with each other but with the Maoris and, by the 1860s, with *rentiers* many of whom were living in the homeland. Numerous regulations imposed a semblance of order on the situation. By the treaty of Waitangi the Crown had the sole right of purchasing land from the Maoris. These Crown lands were sold or leased at low rates, while controls also existed in areas where systematic colonisation by the New Zealand Company or by religious associations had necessitated the establishment of a central authority. In all settlements of untilled lands the first colonists, heedless of the distant authorities making the allotment, determined their own boundaries and dictated the price at which they parted from their holdings. In New Zealand this price was influenced by many factors. Sheep and the institutions of the mother country throve in Canterbury so the demands of well-to-do settlers kept the price of land high. Prospects of gold induced many to brave the austerity, both climatic and social, of Otago and prices rose; while in Southland they fell when attempts were made to finance the building of railways by paying the contractors in land.

Fluctuations in land prices were not overlooked by speculators in England. Though the argricultural interest had seemingly survived the repeal of the Corn Laws, landowners were not quite at ease. Investments in colonial property gave them a feeling of security and the possibility of a fortune if gold were struck. As early as 1850 Charlotte Godley had as a fellow passenger to New Zealand Richard Bulkeley Williams-Bulkeley who, though he thought it 'the right thing to be rough on board ship' and wore 'dirty white trousers turned up to his dirty socks', owned a large property in New Zealand. He probably had some understanding of sheep farming as the extensive family estates were in Wales.[1] Thirty years later Cudbert wrote:

> 'Our neighbours the McGregors have just sold their run to a Mr Campbell in England. He lives somewhere in Gloucester I think, and is a most wealthy man. He has

[1] *Letters from Early New Zealand 1850–1853*, ed. by J. R. Godley, 1951, p. 13.

> any quantity of runs in New Zealand and Australia, beside some splendid properties at home. I don't like the McGregors very much. They are still living up here and are going to manage for Campbell – rather a good billet for them. I don't dislike Mr McGregor. He was a distiller in Scotland, before he came out here. He is not half a bad fellow but Mrs McG. I don't like at all. Her father is a cunning old rogue and was, I believe, either a hotel keeper or dealer in cattle or something of that sort. He had a run adjoining McGregor's; and he went to England to Campbell and sold the lot (his own run, McGregor's and Mr Clerk's and Butler's runs) to Mr Campbell . . . Of course they are gentlefolk out here, anyone with any money at all is that.'

The real rub lay in the last sentence; by 1870 the Thornhills were rapidly losing money and status.

Unfortunately for George and Cudbert Thornhill the Otago gold rush had already sent up the price of land when their run was secured in the spring of 1865. Centre Hill, about seventy miles north of Invercargill, included some bush and stretched over a desolate plain 'exposed to every wind that blows'. The only plants that flourished on the barren soil, 'a mass of large stone and shingle', were tussocks of rigid-bladed grass and towering bushes of flax (*Phormium tenax*). Like the bush and the quickly rising rivers, the vegetation of New Zealand seemed to mock the endeavours of the settlers. Colonists vented their dislike of viciously prickly or sharp-leaved plants by giving them opprobious names: Creeping Lawyer (*Rubus parvus*), Wild Irishman (*Discaria toumatou*), 'a very uncomfortable shrub' according to Butler, and Spaniard (*Aciphylla squarrosa*), presumably so named because of its spinous leaves, which resembled the daggers allegedly carried by Spaniards. Neither the acreage of this Canaan, nor the price paid for it, were revealed in the letters to Minnie. The Thornhills' agent, Cracroft Wilson, eventually bought out the run holder, McAlpine, who seems to have disconcertingly remained on the run until Wilson found a new holding for him in 1867. So quickly was the morning light fading that less than ten years after the arrival of the first settlers in Southland[1] the land agent, or

---

[1] In 1861 Southland separated from Otago, but the two settlements rejoined in 1870.

middleman, was plying his trade as briskly as he had done in the depraved homeland. Settling McAlpine was not easy although he 'could pay down £4000 cash'. It is not unreasonable to suppose that the greater part of this was the sum paid down by the Thornhills who most likely had to pay another £2000 or so in instalments. An enterprising neighbour, Captain Russell, sold his run in 1866 'to two different people; one bought it first for £5,000 cash, another bought it shortly afterwards for £7,000 on the usual terms. The last purchaser has possession at present, but the first is going to send some sheep up to it very shortly.' Prices were certainly rising; by 1867 another neighbour 'sold out for £30,000. Seven years ago he offered the run with 1,700 sheep and 50 cattle for £1,100 and was unable to sell.' Prospects of finding gold, rising wool prices and railway speculations made the 1860s boom years for many landowners. Their debts, inexperience and lassitude kept George and Cudbert from rising on the wave of prosperity. When their energies should have been directed towards improving Centre Hill, the Thornhills were mainly concerned in scraping together enough to 'pay off McAlpine and old Wilson and start clear'. The burden of debt increased rather than lessened with the years. In December 1867 George wrote: 'We are still more than £3000 in debt, but the Bank of New Zealand have taken us up so that there is now no chance of any merchant selling us up; the licence, too, has been transferred to our name, which is a great thing in our favour'. But the rôle of the grasping trader could be played by the banks after 1870 when they were allowed to acquire a valid title to land or property which had been accepted as security.

There is no ill luck like that which dogs the half-hearted. Soon after Centre Hill was purchased George wrote, 'there is every possibility of our sheep being declared scabby; everything seems going against us.' Perhaps George's real grievance was that 'Cud unfortunately has taken the management of the sheep. But I suppose Uncle Cuddy authorised him to do so; therefore I must not complain, thought I don't like being put under a man now who is younger than I am and not more qualified to take over the direction of the station.' Either George or Cudbert might have been qualified to direct a sheep run, but neither were able, or willing, to work on one. Cudbert con sidered: 'Shepherding is about the hardest life in the colony. You are obliged to be out in all weathers, wet or fine, and on Sunday as well as week days. As a general rule a shepherd seldom walks less than 8 or 10 miles a day; on windy days about double that distance. A shepherd's life at home is nothing compared to this.' The shepherd's calendar had no charms for the Thornhills: watching sheep, getting them across rivers, mustering, dipping, shearing, culling and hurdle making all succeeded one another in a 'most confoundedly slow' cycle. The daily monotony was only broken by mishaps and worries about scab, straying sheep, boundaries, servants and above all about money. Dissatisfied with their life and with each other, the young men half-heartedly tried to improve the home station and its immediate surroundings which George planned 'to lay off like the kitchen garden at Lyston'. Wherever the British sojourned or settled they endeavoured to create a familiar ecological niche around them. Despairing of making a garden on the baked soil of the Punjab, Edward Lang gave up one of his bathrooms for growing perennials. In New Zealand settlers in 'preparing strawberry and asparagus beds, and other useful things'[1] introduced a 'stealthy tide of English weeds' which were soon 'creeping over the surface of the waste, cultivated and virgin soil, in annually increasing numbers'.[2]

Despite George's efforts with the kitchen garden Centre Hill did not appear like Lyston to Edward when he arrived in New Zealand early in 1867. He found his brother and cousin living 'in a small room without any carpet; the entrance door opens into it, and consequently in wet weather it is an inch or two deep in mud and slush off people's boots'. The pleasant household comfort at Lyston had depended on servants many of whom, like old Joseph, the groom, and Mrs Jackson had been with the Thornhills since they were children. Domestic affairs at Centre Hill were ordered rather than arranged by a forceful character whom George described as 'a pretty fair cook, but a very coarse man. He is a "man of wars man" and served in the

[1] Lady F. N. Barker, *Station Life in New Zealand*, 1870, p. 63.

[2] *The Natural History Review*, January 1864, No. XIII, pp. 123–7, J. D. Hooker, 'Note on the Replacement of Species in the Colonies and Elsewhere'.

Crimea, China and several other places, and is fearfully con-
ceited. He came in this evening and said he should leave, but
at last said he would stop for 22s 6d a week.' A man who had
survived the Crimean and several other campaigns had some
right to think well of himself and also to keep up 'such tremendous fires' that the chimney caught fire twice in one week. It
was to immigrants like the 'man of wars man' and the house-
maid at the Barkers' station who, starting with 10s a week,
declared her intention of becoming a 'first-rater' that New
Zealand was a land not only of promise but of fulfilment. For
them a new life did start when the emigrant ship docked, and
they sniffed the heady air and saw on the quay the crowds
waiting for a chance to secure servants. By the 1880s societies
were assisting the emigration of girls whose jubilant letters
home showed how easy it was to secure a horse, a bank balance and a husband. Though thousands of servants at home
were unlikely to secure these blessings, they were encouraged
by such accounts to assert themselves and 'to make the kitchen
fire too hot for the missus and too cold for the sirloin.' As early
as the 1870s the underswell from the basement was rocking
every household Minnie visited.

Squalor at home and gales abroad did not ease the relations between Cudbert and the two brothers. Sensing, too, that
his control of the run was resented, Cudbert moved to
share with the shepherd the newly-built out-station. Though
satisfied with the new arrangement George still had a grievance, 'it is better it should be so for Ned and I have the home
station to ourselves. The other place is far the best, though, for
it is close to the bush and well sheltered. This place is out on a
plain without a tree or any kind of shelter near.' Cudbert was
not long alone as early in 1868 he was joined by his brother. William had hardly finished extolling his fiancée when Mrs
Russell's letter arrived breaking off her daughter's engagement. Now he had to try his luck again at the local balls. His
hair was curled 'with a pair of irons' by Cudbert, but to little
avail for William found the balls 'horribly mixed' and the pro-
grammes half a century out of date. The truth was that girls
were in such short supply that the young and pretty were
obliged to share one dance with two partners. Edward, too,
became anxious, but not pressingly so, about his matrimonial

prospects: 'I will send my photograph home in about another year and a half's time. You, Minnie, can go with it and hunt out some pretty heiress for me. If you're successful I'll come home and have a look at her. Nothing under £20,000 will do for me, though, mind that. Then I might manage to start a good run of my own.' Edward never secured either a wife or a run.

When their juniors arrived George and Cudbert had struggled through five years of sheep farming without becoming interested in the work or, despite the boom of the 1860s, making it pay. Both, therefore, were singularly ill-equipped to face the depression of the 1870s. Cudbert tried to explain the situation, 'when Cracroft Wilson bought the run for us [1865–6] sheep were worth about 20 to 25 shillings a head. Now [July 1871] they are worth 5 to 6 shillings, which makes a considerable difference I can assure you; and a very bad one for us.' Neither William nor Edward, both of whom had left England under a cloud, were likely to re-animate Centre Hill activities which were creaking to a standstill. As the economic clouds gathered, the Thornhills took refuge in the Swiss-Family-Robinson ploys which had absorbed them at Lyston. Edward discovered 'a splendid way for taming wild kittens'. As a result Lily, Smut and Ugly, instead of racing about and screeching under the hut, learned to sit like 'statues before the fire'. The tamed magpie remained silent, but the white cockatoo was persuaded to say 'pretty Cocky'. Numbers of ducks, including a handsome Paradise duck, picked up scraps in the yard. The cry of these birds exactly expressed the predicament of the Thornhills. The warning cry of the Paradise drake sounded like, 'hook it, hook it', while the duck despairingly answered, 'where, where?'[1] Centre Hill with tame birds fluttering around the home and out stations, presented an idyllic picture of colonial life to visitors. One of these was Baron Anatole von Hügel whom Edward described as having 'something to do with the British Museum; he is out here for his health and is spending his time collecting the different birds and plants of New Zealand.'[2] Von Hügel was only just in time to find the indigenous fauna and

[1] T. H. Pott, *On Recent Changes in the Fauna of New Zealand*, 1872, 12 pp.

[2] Anatole von Hügel (1854–1928) on his return from the Antipodes became curator of the Cambridge University Museum of Archaeology and Ethnology.

flora of New Zealand. Not only were English weeds overrunning the countryside, but English birds were being introduced by settlers. With song thrushes in the bushes and their own flocks of sheep on the pastures, settlers could feel they had the best of the Old and the New Worlds. They forgot that to their New Zealand-born children the native birds, which the parents so ruthlessly slaughtered, would be the home birds. A Rangitata sheep farmer sadly noted in the 1870s that 'the disappearance of the native fauna is the natural sequence of Anglo-Saxon colonisation' and wondered how many among 'the busy swarm of men pressing onward in the struggle for wealth or position . . . would think of turning aside' to save either the fauna or flora of their adopted land.[1]

In the 1860s the efforts of individuals to change the antipodean environment to meet their own needs and inclinations were being reinforced by those of acclimatisation societies. In May 1867 George Thornhill wrote: 'An Acclimatisation Society has been started in Southland for the purpose of stocking the rivers with fish and the forests with game. There are plenty of rabbits in some places; a few deer and Kangaroo have also been turned out, but they will not afford any sport for some years. I have written to Willy to ask him to try and get me some French partridges. They are very hardy birds and ought to thrive very well here as there are plenty of berries on the ground in winter, and any quantity of insects and seeds during the rest of the year.' A partridge from India (*Alectoris graeca*), not from France, was eventually acclimatised in Southland. Within a decade the rabbits, which George approvingly noted were plentiful in some places, had undermined the prospects of many run owners. In 1875 Edward wrote, 'We have got an immense number of rabbits at Centre Hill now, they have completely overrun the country'.

The formation of acclimatisation societies in the mid-nineteenth century was man's response to the demands of rapidly increasing populations in deteriorating environments. The most pressing need in the United Kindom was to feed a determinedly carnivorous nation. The soaring imagination of the naturalist, Frank Buckland (1826–1880), envisaged that the herds of Shorthorns and of Southdowns on English pastures

[1] T. H. Pott, op. cit.

should be reinforced by the bison, eland and llama. Buckland, however, came down to earth when he introduced trout from English chalk streams into the rivers of New Zealand, and bumble bees to pollinate the antipodean fields of red clover. When George Thornhill returned to New Zealand in 1878, after a fruitless search in England for 'a good berth', his only assets were the bumble bees entrusted to him by Buckland. These might improve the prospects of the colony, but did little to help his own. The fauna and flora introduced into New Zealand by the settlers gave rise to a Maori saying, 'as the white man's rat has driven away the native rat, so the European fly drives away our own, and the clover kills our fern, so will the Maoris disappear before the white man himself.'[1]

By the 1870s, however, the white man himself was retreating before the rabbits he had introduced as game. The rabbit pest and the depression were emptying hundreds of runs and threatening the whole future of sheep farming in New Zealand; and in the face of mounting disasters outside the Thornhills took to reading indoors. Since they constantly demanded from home travel and historical books rather than 'trashy' novels, this indulgence could be camouflaged as self-improvement. But after the severe winter of 1874 the realities of crippling debts, falling prices and the rabbit pest could no longer be ignored. With money left by their father, who had died in 1868, Cudbert and William took another run at Venlaw, nearer Invercargill; and left George and Edward in possession at Centre Hill. Since the most hardworking and experienced run owners could not make sheep farming pay in the mid 1870s, debts only accumulated at Centre Hill and started building up at Venlaw. First Cudbert and then George went to England to see if relations were prepared to save the sheep runs or provide for other openings outside New Zealand. When he was returning disappointed to New Zealand, Cudbert met an Anglo-Indian coffee planter from the Nilgiris. He married the planter's daughter and secured a share of the plantation where he lived for the rest of his life. The rigours of New Zealand were forgotten among the rolling hills where the sweet-scented Nilgiri Lily abounded, and heliotrope flourished in the

<hr>

[1] *The Natural History Review*, January 1864, No. XIII, pp. 123–7, J. D. Hooker, op. cit.

hedgerows. Just before his death in 1904 he was visited by his younger brother, Henry, who had not seen him for forty years. Henry found Cudbert, 'looking very thin, but without any gray hair! And younger and better than he expected'.

The years did not deal so kindly with George. During his London visit (1877–1878) relations admired and pitied, his fascinating, but delicate bride, Esther McIvor; but financial aid only came from his ever compassionate sister who, though without a home herself, parted with £1,500 to save Centre Hill.[1] Left in charge of the run, Edward occupied himself by practising the violin and observing the transit of Venus. He was often joined by William who had only been kept at Venlaw by Cudbert's steadying influence. When the embittered George returned to New Zealand, Centre Hill was past saving. His sister's money was not enough to enable George to realise his adolescent longing, which he never outgrew, of making a fortune by speculation rather than work.

Venlaw and Centre Hill were abandoned; the settlement of the Centre Hill estate brought George about £45, so he fell back on his wife's family, the McIvors. Less fortunate, Edward and William had to fend for themselves, and both drifted into towns. William found clerical work in Invercargill with 'a fair screw' that enabled him to marry Nora Williams, a doctor's daughter. George found her 'an insignificant little thing and I'm afraid not very amiable'; but by this time few welcomed George, always in search of a loan. A wife and family of girls, one of whom had Ellen's beautiful auburn hair, could not anchor William. He drifted from job to job; was in charge of a Fish Hatchery in North Island, dabbled in electioneering work and was even reported in 1912 to have obtained a 'government appointment.' But by 1913 his young brother, Henry, was writing, 'no one seems to hear from our Will (who was a rum old bird by all acounts)'. The jaunty boy who had been so careful of his appearance had long ceased to care what anyone thought of him. Edward, who had probably received some small sum from the sale of Centre Hill, listened to the enticements of 'a bad crowd' and started digging for gold near Riverton. The claim was a good one but failed from

[1] This sum and Mrs Siddons' diamond ring was left to Minnie by her grandmother Siddons who also left George and Edward £500 each.

bad management, and Edward found employment on the Riverton tramway. By 1910 he had not become one of the city fathers but was a person of some consequence in the now thriving town: 'I am the owner of a large Billiard Saloon here, but don't get the general impression that most people do that it is low down. I am received and welcome to the houses of the best families here, among them the Parson of the Church of England, where I am due for a garden party on the 9th of next month [February 1910] . . . I have taken on the game of Bowls and have become very fond of it.' The 'Radley tone' was still faintly ringing in Edward's ears. His last letter to Minnie in October 1915 announced the death of George and complained of the funeral expenses.

George was no more successful at managing for the McIvors at Victoria Park Farm than he had been at Centre Hill. The windfall of £500 left him by his grandmother did not help as 'much against the advice of his friends, George put all he had in mining and lost everything.' Worn out by the strain his wife, Tassey, with her two children, Robert and Hazel, returned to her parents.

George lived by doing odd jobs, such as rabbiting, chopping wood and harvesting; and spent his leisure writing long and complaining letters to his sister: 'I often think what on earth I was created for, and why I have such good health when other far better men die off like rotten sheep.' Even his good health was a grievance to George, and even greater grievances were the successes or good fortune of others. When he heard of his sister's engagement in 1880 to Charles Pearson Downe (plates 36 and 37) his congratulations took a strange form: 'I can't write to Mr Downe for I should be sorry to let him know he was marrying the sister of a beggar'. George's attacks on his relations who seemed to be having 'a pretty good time of it' were particularly venomous. The radicalism of his vinegar-manufacturing cousin, Mark Beaufoy, was assumed 'no doubt only for the sake of popularity'; while the conservatism of Mark's mother was equally at fault since little of her wealth found its way to New Zealand. George wrapped himself in a cocoon of self-pity, 'no one would ever think, even if they knew Aunt George had relations, that starving wretches like us could possibly be them . . . the best I can hope for is that we shall be utterly forgotten in a very short time.' But Anne Beaufoy, who had made her way against hardships as great as any George had faced, held her own until the end of her life. All those who remember her in old age at Frimley stress her presence and vital personality. Shortly before her death in December 1894 her daughter, Rita, wrote to Minnie: 'Mother is gradually getting weaker, but by slow degrees . . . the doctor thinks she cannot live more than two or three days; but her vitality is so wonderful that he says no one can predict when the end is likely to come. She is still conscious when really awake. She quite knew you had come and talked of you afterwards.'

Like his drifting cousin, John, George Thornhill attributed his misfortunes to 'the general cussedness of an upside-down world' which favoured the undeserving who ranged from royalty to working men. When Prince Alfred visited New Zealand after the suppression of Maori unrest, George wrote: 'The Prince has been causing great excitement in Dunedin. He was drunk about half the day, and one or two men from this part (fearful cads) had the honour, as they thought it, of losing bets to him. The Maoris are more quiet in the north; some of the Friendlies sent an address to the Prince, but I don't suppose it means much.' If the prince did not merit his good fortune, neither, in George's opinion, did the working-class immigrants who easily secured work. He complained: 'If I could conduct myself like an ordinary working man, I, no doubt, could get work; but somehow I can't do that yet, but may sink to that level later on. Employers will give working men a job before a broken down swell, although the latter may be just as well able to do the work . . . New Zealand is rapidly recovering from the depression that for so long kept it down, and I only hope we may rise with it. The present government, though, are a queer lot but in all probability there will soon be a change.'

This was written in 1893 and the Liberals in New Zealand were to remain in power another eighteen years. Largely thanks to their benevolent étatism George's children were able to rise; but George and the many of his contemporaries who had failed to thrive in a new social climate were past rehabilitation. George's last words were to call for his boots so that he might get up in the morning; but it was too late for him to rise to the level of 'an ordinary working man'.

The lives of the misfits who settled in New Zealand in the 1860s were not wasted; their children, nurtured amid hardships, throve when better times came. Travellers to New Zealand in the mid-nineteenth century were struck with the healthiness of the children and with their 'pert and independent' ways. Many, like George's children, had to be early wage earners and their know-all attitude was the inevitable corollary of their parents' supineness. From an early age Robert and Hazel Thornhill helped support their mother and then trained themselves for careers as an engineer and photographer. Hazel married well and happily; her letter to Minnie, written in August 1916, triumphantly rebuts her father's prognostications that his whole family would be 'wiped out . . . and utterly forgotten in a very short time':

> 'I am sure my father's death would be a great shock to you as it was to us all. It was so sudden . . . As you say it might have all been so different but, Auntie dear, you probably only heard one side and there may have been faults on both sides. Naturally I side with my mother . . . her life has not been a bed of roses by any means . . . Neither has mine for that matter; but thank goodness, I've always been able to hold my own and keep my head up in spite of the knocks and bruises. Such is Life, Auntie, isn't it? But I hope to be as happy as I can be now, with a man who is 'one of the best' [Harold McDowell Smith] . . . Hal is doing very well down here; he has only been down three years and has already done the biggest buildings ever built here as yet, against a lot of opposition . . . Robert has enlisted. . . I do not know of a family here, Auntie, that has not sent someone; and such numbers of them were killed at the Dardanelles and all seemingly wasted . . .'

Two years later Hazel's husband, Private H. McDowell Smith in the New Zealand Expeditionary Forces, was in England. He and over 100,000 of his countrymen were repaying the debt they owed the mother country whose policy, though often uncertain and sometimes unwise, had furnished the misfits, the ambitious and the needy with opportunities for betterment which were lacking at home. The exodus of young men after 1914 provided Edward Thornhill with his last grievance:

'Almost half the young fellows have left here for the Front and it makes a great difference to my business'.

It is fitting that a story which began with the mercantile audacity of Captain Cudbert Thornhill and with the Commercial astuteness of Mark Beaufoy at Cuper's Garden should end with the wanderings of their descendants in New Zealand. In securing maritime and industrial supremacy Britain pledged future generations to rootless lives. By the mid-nineteenth century a nation of Ishmaelites was on the move. Railways carried villagers to industrial centres, tourists and emigrants to ports and servants from one situation to another. Wherever men sojourned or settled they endeavoured to create the surroundings with which they were familiar. Countrymen tended their pots of pansies and caged song birds in city squalor. Seedsmen were pestered by Anglo-Indians demanding perennials suited to hot climates, and by settlers in New Zealand wanting vegetables. Throughout the world Britons were seeking to strike new roots in alien soils.

The lives of the Thornhills who left Lyston to wander from country to country and from difficulty to difficulty tell the whole story of their generation.

NOTES ON SOURCES USED IN CHAPTER ONE

It is convenient to place under this heading works which have been frequently used for every chapter. My debt is great to the following:

Gwendolyn Beaufoy, *Leaves from a Beech Tree*, 1930[1]

W. L. Burn, *The Age of Equipoise*, A Study of the Mid-Victorian Generation, 1st ed. 1964, 1968 ed. used.

J. Burnett, *Plenty and Want*, 1966.

R. C. K. Ensor, *England 1870–1914*, 1930.

Gertrude Himmelfarb, *Victorian Minds*, 1968.

James Morris, *Pax Britannica*, The Climax of an Empire, 1968.

With authoritative works it is useful to consult the writings of contemporaries who were not always conscious of the import of events taking place around them. Foremost among these is *Punch* whose views were decided and often idiosyncratic on every contemporary issue. I am very grateful to the directors of *Punch* for permission to use quotations. Equally informative are the *Boy's Own Paper* (1879–1966) and the *Girl's Own Paper* (1880–1947). Both were concerned to instil practical virtues into the young with whose romantic aspirations neither publication had much sympathy. Two examples, taken from answers to correspondents, will suffice to indicate the trend of the editors' outlook:

> *Boy's Own Paper*, 11 November 1880, 'You are a sensible boy, Rufus. While other lads keep rabbits for pleasure alone, you want to combine profit. We will answer you as you deserve.'
>
> *Girl's Own Paper*, 2 April 1887, 'A schoolgirl of fifteen should devote her thoughts and energies to her education . . . Have you no common-sense nor self-respect? We do not know what "a griffen-like style of

[1] This printed selection from the Beaufoy and Siddons documents is invaluable since many of the family records were destroyed by enemy action in the Second World War.

244

beauty, awfully handsome", may be. That of some ferocious, murdering bandit, perhaps. You have no business
to be looking at strange men at all, bandit or not.'

This reply suggests that Byron was still being hidden under
schoolgirl pillows. Two works concerning Byron have been
consulted:

Thomas More, *Letters and Journals of Lord Byron*: with
Notices of his Life, 2 Vols., 1830.

Peter Quennell, *Romantic England*, Writing and Painting,
1717–1851, 1970.

On the life and art of Sarah Siddons the following have been
used:

J. Boaden, *Memoirs of Mrs Siddons*, 1837, 2 Vols.

Yvonne Ffrench, *Mrs Siddons: Tragic Actress*, 1936.

Nina Kennard, *Mrs Siddons*, 1887.

Elizabeth Mair, *Recollections of the Past*, 1877.

R. Manvell, *Sarah Siddons*, 1970.

Florence Parsons (Mrs Clement Parsons), *The Incomparable
Siddons*, 1909.

Writing between the total involvement of Boaden and the
wider researches of the later writers, perhaps Mrs Kennard
gives the most complete picture of the actress and her times.

I am very grateful for kind help I have received from libra-
rians and archivists at:

The India Office Library and India Office Records, where
permission was given for the reproduction of the illustration of
Calcutta.

The Royal Institution of Naval Architects.

The Trustees of the Victoria and Albert Museum who gave
permission to reproduce the portrait of Sarah Siddons.

The Trustees of the British Museum who allowed the reproductions of the mezzotint of Gainsborough's Mark Beaufoy.

Also I am indebted to Mr G. J. Leversuch of the Stanmore,
Edgware and Harrow Historical Society for information concerning the memorials in St John's Stanmore; and for directing me to Mark Beaufoy's obelisk at Bushey.

NOTES ON SOURCES USED IN CHAPTER TWO

For help in this chapter I am much indebted to officials of the Record Offices of Essex and the Greater London Council; particularly for the production of Tithe Apportionments, Land-Tax Returns and other records for Lyston and Stanmore; and also of the Public Record Office for the relevant Census Returns.

Information was also kindly sent by the West Suffolk Record Office.

I am most grateful for help given by Foxearth and Lyston inhabitants:

Mr and Mrs H. Clover of Long Melford who had close associations with Lyston.

Mr and Mrs E. Gardiner of Lyston Hall, both of whom come from families long settled in the district.

Canon James Pennell, lately rector of Foxearth with Pentlow, curate in charge of Lyston with Borley.

The late Miss R. Plumb of Lyston Gardens whose father, Albert Plumb, worked in the gardens of Lyston Hall before the Second World War.

NOTES ON SOURCES USED IN CHAPTER THREE

In his *A Priest to the Temple; or the Country Parson, his Character, and rule of Holy Life*, written in 1632, published in 1652, George Herbert wrote a handbook for rural incumbents who probably in his lifetime, and certainly later, maintained a determined independence of conduct and outlook.

That the green mould so widely discussed in the debate on 'The Church in Relation to the Rural Populations' at the Church Congress of 1886 (pp. 118–142) was not the touch of nature making country parsons kin is indicated by works such as:

J. Hervey, *Meditations and Contemplations*, including Meditations among the Tombs, 26th ed., 1799.

A. Huxtable, *The Present Prices*, 1850.

F. Kilvert, *Diary 1870–9*. ed. W. Plomer, London, 1944.

G. White, *The Natural History of Selborne*, 1st ed. 1789, 1908 ed. used.

J. Woodforde, *Diary of a Country Parson*, 1758–1781 World's Classics ed. 1949, used.

Even Anthony Trollope, whose bluff, active and far from bookish parsons were hailed by his contemporaries as typical, realised the gulf which separated Josiah Crawley from Archdeacon Grantly.

A full and most entertaining summary of the curate's position in the nineteenth century is given in A. Tindal Hart's *The Curate's Lot*, 1970; and church music during this period is described by B. Rainbow, *The Choral Revival in the Anglican Church 1839–1872*, 1970.

Those who have given much kind help include:

The archivists of the Essex Record Office, where information was obtained concerning the Lyston and Foxearth churches, and of the Dorset Record Office where the family papers of the Bowers of Iwerne Minister are deposited.

I am very grateful to:

The Librarian of the Peterborough Public Library and to officials in the office of the *Peterborough Gazette* for much kind assistance.

The Reverend Mother Superior of the Convent of St John the Baptist, Clewer, kindly allowed inspection of the chapels and some of the convent buildings and grounds; and also searched the records for Sophia Russell of South Lambeth whose bid for independence in entering the sisterhood in the 1860s does not appear to have succeeded.

NOTES ON SOURCES USED IN CHAPTER FOUR

In this chapter great use has been made of the Beaufoy letters and papers, published by the wife of Mark H. Beaufoy's eldest son, Henry Mark:

Gwendolyn Beaufoy, *Leaves from a Beech Tree*, 1930.

The vinegar-brewing activities of the Beaufoys at South Lambeth have been fully described by:

A. W. Slater, 'The Vinegar Brewing Industry', in *Industrial Archaeology*, August 1970, Vol. 7, No. 3, pp. 292–309.

For personal reminiscences of Caron Place at the turn of this century I am most grateful to Mrs Hilda Clowes, the daughter of Mark Hanbury Beaufoy (1854–1922), who kindly provided the election photograph of her father, probably taken in 1892.

In the early nineteenth century horticulture was the interest of many of the nobility and market gardening the means of livelihood for large numbers of families living on the outskirts of London. Most of the leading gardeners committed their theories and criticisms of fellow horticulturalists to paper.

'At the particular request of many respectable florists' James Maddock of Walworth wrote:

> *The Florist's Directory . . . to which is added a Supplementary Dissertation on Soils, Manures etc. with . . . An Appendix . . . by Samuel Curtis* [son-in-law of William Curtis], 1822.

Thomas Hogg stated that Maddock's work was 'a very extensive compilation of pirated extracts from Justice, Emmerton, and Hogg' in his:

Concise and Practical Treatise on the Growth and Culture of the Carnation . . . including a Dissertation on Soils and Manures, . . . 1824.

More canny or generous, Charles McIntosh praised the efforts of all his eminent fellow gardeners in:

The Practical Gardener and Modern Horticulturalist, Vols. I and II, 1828.

Like the gardening authorities the topographical writers on London in the early nineteenth century were inclined to copy, and not always accurately, information from earlier works. The exuberant account of Beaufoy's vinegar yard in Cuper's Garden given by T. Pennant in his *Some Account of London*, 1813, was copied with a few variations, by:

Priscilla Wakefield, *Perambulations in London . . .* 1814.

T. Allen, *The History and Antiquities of the Parish of Lambeth* . . . , 1826,
and even by E. W. Brayley in his *Topographical History of Surrey*, 1850, Vol. III, although by that time the Beaufoys had been established in the South Lambeth Road for thirty-eight years. The correct location of the vinegar yard was established by J. Tanswell in his *History and Antiquities of Lambeth*, 1858. Though like many of his contemporary topographers Tanswell was most interested in antiquities, he included accounts of the workhouse, Beaufoy's Ragged School and industrial undertakings. Antiquarian interests also predominate in Walter Besant's *South London*, 1899. But Besant did take a long look at contemporary South London which he considered, 'a city without a municipality, without a centre, without a civic history . . . its residents have no local patriotism or enthusiasm – one cannot imagine a man proud of New Cross'. Writing earlier and having marked theatrical interests, Edward Walford in his *London Old and New*, 1873, Vol. VI took a more sympathetic view of the South Bank where 'sensational drama' flourished.

The immense labour of sifting the accounts of early London topographers and of describing existing buildings of architectural interest was undertaken by the London County Council and incorporated in the monumental *Survey of London*; the volumes which deal with Lambeth and its environs are: Volume XXIII, part 1, 1951 and Volume XXVI, part 2, 1956.

Topographical and historical accounts of a district indicate the main trends of development. The day-to-day concerns of the inhabitants can be gleaned from deeds, registers, newspaper reports, business histories and, perhaps most important, from the recollections of those long associated with the district. In the course of the study of Lambeth numbers of people have been bothered with queries and I am most grateful for all the help so kindly given by the following organisations and individuals:

William Bloore and Son Limited, 55–77 South Lambeth Road, SW8. As well as giving an account of his early recollections of South Lambeth, Mr R. G. Bloore kindly showed me over the offices and timber yard.

Brand and Company Limited, now at Greatham Hartlepool, Durham.

British Vinegars Limited, 87 South Lambeth Road, SW8. Mr G. F. Bond kindly gave information and also permission to see over the works and to take photographs.

Price's Patent Candle Company Limited, Belmont Works, Battersea, SW11. Established in the 1840s at Vauxhall, the Company moved in the 1860s to Battersea where the name Belmont was retained.

Seager, Evans and Company Limited, 20 Queen Anne's Gate, London SW1.

The headmaster of the City of London School, Victoria Embankment, Mr J. A. Boyes, who also kindly gave permission to photograph the bust of Henry Beaufoy.

The executive secretary, Mr T. O'Grady, of the Linnean Society of London, Burlington House, Piccadilly, London W1.

The archivist, Miss Y. Williams, The Minet Library, Knatchbull Road, Brixton, SE5.

The archivists of the Public Record Offices of Bristol and the Greater London Council.

The Reverend P. E. Naylor, vicar of St Anne's, South Lambeth and Mr Michael Gaunt, Archivist of St Anne's.

Miss H. Butler and the members of the St Anne's Evergreen Club for Old Age Pensioners, South Lambeth.

Mr R. J. Wood of the London Fire Brigade, who provided information concerning Frederick Hodges, renowned distiller and fire-fighter in South Lambeth during the 1860s. Evidences of his exploits may be found in the Museum of the London Fire Brigade at Winchester House, the most fascinating of the smaller London museums.

For kind permission to reproduce prints, drawings, and paintings, I am very grateful to:

The Keeper of Prints, Guildhall Library.

The Trustees of the British Museum and the Victoria and Albert Museum.

NOTES ON SOURCES USED IN CHAPTER FIVE

All those who find difficulty in penetrating the thickets of religious controversy in the last century must be grateful to:

O. Chadwick, *The Victorian Church*, Part I, 1966, Part II, 1970.

That many of the controversial issues were influenced by movements on the Continent and were often pursued to the exclusion of social problems is suggested by:

C. Booth, *Life and Labour of People in London*, Series 3, Religious Influences, 1902.

K. S. Inglis, *Churches and the Working Classes in England*, 1963.

A. R. Vidler, *The Church in an Age of Revolution*, Vol. V, The Pelican History of the Church, 1961.

The religious scene has also been viewed in retrospect with reference to specific issues by:

B. L. Clarke, *Church Building in the Nineteenth Century*, 1938.

Joyce Coombs, *Judgement on Hatcham*, the History of a Religious Struggle 1877–1886, 1969.

That the High, Low and Broad Church parties shared more ideas in common than was generally believed is suggested by:

N. Dearmer, *The Life of Percy Dearmer*, 1940.

C. L. Eastlake, *A History of the Gothic Revival*, 1872.

E. Hodder, *The Life and Work of the Seventh Earl of Shaftesbury*, 1886, 3 Vols.

W. H. Hutchings, *Life and Letters of T. T. Carter*, 1903.

C. Kingsley, *Scientific Lectures and Essays*, 1880.

F. Kingsley, *Charles Kingsley, His Letters and Memories of His Life*, 1876.

F. Maurice, *The Life of Frederick Denison Maurice*, chiefly told in his own letters, 1884, 2 Vols.

The church studies in this chapter are in such a minor key that wide use has been made of popular and fictional works.

C. Bede, *Mattins and Mutton's*; or, The Beauty of Brighton, 1866, 2 Vols., though coming out in favour of morning service rather than mattins, Bede gives an entertaining and not unfair assessment of the popular Brighton churches.

Charlotte Elizabeth Tonna confessed to having succumbed to 'the terrible excitement of Shakespeare'. That she was not unacquainted with Byron is suggested by the titles of some of her tracts: *Zadoc, the Outcast of Israel* (1825), *Izram, a Mexican Tale* (1826), and *The Convent Bell* (1845).

Although *The Guardian* 1846–1949 was the mouthpiece of moderate High Churchmen, the reporting in this paper on home, foreign and church affairs was marked by an honest endeavour to ascertain the truth rather than to score controversial points.

In describing the Christian beliefs of the *London Labour and London Poor*, 1851, and of the middle classes in *The Greatest Plague of Life*, 1841, written with his brother Augustus, Henry Mayhew was concerned to separate the basic Christian tenents from the contemporary religious chauvinism. This concern was his legacy to *Punch* for the appearance of which as a 'Cleanly Comic' in 1841 Mayhew was responsible.

Mayhew's association with *Punch* was described by his son: Athol Mayhew, *A Jorum of 'Punch'*, 1895.

Also concerned with the 'dark populations' was Thomas Holmes who in the 1870s started work as a police-court missionary in Lambeth. His *Pictures and Problems from London Police Courts*, 1900, are less harrowing than Mayhew's, but the 'slain souls' among whom he worked haunted Holmes all his life.

In the second decade of the nineteenth century the moral authority of churchmen was shared by laymen, like Samuel Smiles, preaching the efficacy of self-help. Among the most popular of these writers was:

W. H. Davenport Adams, *The Secret of Success; or, How to Get on in the World*, 1879.

On the question of religious reading Davenport Adams concluded with the observation: 'A constant study of the Bible we take for granted.'

Those who have given much kind help include:

The Archivists of the Greater London Record Office, where the memoranda book of W. A. Harrison has been deposited.

The Rev. P. Naylor, vicar of St Anne's, South Lambeth.

Mr M. Gaunt, the church archivist who kindly supplied the photograph of W. A. Harrison.

Miss H. Butler with members of the Evergreen Club, a

member of which, the late Mrs Curtis, kindly supplied the photograph of W. A. Morris under whom she served in the Guild of Perseverance.

For permission to reproduce prints and drawings I am grateful to:

The Keeper of Prints, The Guildhall Library.

The Trustees of the Victoria and Albert Museum.

I am also grateful to Dr J. S. Lawton, the Warden of St Deiniol's, for the use of the excellent facilities of the Residential Library at Hawarden.

NOTES ON SOURCES USED IN CHAPTER SIX

The book most used to obtain some background for the resorts visited by the Beaufoys and Thornhills has been:

A. B. Granville, *The Spas of England and Principal Bathing Places of England, 1841*, 2 Vols.

Though he investigated most assiduously the social, sanitary and medical amenities of all the resorts (among which he mentioned Manchester) he visited, the lively doctor felt the real drawback to them all was the stolid English visitors.

Information concerning Eller Close and the places visited by the Beaufoy party during their stay at Grasmere was very kindly collected in the Lake District by the Misses N. and K. O'Driscoll.

I am also indebted to the late Mrs C. A. H. O'Driscoll for information concerning Bournemouth as a resort at the turn of the twentieth century.

Brother Michael Sherry, of Hopwood Hall, Manchester, kindly let me see the MSS of his two articles, 'Bournemouth – A Victorian Town' and 'The Past and Present Holiday Industry of Bournemouth'.

NOTES ON SOURCES USED IN CHAPTER SEVEN

In the second half of the nineteenth century travel handbooks and guides were legion; and large numbers of travellers returned the compliment by recording their adventures and impressions. It has, therefore, only been possible to consult a few of these authorities.

THE RIVIERA

The praise accorded W. Miller, *Wintering in the Riviera* with Notes of Travel in Italy and France and Practical Hints to Travellers, 1879, indicates the widespread need for such a book:

> 'Mr Miller has fortunately remembered that there are still a few men and women left who have not been all over Europe, and he has not disdained to give particulars which some less considerate writers pretend to think unnecessary'.

Manchester Guardian

NORWAY

William Dawson Hooker, *Notes on Norway* or a brief Journal of a Tour made to the Northern Parts of Norway in the Summer of 1836, published privately Glasgow, 1837 and 1839, and Thomas Robert Malthus, *The Travel Dairies*, including The Scandinavian Journal, 1799, The Continental Tour, 1825, and The Scottish Holiday, 1826, 1966 ed. by Patricia James set a high standard which was not always reached by succeeding travellers who published their adventures and impressions. The most individual, if not the most informative, among these are:

Lieut. W. H. Breton, R.N. *Scandinavian Sketches*, 1835.

John Milford, *Norway and her Laplanders in 1841*, with a few Hints to the Salmon Fisher, 1842.

J. C. Phythian, *Scenes of Travel in Norway*, 1877.

Lizzie Vickers, *Old Norway and its Fjords*, or a Holiday in Norseland, 1893, gave an account which well illustrates the outlook of enlightened middle-class Liberals with whom travel in Norway was very popular.

W. Mattieu Williams, *Through Norway with a Knapsack*, 1859.

The modern book on northern Norway which has been most consulted is an excellent account:

F. N. Stagg, *North Norway*, 1952.

I am very grateful for much help given in the public libraries of Bergen and Trondheim, particularly for the opportunity to consult the following excellent town histories:

Bergen 1814–1914 ed. Carl Geelmuyden, 1914, 3 Vols.

Trondheim Bys Historie, ed. J. Shreiner, Vols. III and IV, 1955 and 1958.

TRAVELS IN SOUTH-EAST EUROPE

The Danube

W. Beattie, *The Danube*, 1844. This follows the course of the Danube from source to mouth, and is illustrated by W. H. Bartlett (1809–1853) whose drawings helped to popularise travel in Holland, Switzerland, Egypt and the Holy Land.

R. T. Claridge, *A Guide along the Danube*, 1837.

C. B. Elliott, *Travels in the Three Great Empires of Austria, Russia and Turkey*, 1838, Vol. I.

Murray's Handbook for Travellers in Southern Germany, 1838, has a section on the Danube from Ulm to the Black Sea; but, as William Denton observed, from Semlin (Zemun) downstream guide books tended to 'grow chary of information'.

M. J. Quin, *A Steam Voyage Down the Danube*, 1836. Quin was the first Englishman to publish his impressions of travel down the Danube; and wondered that 'this noble river . . . was so little known to Europe'.

Serbia

J. Cvijić, *La Peninsule Balkanique*, 1918, Jovan Cvijić (1865–1927), the great Serb geographer, dealt fully with the influence of historical events and of the terrain on the development of Serbia.

W. Denton, *Serbia and the Serbians*, 1862.

Mary Durham, *Through the Lands of the Serb*, 1904. This account opens with the author stressing the difficulties facing a tourist in Serbia. 'He seldom needs to complain that he has heard one side only; but there is a Catholic side, an Orthodox side, a Mahommedan side, there are German, Slav, Italian, Turkish and Albanian sides; and when he has heard them all he feels far less capable of forming an opinion on the Eastern Question than he did before.'

Mary Durham, *The Burden of the Balkans*, 1905. *Twenty*

Years of Balkan Tangle, 1920.

W. T. Greive, 'The Church and People of Serbia,' article in *Vacation Tourists* 1862–3, ed. F. Galton.

Georgina Mackenzie and Adeline Kirby, *The Slavonic Provinces of Turkey-in-Europe*, 1877, 2 Vols.

In his preface W. G. Gladstone wrote: 'I do not mean to disparage the labours and services of others when I say that in my opinion, no diplomatist, no consul, no traveller, among our countrymen, has made such a valuable contribution to our means of knowledge in this important matter, as was made by Miss Mackenzie and Miss Irby, when they published in 1867 [*The Turks, the Greeks, and the Slavons*] their travels in some of the Slavonian Provinces of European Turkey.'

Julia Pardoe, *The City of the Magyar*, or Hungary and her Institutions in 1839–40, 1840, 3 Vols. The romantic Miss Pardoe was fervently pro-Magyar. Concerning Slav ambitions she wrote: They 'have even begun to cherish dreams of establishing in the country of the Magyars a Sclavonic Monarchy! A wild vision, which arouses the ridicule of the Hungarians'.

H. de Windt, *Through Savage Europe*, 1904.

NOTES ON SOURCES USED IN CHAPTER EIGHT

The main sources for British activities in India during the late eighteenth and early nineteenth centuries have been:

The Cambridge History of India, 1929, Vol. V.

J. W. Kaye, *The History of the Sepoy War in India 1857–8*, 1865–1876, 3 Vols. *Lives of Indian Officers*, 1867, 2 Vols.

Though sometimes his rolling periods carried him away, Sir John Kaye (1814–1876) did believe, as he wrote in his introduction to Volume III: 'If it be not Truth it is not History, and Truth lies very far below the surface . . . For History is not the growth of Inspiration, but of Evidence'; and he sifted his sources, many of them the private papers of his contemporaries, thoroughly. That his thirteen years in India had not left him unaffected by the prevailing Anglo-Indian choler is suggested by his view that: 'The Historian who shrinks from controversy has mistaken his vocation.'

That the controversies of the mid-nineteenth century, especially as regards land tenure and *zamindari* have not yet been settled is clearly shown in:

Doreen Warriner, *Land Reform in Principle and Practice*, 1969. Chapter VI, India, pp. 136–218.

The changes in the Indian countryside that charmed Mark Thornhill are suggested by:

O. Spate, *India and Pakistan*, 1st ed. 1954, 2nd ed. 1957 used.

Mark Thornhill's poetic vision and command of prose gave him a lead in the over-crowded field of books on India. His works on which this chapter is largely based are:

The Personal Adventures and Experiences of a Magistrate during the Rise, Progress and Suppression of the Indian Mutiny, 1884.

Indian Fairy Tales, 1889.

Haunts and Hobbies of an Indian Official, 1899.

I am grateful to Miss Brenda Lang of Charmouth for allowing me to use the MS letters of her grandparents, Edward and Hebe Lang, written from India 1870–1874. These letters have been carefully annotated by the late Dr W. D. Lang, F.R.S. (1879–1966).

I am also grateful to Mrs Penny of Mappowder who kindly allowed me to reproduce the photograph of skinning a tiger, and also a drawing by her uncle, Major Littleton Albert Powys of the 59th Regiment, who died 'regretted by officers and men' on 6 August 1879.

In India as in other countries, social patterns whether in villages or among European communities began to change rapidly after 1918. Those who remember India before the First World War can bring to mind ways of living which in the villages had remained unchanged for centuries and among the European communities had been established in the 1860s. Accounts of life in India on the eve of the First World War were supplied by my uncles, F. H. W. Kerr (1885–1958), missionary and botanist, Dublin University Mission, Hazaribagh and W. J. Kerr (1880–1956), chief engineer of the Public Works Department, Bengal; and by the late Mrs Norah Trevor who as a child was taken to visit a shrivelled old man, General H. G. Delafosse. Mentioned by Kaye (II, pp. 343–8), Delafosse was one of the four survivors from Cawnpore garrison, which capitulated 25 June 1857.

I have to thank the assistants in the India Office Records and Library, and Print Room for assistance.

The Hindoo Text Seller from H. Mayhew's *London Labour and the London Poor* (1851) is reproduced by permission of the Trustees of the British Museum.

The postcards reproduced in this and the succeeding chapter were sent home by members of my family early in this century.

NOTES ON SOURCES USED IN CHAPTER NINE

When by the end of the nineteenth century the jungle ways had been cleared for Europeans, they were trodden by thousands of officials, memsahibs, missionaries and fact-finders from Britain who were determined to publish their views. Among the accounts by women one is outstanding for its fairness, astringency and humour:

Sara Duncan, *The Simple Adventures of a Memsahib*, 1893, Nelson ed., 1908, used.

In the late eighteenth and early nineteenth centuries women in India lacked the energy or the inclination to publish their impressions, but many wrote home at length. Some of these letters and also parts of the journals of Emily Eden, have been excellently edited by:

J. K. Standford, *Ladies in the Sun*, The Memsahib's India, 1790–1860, 1962.

The backwash of the Revolution accounts for the prevalence of literary ladies in the 1830s and 1840s, and India was well served by two of these. The Honourable Emily Eden, sister of Lord Auckland, Governor-General 1836–1841, took a long, cool look at Indian affairs in:

Emily Eden, *Up the Country 1837–1840*, 2 Vols., 1866.

Lady Florentia Sale was equally dispassionate about the confusion, mismanagement and horror of the retreat from Kabul; she wisely concluded her published diary with the words: 'Where the blame rests, it is not for *me* to determine.':

Lady Sale, *A Journal of the Disasters in Afghanistan 1841–2*, 1844.

Between the accounts of the redoubtable Florentia Sale and

the clear-sighted Emily Eden and those of the women who took India in their stride in the late nineteenth century there are comparatively few published records by, or about, women in India. A woman's view of the Mutiny was given by:

Lady Julia Inglis, *The Siege of Lucknow*, A Diary, 1893.

The letters of Tal and Ellen Thornhill and of Hebe Lang cover the 1860s and early 1870s when women in India had ceased to be pioneers and had not yet started to record their careers, or their travellers' tales for the popular press. An account of an early woman missionary in India appears in:

Agnes Giberne, *A Lady of England*, The Life and Letters of Charlotte Tucker, 1895.

Agnes Giberne was an Anglo-Indian child who made good in England as a writer of popular scientific books.

I am most grateful for kind assistance and informatiom from:

The Librarian, P and O Steam Navigation Company Beaufort House, Gravel Lane, London E. 1.

Mr L. Kimpton sent full records of the P and O captains and the ships appearing in the Thornhill and Lang papers.

The Departmental Records Officer, Post Office Records.

Mr R. S. Davidson, director of the Army and Navy Stores gave information and permission to inspect early catalogues. In 1971 The Army and Navy Stores Ltd. produced an excellent centenary account of Captain McCrea's venture and its development.

NOTES ON SOURCES USED IN CHAPTER TEN

When an attempt is made to describe life in an unvisited land, the dependence on written sources must be great. Throughout the chapter the following authorities have been invaluable:

E. S. Dellimore, *The New Zealand Guide*, 1952.

R. M. Laing and E. W. Blackwell, *Plants of New Zealand*, 1st ed. 1906, 7th ed., revised by E. J. Godley, 1964.

P. Moncrieff, *New Zealand Birds*, 1st ed., 5th ed. 1957.

Keith Sinclair, *A History of New Zealand*, 1959.

Descriptions of conditions in the 1860s have been taken from two published sources, which were selected as the authors had only one common characteristic – a willingness to make the best of life in a new country. Because of the diverse tastes of the authors nearly all aspects of a settler's life in New Zealand were covered by:

Lady F. N. Barker, *Station Life in New Zealand*, 1870.

S. Butler, *A First Year in Canterbury Settlement*, 1863.

As Radley College was so closely connected with the settlement of New Zealand in the 1860s, the influence of the founder, William Sewell, is of great interest. The work of Sewell and the development of the College have been admirably and entertainingly described by:

A. K. Boyd, *A History of Radley College, 1847–1947*, 1948.

By the kind courtesy of the Warden of Radley College, Mr D. R. W. Silk, buildings, archives and registers were inspected. I am also grateful for much help from Mr P. Crowson and Mr J. E. A. Morton.

An attempt was made to read William Sewell's *Sermons to Boys, Preached in the Chapel of St. Peter's College, Radley*, 1854; but, however impressive in the pulpit, Sewell's relentless piling of clause upon clause makes his addresses practically unreadable.

Some of the men who directed the destiny of New Zealand are described in:

W. Gisborne, *New Zealand Rulers and Statesmen, 1840–1897*, 1897.

H. E. L. Mellersh, *Fitzroy of the Beagle*, 1968.

The most able and the most unfathomable of those directing New Zealand affairs was Sir George Grey (1812–1898). He could commune with notables like Carlyle or the Maori chieftain, Heke, but he could not make himself intelligible to his less exalted contemporaries or to posterity. An admiring journalist attempted to pin down Grey's philosophy and describe his life's work of 'hammering up hearths for the Anglo-Saxon' in:

I. Milne, *The Romance of a Pro-Consul*, 1911.

Line engraving drawn by W. Hamilton of Sarah Siddons as a young woman.

2. Pierre Fombelle (1731–1802) with his grand-daughter Mary Fombelle (right), who married Mrs Siddons' son, George John, a servant of the East India Company.

3. Watercolour of Calcutta in the 1820s by J. B. Frazer.

Increasing numbers of home-keeping Britons were drawn within the Indian orbit in the early nineteenth century. Mrs Siddons had dreams of sailing to Calcutta to join her son.

4. Mark Beaufoy (1718–82), founder of the vinegar-making dynasty at Lambeth, mezzotint from a painting by Thomas Gainsborough.

5. Bust of Henry Beaufoy (1786–1851) in the entrance hall of the City of London School.

6. Mark Hanbury Beaufoy (1854–1922), from an election manifesto probably dated 1892.

7.   The Bensley and Thornhill grave in the ruined old St John's Church, Stanmore.

8.   Painting by Henry Eldridge (1769–1821) of a scene near Little Bushey with a view of St Albans Cathedral, the bearings of which appear on the obelisk erected nearby by Mark Beaufoy (1764–1827).

9.   Lyston Hall, Essex, as rebuilt after the fire of 1870.

John Wilson

10.   One of the two wings of Lyston Hall which remained in 1969 of the reconstructed mansion built by William Campbell two centuries earlier.

11. Lyston Church in 1969, showing the exterior which, unlike the interior, was little changed by restorers in the mid-nineteenth century.

12. Foxearth Church in 1969, 'restored and beautified' by John Foster (1815–92).

13. Donhead Hall in 1970, built at the turn of the eighteenth century by Godfrey Kneller, grandson of the painter.

14. Coombe House in 1970, built in the 1880s by Mark Hanbury Beaufoy.

Both houses were built from local greensand in the broken terrain west of Shaftesbury, but Donhead was an integral part of the landscape with which Coombe did not entirely harmonise.

15. The Beaufoy coat of arms which still stands over the one remaining entrance lodge to Caron Place, and proclaims the family's descent from a chaplain of William I.

16. Beaufoy's vinegar yard in the South Lambeth Road, 1969; remains of Caron.

17. Line engraving showing how Mark Beaufoy made use of the pleasure-ground buildings at Cuper's Garden.

18. Part of a lithograph showing the rural aspect of the South Lambeth riverside before the industrial onslaught.

19. The villas of Lansdowne Gardens, built in the mid-nineteenth century as South Lambeth expanded southwards away from the industrial squalor of the riverside.

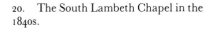

20.   The South Lambeth Chapel in the 1840s.

21.   St Anne's Church, Lambeth, built on the site of the South Lambeth Chapel.

22.   The South Lambeth Dispensary (in 1969), the foundation stone of which was laid by General George Lawrence in 1866.

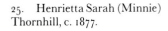

Archivist of St Anne's, Lambeth

23. William Anthony Harrison, Vicar of South Lambeth from 1867 to 1891.

24. William Alexander Morris, Vicar of South Lambeth from 1891 to 1903.

25. Henrietta Sarah (Minnie) Thornhill, c. 1877.

The work of W. A. Harrison and of his Sunday-School teachers, who included Henrietta Sarah Thornhill, made possible the outstanding achievements of W. A. Morris.

26. A group at Eller Close, Grasmere, in August 1868. Left to right: Louey Lean, John Gooch, Aunt George (seated), Mark Beaufoy, Anne Mercier, Minnie Thornhill, Rita Beaufoy.

27. Kaafjord, near Hammerfest. A drawing by W. D. Hooker from his *Notes on Norway*, 1839, to illustrate 'this remote country, which few travellers have ever seen'.

Two aspects of holiday-making in the mid-nineteenth century: billiard-playing at Grasmere, and the search for solitude.

John Wilson

28. Wooden houses at Bergen, of a type which predominated when British tourists started to arrive in the 1850s.

John Wilson

29. Bergen houses of the 1890s, owing not a little to British architectural influences.

In striving to fulfil the expectations of British tourists, Continental resorts tended to lose their architectural individuality.

30. The Hindoo tract-seller, from H. Mayhew's *London Labour and the London Poor*, 1851.

31. Christ Church and the Town Hall at Simla in the early twentieth century, showing the Anglo-Indian determination to create a familiar environment.

Attempts at acclimatisation: Victorian Gothic architecture in Simla, and the boots of the Hindoo tract-seller in London.

32. Daguerreotype of Robert Bensley Thornhill (1818–57),
two of whose brothers survived the Mutiny in the fort of Agra.

Moti Masjid and the great Court Yard in the fort Agra.

33. The Moti Masjid mosque as it appeared early in the twentieth century.

7391.   Landour Bazaar, Mussoorie, Landour in Background.

34.   Mussoorie in the early twentieth century.

35.   Skinning a tiger in the 1870s.

Two aspects of Anglo-Indian life in the mid-nineteenth century: shopping in the bazaars and big-game shooting.

36. Charles Pearson Downe (1840–1912).

Museum of Costume, Bath

37. The wedding dress 'of a very deep red street velvet' presented by Aunt George to Minnie Thornhill for her marriage on 10 May 1881

38. Edward Thornhill, photographed in New Zealand, probably at the end of the nineteenth century.

Index

INDEX OF PLACE NAMES

INDEX OF SUBJECTS